BANZEIRO ÒKÒTÓ

Also by Eliane Brum

The Collector of Leftover Souls:
Field Notes on Brazil's Everyday Insurrections

BANZEIRO ÒKÒTÓ

The Amazon as the Center of the World

Eliane Brum

Translated from the Portuguese by Diane Whitty

Graywolf Press

Originally published in Portuguese as *Banzeiro Òkòtó: Uma viagem à Amazônia Centro do Mundo* by Companhia das Letras, São Paulo, Brazil, 2021.

Earlier versions of "the amazon is a woman" and "fierce life" first appeared in *Atmos* magazine. "in betweens of the world" first appeared in *BOMB*.

This publication is made possible, in part, by the voters of Minnesota through a Minnesota State Arts Board Operating Support grant, thanks to a legislative appropriation from the arts and cultural heritage fund. Significant support has also been provided by the National Endowment for the Arts, the McKnight Foundation, the Lannan Foundation, the Amazon Literary Partnership, and other generous contributions from foundations, corporations, and individuals. To these organizations and individuals we offer our heartfelt thanks.

Published by Graywolf Press
212 Third Avenue North, Suite 485
Minneapolis, Minnesota 55401

All rights reserved.

www.graywolfpress.org

Published in the United States of America

ISBN 978-1-64445-219-6   (paperback)
ISBN 978-1-64445-220-2   (ebook)

2 4 6 8 9 7 5 3 1
First Graywolf Printing, 2023

Library of Congress Control Number: 2022938790

Cover design: Frances Baca

Cover photo: Lilo Clareto

For Jon Watts,
who is Amazonizing with me, in me.

contents

BANZEIRO ÒKÒTÓ

11. where does a circle begin?

Banzeiro   this is what the people of the Xingu call places where
the river goes savage. Where, if you're lucky, you make it through;
where if you're not, you don't. It is a place of danger between where
you're coming from and where you want to go. If you're rowing, you
wait for the banzeiro to retract its claws or calm down. And you
grow quiet, because your boat might suddenly flip over or get
sucked in. You grow quiet so you won't stir the river's wrath.

There are no synonyms for banzeiro. Nor any translation.
Banzeiro is the one that is. And is only where it is.

Since I moved to the Amazon rainforest in August 2017, the
banzeiro has moved from the river to somewhere inside me. I
don't have a liver, kidneys, or stomach like other people do. I have
a banzeiro. Overcome by the whirlpool, my heart beats in con-
centric circles, sometimes so fast it won't let me sleep at night.
And it misses the pitch, goes off key, like a dissonant symphony.
My doctor says it's arrhythmia, but doctors don't know about
bodies that mix. White people's doctors are obsessed with borders; they see the world like the European diplomats who sliced
up Africa at a negotiation table in Berlin in 1885. Give me this
heart here, they say, you take the kidney, in exchange for this leg
I'll let you have the liver and spleen.

With this heart that forgets how to beat in the conventional
rhythm, my insomnia sails me along. My blood has turned to
water and sometimes I feel a fish tickling my pancreas. Other
times, I'm poisoned through and through by the mercury that
gold miners dump in the river's veins and in their own. I squirm,
go mutant, and my gills rot away.

3

This didn't happen suddenly; it set about happening. And still does. I don't think it'll ever stop. The Amazon isn't a place you can go to and simply carry your body along with you, this sum total of bacteria, cells, and subjectivities that are you. That's not how it works. The Amazon leaps inside you like an anaconda striking, crushing the backbone of your thoughts and stirring you in with the planet's marrow. You no longer know your own *I*. People still call you by your name, and you answer; apparently your identity is intact—but what you are, you just don't know anymore. What you've become has no name. Not because it doesn't have one, but because you don't know its language.

You might have noticed that all my metaphors are corporeal. They aren't even metaphors. The Amazon literalizes everything. I can no longer follow Cartesian logic, because the body is everything and dominates everything. People who enter the forest for the first time don't know what to do with the feelings they feel, with the body parts they didn't know they had and that suddenly will never leave them. At some point they fall ill, because their city body, accustomed to pretending it doesn't exist so it can robotize itself in front of a computer, doesn't know what to do with itself.

This body used to occupy 10 percent of itself, because so much was repressed, and now all 100 percent comes on at once. And the body sweats so much it drips on the ground and itches from blackfly bites and gets cut on spiny *tucum* palms and shivers from river water and is drenched in desire for bodies that weren't on the menu before. It's so much of an everything-all-at-once. City people get sick on their first forays into the Amazon because they overdose on body. They confuse malaria with desire for a body that didn't know itself.

This happened to me over twenty years ago, in the late 1990s, during the first times I went to the Amazon as a reporter. I was going to and from. And when I first went back to Porto Alegre, and then to São Paulo all the other times, I turned the key inside myself until my body was once again framed within the apartment it had conformed to, because it knew the layout by heart. My body converted back into a middle-class two-bedroom apartment, but the beast who lives deep inside had had a taste. And wouldn't let itself forget. Then I'd go back to the Amazon. I'd come and go, back and forth, pondering. One day in January 2016, a girlfriend and I were walking through the city of Altamira, in Pará. It was tho rainy ocaoon, but it was dry. The Yudjá people, from Volta Grande do Xingu, called 2016 the Year of the End of the World. I'll explain why on another turn of the banzeiro. Unless I drown first. It's easy to drown writing. What's hard is not to.

I was escorting a friend, the psychoanalyst Ilana Katz, and a small group of people who were meeting with folks from socio-environmental movements in Altamira. We wanted to create a clinical experience centered on listening to the suffering of the refugees of Belo Monte, the hydro dam project that killed part of the Xingu River's body. Ever since the dam imprisoned the river, the Xingu carries dead pieces along with it. In some stretches, it painfully drags its motionless arms and legs, the ones people call reservoirs or artificial lakes. In other spots, as in the region of Volta Grande do Xingu, its body dries up and whole universes are asphyxiated. The fish try to swim and spawn but they end up dying, joining the other corpses there. Death doesn't like to die alone. It dies in a chain. It likes all peoples—fish, mosquitoes, trees, us humans.

There among the ruins of the most violent city in the Amazon, the sun weighing down on my head like a lead crown, I told my friend: I'm going to move to Altamira. Not even I knew where that voice was coming from. But the words were said. And what is said comes into being.

31. destructuring

I'm a journalist. And like all journalists, I was trained to ask my interviewees their age. What we call "Western civilization" develops in linearity. It starts at zero and from there divides us into age brackets. Everything is built around this convention: statistics, what we should feel, what happens to our body and mind, quality of life, the moment you expect to die. It all goes from zero to somewhere in a straight line. The higher a nation's life expectancy, supposedly the more developed the nation. People think about themselves in these numbers, marked by birthdays registered on paper and now in the cloud as well. This convention structures thought, and a structure is also a prison.

Moving to the Amazon destructured me, and I went to pieces. Most people think of going to pieces as a kind of personal catastrophe, but I think that's a very limited way of looking at life. When this happens to someone, it's because the structure that held them grew unbearable, and sometimes they don't even know why. Every effort will be made so the person goes back to belonging, to their own, on track. They'll try everything possible to return to their old form, conform their bodies, conform themselves. But their body—and body is what we are—will rebel. They'll think they have a mind and a body, because Descartes was terribly convincing and very convenient for modernity. And who knows what was happening with his testicles when he invented this partitioned human. But there are no partitions, because there are no parts. This—what people are—screams, hurts, and loves all mixed together.

Women in the Western world know this more than men because

they bleed, and during this period they are treated like anomalies, so the theory will still stand. Don't speak to them, they're crazy. They're crazy because they've become body. I have a friend, a photographer, who threw a bag of menstrual blood in the Vatican years ago. She hopped on a plane in São Paulo and flew across an ocean to do it. Her period, however, did not match up with the performance date, and she had to borrow another woman's menstrual blood. No problem. There are always enough of us around bleeding from our vaginas. Duly supplied, she went to the pope's house and bloodied that which is holy.

She took her pictures. And wasn't arrested. I remember that back then I thought her act might have been a bit exaggerated, but later, no. Given the offensive launched in the late 2010s by the world's ruling white machos, such as Donald Trump and Jair Bolsonaro, I like to imagine a movement where all of us— Black, Indigenous, and white women—would menstruate together at the White House, at the Palácio do Planalto in Brasília, in all those seats of power. We would redden it all up. So long as Francis continues to stand up to the conservatives, I'd leave him (temporarily) immaculate.

I destructured in the Xingu and went to pieces. And going to pieces is risky, because once it happens there's no going back. It means you can no longer conform to a single-minded structure, and so you'll never go back to feeling comfortable, perhaps you won't even go back to being coherent. You'll find yourself disconformed. Before, you had been deformed by form, but once you are dis-conformed, you can transmute into multiple forms, and this is amazingly scary. I didn't know this loss of bones was happening to me. I wanted it but didn't know it.

Shortly after I decided to move to the Amazon, my father died. I used to talk on the phone to my father and mother at the same time, each of them on a different extension. On that last call, he told me he was dying. My mother swears he didn't, but I'm sure of what I heard. And then I left São Paulo, where I lived at the time, to go to my parents' home, to the town where I was born, in far southern Brazil. A six-hundred-mile trip requiring a plane ride and then another six hours on a bus. When I got there, my father had already died. It was supposedly sudden, a stroke. But no.

I'm telling you this because I had already begun dis-conforming and no longer knew what I was. Not who, but what. Grief exacerbated this process. At the time, I was married to a writer of children's books, and he gave me a book called *The Five Misfits*. Each character had a different body form, and I remember feeling at peace when I identified with one of them, a floating body full of holes. That was how I felt, each grief a hole. And I realized it was possible to go through the world full of holes. I was still searching for a form, even if it wasn't conventional.

Another time, I was giving a talk at the Festival of Literature from the Peripheries, in Rio de Janeiro. I was in Mangueira, known worldwide as the birthplace of one of the best-loved samba schools from Rio's Carnival. When I need to give a talk, I write my text down and read it. Writing anchors me; visible words are the force of gravity holding me to the ground. On that occasion, I don't know why, I decided to speak without having anything written down. And then I felt myself floating, as if I had no borders, no separation between me and the words. When it was over, one of the organizers told me, "I thought you were going to dissolve right in front of us." And I replied, "I do almost dissolve, but 'almost' makes all the difference." What still gives me borders in this world? That's a question I don't know how to answer.

I realize now that I don't know why I chose this path to tell the book's story. But I've learned not to lose out on any chance to get lost. I started by writing about age here, because this is the first sign given by the peoples of the forest that their worlds don't conform to linearity. I would ask someone how old they were, and they would look at me, a bit startled, but always very willing to give me what I wanted, and they would reply, "Sixty-five." I would find it odd. Later, sometimes years later, I would ask again, "How old are you now?" And the same person would reply, "Twenty-three." You want a number, they'll give you a number. But without ever abandoning coherence. It will be a different number every time, and not necessarily a bigger one. A kind of a negotiation: I'll give you what you want but I'll stay whole.

Age measured in numbers, in a straight line, makes no sense whatsoever for someone who lives in the forest and moves through dry seasons and rainy seasons, through the cycles of all other people, human and nonhuman, to whom they are intimately connected, in part because they eat each other. Why would you need to know someone's age if you know what they feel, what they can do, and what they desire?

Peoples of the forest find white people very bizarre. But they go along with it when they accompany us on our "expeditions." In addition to the extra income this brings and the alliances that are forged (which have become necessary given the various offensives being waged against the Amazon), I also think they accept our presence in some communities out of a kind of anthropological curiosity—if the word *anthropological* made any sense to them. Anthropologists and journalists think of themselves as observing, but they are the ones being observed all the while, and with great amusement. We're the guinea pigs for these peoples who are Others. These peoples for whom we, "the whites," are Others.

I think I owe you an explanation about what "white" means in this book. I am borrowing the view of the Yanomami people, who use the word *napë* for "enemy." "Enemy" and "white" in fact share the same word, their meanings not separate but merging. They turn into Others who are the same.

"White," in this case, does not depend on color but refers to those who belong to what Davi Kopenawa, shaman and diplomat of the Yanomami people, calls the "commodities people," or "forest eaters." If all original peoples are sometimes called "Indians"—as if we could use one word alone to encompass more than three hundred peoples who speak more than two hundred different languages, and this in Brazil alone—then nothing is more symmetrical than returning us the favor by calling us all "white." We whites, in this sense, like to think of ourselves as universal, so much so that we don't need to be named, unlike everyone else, who has to be identified, because they don't belong to the club. Identified so they can't get through the door, plainly put. Using the word *white* here is also a way of rejecting this purported universality, looking at whiteness instead as a specific identity.

Years ago I began unraveling the whiteness in me as well, meaning I began problematizing white political-racial identity as a producer, reproducer, and sustainer of privileges, among them the privilege of universality. This topic demands a much longer conversation. But what I would like to introduce here is a concept I developed through my own confrontation with being white in a structurally racist country: the concept of "existing violently."

No matter how ethical we whites may manage to be on the individual level, the fact that we are white in a racist country propels us into a daily experience where we are violent merely by existing. If I am born in Brazil rather than Italy—because Brazil's elites decided to whiten the country by importing white men and women like my great-grandparents—I am already violent when I am born. When Black people around me have the worst jobs and worst wages, worst health, worst education, worst housing, worst life, and worst death, I, as a white, exist violently even if I am not a violent person.

In 2014, I wrote an article in which I said that in Brazil—and I believe in the United States and other structurally racist countries as well—the best white person can only manage to be a nice slave master. Because, yes, we are still slave masters and mistresses, even when we try to be egalitarian. Racial inequality is our daily condition. And the experience of existing violently, or of being violent even without actually being violent, is something that has always eaten away at me.

It is tough to acknowledge that I exist violently and to feel it in my bones every day. I can't choose not to, because this is the condition that was given to me at this historical moment. But there is something I can choose, which is to fight so my grandchildren can live in a country where a white person doesn't exist violently merely because they are white. And to do this I must listen. And mainly give up privileges. One of the most crucial questions has to do with how much we're willing to lose in order to be with all others. Because whites must lose for Brazil to move, for the world to move.

Sometimes the hardest privileges to lose are the subtlest, as well as the most subjective. For centuries, whites have practically talked only to themselves, and this includes talking about what culture is and what belonging is. Whites have practically talked only to themselves even about Black people's "place." But the first privilege we lost when Black voices began resounding farther was the illusion that our hands are clean because we're not racist. Our hands are not clean. Because there's no way to be white and likewise blameless in countries where Black people live worse and die first. This is what I call existing violently.

In acknowledging I am "white," I am taking a stance in this book. Davi Kopenawa describes white people's books as "paper skin" where words are imprisoned. Nothing could be more accurate. In this skin, I stand alongside the Indigenous in the fight for the Amazon, which here encompasses much more than the forest per se. Here, the Amazon expands into a battle for a world understood from another perspective, a perspective where humans are not at the center.

While I stand alongside the Indigenous, however, I realize this is not enough to absolve me from my status of *napë*, of enemy. The banzeiro casts me into this state of ambivalence as well. Only by admitting this can I write this book, a narrative where I attempt to don different skins, but where despite all my efforts, I am left with mine, a skin that grows ever more uncomfortable and too tight for a body that is dis-conforming. No transmutation is possible. When a *napë* enters the Amazon, in the deepest sense, they have to know they will never again fit inside their own body, yet they will never manage to fully assume an other either. In this sense, they become where-less, home-less. A foreigner in, of, and to themself. "Foreigner" is the other meaning the Yanomami ascribe to the word *napë*.

I haven't quit asking the people of the forest how old they are. I've gradually learned that asking someone their age doesn't provide me with any information—about age. But it has helped me get at something more important: how much the person has deforested themself. If they tell me their precise age, without hesitating, and the next year they are one year older, the city has already entered them like a steel chisel. They are undergoing a rapid process of un-merging themself from the earth. They are deforming themself to conform. I was to find many people deformed by form in Altamira. Some died from the force of an uprooting that ended in emptiness, dissolving all flesh beneath the skin. Not a death like before, the kind of death they knew and that was transformation, the one where they continued to live as another, but death without a coming to be, dead death.

2. the clitoris and the origin of the forest

Shortly after I landed in Altamira to live for a year, carrying a suitcase and enough funding to continue my reporting projects during that time, I went on an expedition organized by William Balée, a professor of anthropology from Tulane University, in the United States. Bill, as he is better known, is one of the main exponents of the concept of historical ecology, the field of study that explores how humans have interacted with the environment across space and time. This interaction forms "landscapes" but not in our usual understanding of the term. "Landscapes are . . . encounters of places, humans and nonhumans whose histories are imprinted in the environment," Balée wrote poetically. What each of us sees is not the same, ever. When Bill looks at the forest, he tries to uncover the conversation among the trees, bushes, vines, and everything classified as botany and the people who lived there centuries or millennia before. He wants to comprehend the landscape they created, beyond what meets the eye today. And also comprehend what this landscape can tell us about the future.

Bill was investigating the hypothesis that this part of the Amazon rainforest was planted by the ancestors of today's Indigenous people and that the presence of contemporary traditional societies isn't incompatible with forest conservation principles. Most whites believe that when the European colonizers encountered the world's largest tropical forest, it was a creation free of human fingerprints. A kind of fifty-million-year-old "virgin." This belief has no basis in the reality laid bare through the research of scientists like Bill Balée. Part of the Amazon is a cultural forest,

15

meaning it has been sculpted over the course of thousands of years, mainly by humans, but also by nonhumans, the ones we call "animals," through their interactions with the environment. And not by all human persons, but by the same ones who ensure that the remaining forest still stands and who are shot to death for it: the Indigenous and, in more recent centuries, the members of traditional forest communities known as *beiradeiros*, along with *quilombolas*, the descendants of runaway slaves.

Archaeologists like Eduardo Neves, a Brazilian, have proven that the forest was much more inhabited by humans in the past than today. "The Amazon has been occupied for more than ten thousand years, in some cases by populations of thousands of people," says Eduardo, one of the most endearing white men to pilgrimage through the forest in search of "terra preta," the dark earth that signals human occupation, rich soil darkened by layers of intense, intelligent interaction with this place.

It's impossible to understand the natural history of the Amazon without taking the influence of human populations into account. Similarly, you can't understand the history of the Amazon peoples without taking into account the relationships they established with nature. In addition to its natural history, the forest that now overlies archaeological sites has a cultural history.

The reduction of the number of human inhabitants in the Amazon (original peoples, clearly put, because the number of whites just keeps growing) has been the result of European colonization, at least in more recent centuries. Invaders exterminated a large percentage of these peoples through the viruses and bacteria loaded on their bodies and also through the violence of their onslaughts. When researchers like Eduardo and Bill investigate and demonstrate the Amazon's human past, they are joining the forces of resistance that oppose the destruction of the forest and its peoples and that also oppose the preservationist groups that want to remove from the forest the traditional communities who reached the Amazon in recent centuries, like beiradeiros, all in the name of preserving the ecosystem. But humans—this generic term invented to conceal asymmetries—are not a threat to the forest; rather, some humans are. Others interact with it, transform it, and even plant it.

This language is white, because I'm writing mainly to the non-Indigenous, just as researchers write to the non-Indigenous. For the original peoples, there is no nature and humans, one thing and the other. There is only nature. Indigenous people aren't in the forest, they *are* forest. They interact with what whites call "forest," just like nonhuman persons interact with it. The forest is everything, visible and invisible.

Davi Kopenawa explains the forest much better than a white woman like me can:

> In the forest, we human beings are the "ecology." But it is equally the *xapiri* [spirits], the game, the trees, the rivers, the fish, the sky, the rain, the wind, and the sun! It is everything that came into being in the forest, far from the white people: everything that isn't surrounded by fences yet.

In his interviews with the French anthropologist Bruce Albert in the magisterial book *The Falling Sky*, Kopenawa says that words of the creator deity Omama are "the center of what the white people call ecology." When the Yanomami leader began traveling to cities like New York, London, and Paris to talk about the destruction of the forest, he realized whites used another name for something that had been passed down by the ancient ones "since the beginning of time."

> This is why we understood these new white people words as soon as they reached us. I explained them to my kin and they

thought: "*Haixopë!* This is good! The white people call these things 'ecology'!" As for us, we say *urihi a*, earth-forest, and we also speak of the *xapiri*, for without them, without ecology, the land gets warmer and lets the epidemics and the evil beings get closer.

Intrinsic to the very existence of Indigenous peoples, ecology has reached whites only recently.

In the past, our elders were not able to make their words about the forest heard by the white people because they did not know their language. And when the white people first arrived at our elders' houses, they did not yet speak about ecology. They were more eager to ask them for jaguar, peccary, and deer skins! At that time, these white people did not possess any of these words to protect the forest.

For thinkers like Kopenawa, "the white people's thought remains full of forgetting"; they don't perceive Earth as a being that "has a heart and breathes." Or, in the words of Viveiros de Castro, they don't know "what it is to *be* in your place, in the world as a home, shelter, and environment." The white-centrism denounced by Kopenawa underlies a misconception shared even by respected academics: the idea that the Amazon is a kind of "virgin." From this ill-informed viewpoint, the solution to keeping the forest alive is to get rid of all humans, as if they were all predators. Both the original peoples (Indigenous) and traditional communities (beiradeiros, quilombolas, etc.) are forest peoples. With the white people's offensive, they have become the forest's greatest stewards as well, placing their very existence and bodies as obstacles to the destruction not only of their home but also of what they are collectively. Brazil is among the countries that kill the highest number of environmental defenders, representing the systematic execution of humans who are nature. In its hegemony, what white-centrism erases is the fact that not all humans have white minds. Or, to echo the words of Davi Kopenawa once again, not all human persons have their thought filled with forgetting.

The purpose of the first scientific expedition to Terra do Meio Ecological Station, in 2017, was precisely to combat white people's forgetting. The researchers were in search of possible pasts—to reach possible futures.

Very white, and overweight, Bill evoked the foreign naturalists who traveled the Amazon's rivers in the nineteenth century, except a heartier version. When the forest dwellers laid eyes on the "professor" for the first time, they had major doubts about his ability to withstand the omnipresent Amazon sun, the legendary hunger for fresh flesh shown by the Amazon's voracious blood-sucking mosquitoes, and the trails where you sometimes have to rappel from one spot to another. Not to mention the times you have to take flight or scramble up a tree because hundreds of peccaries are traversing the forest. Their hooves sound like the end of the world, and if you can't get out of their way as nimbly as a spider monkey, you're pounded to pulp.

When the beiradeiros first saw the curious human specimen named Bill Balée, they concluded: "Yeah, right . . ."

And right they were. On his first expedition alone, Bill lost over twenty pounds. In October 2017, he traveled in the company of two archaeologists, Vinicius Honorato and Márcio Amaral. It was the first time a group of scientists had investigated the region of this ecological station from the perspective of either historical ecology or archaeology. Evidence of a remote human past is a truism for the forest peoples, but not for science, since little scientific research has been done in Terra do Meio—just as little research has been done in most of the Amazon, which is being destroyed by large hydroelectric dams, mining projects, railroads and highways, cattle and soybeans. All the marks inscribed on the forest by a human history thousands of years long are being swept away, along with the forest itself.

Exploitation by white people in the name of "progress" is a political operation meant to erase everything that existed before they crushed life in the tropics under their boots. Whites have the galling obsession of thinking every history begins with their own arrival. But what generally happens is that their boots, chain saws, and weapons put an end to these histories.

For archaeologists like Vinicius and Márcio, a people's infrastructure does not consist solely of clay pots or ceramic vases but is everything living as well. Like trees. What today's white people see as infrastructure and agriculture, for example, is not how the ancient peoples of the forest saw things. Theirs is another way of being and becoming in the world, a narrative told by other "artifacts," in this case living ones.

This understanding that archaeological riches are limited to huge monuments or vast treasures, like those of the pharaohs or the Aztecs, Mayans, and Incans, has become a commonplace with the help of Hollywood and its various iterations of Indiana Jones—the most violent, colonialist, and likewise incompetent archaeologist in all of fiction. This deliberately distorted viewpoint leaves the Amazon devoid of any apparent archaeological interest for most. And it feeds a fabrication that has served various interests and ideologies.

The business-military dictatorship that oppressed Brazil from 1964 to 1985 and consummated the first great project of massive forest destruction expanded on this fabrication, strengthening and taking great advantage of it. To this end, Brazil's generals launched an ad campaign that solidified an imagination still reigning in many people's minds today: the idea of the Amazon as a virgin untouched by humans. The dictatorship spread this intentional ignorance through terms like "human desert" and "green desert" to justify the operation of invading and destroying the forest, with the purported goal of "*integrar para não entregar*," of integrating to avoid handing over—integrating the rainforest into the only civilization they deemed valid, the civilization of white exploiters, supposedly to avoid handing anything over to foreign white exploiters.

The generals defended—and still defend—a strategy of war: occupying territory in the name of national interests. They wanted to be the first to "devirginize" the forest and thus guarantee their dominion. The most appalling slogan of the era was "the Amazon—a land without men for men without land." The message was clear: for the dictatorship's generals, the original peoples who occupied the forest before the existence of this convention called Brazil did not fall into the human category.

In an epochal special edition on the Amazon published in October 1971 by the magazine *Realidade*, the large construction company Queiroz Galvão—one of those then thrashing the forest to build the Transamazonian Highway—published an explicit ad that speaks to the ideology driving this destruction. The caption alongside an image of a newborn dangling upside down from an obstetrician's hand read: "Minister, Transamazonian is doing well." This message followed:

His full name is Juarez Furtado de Araújo Transamazonian. HE IS THE FIRST BOY BORN IN THE BRAVE NEW WORLD we are helping to build—erecting it within the biggest green space on Earth. Where nothing existed but woods. And legends. Myth and fear. The other day, the message was delivered straight to Minister Andreazza himself by the settler Joaquim Félix Araújo, the father of Transamazonian—this big boy [is headed to] the year 2000. He was born precisely where we are starting out. Better put: where Brazil is being discovered again. God bless you, Transamazonian!

Fifty years later, now in the twenty-first century, Brazil's armed forces show through their actions and statements that they still consider, and treat, the original peoples and traditional communities of the forest as less than human. In 2020, Jair Bolsonaro actually said "more and more, Indians are becoming human beings just like us." The antipresident tried to convince his listeners that the greatest dream of the Indigenous peoples is to open their lands to livestock, soybeans, and mining. Hence, they would complete their humanization by embracing predatory capitalism's project and leasing or selling their ancestral lands—by beginning to treat the forest as a commodity.

The landmark construction of the Transamazonian Highway, a pharaonic project that symbolized "the conquest of this gigantic green world," is emblematic of the generals' phallic relationship with the forest. Emílio Garrastazu Médici (1905–85) was president of Brazil during the bloodiest period of the dictatorship, when more than eight thousand Indigenous people and hundreds of white resisters were killed and thousands of others tortured. In 1970, the dictator traveled to Altamira to commemorate the inauguration of highway construction and produce images of the conquest of the Amazon for those in the press who were submissive to the generals. Intended to demonstrate humankind's power over nature—and so typical of modernity—Médici's symbolic act was to chop down a Brazil nut tree towering more than one hundred sixty feet. We can interpret this gesture as an allusion to the regime's power over the bodies then being butchered in dungeons, their very subjecthood drained from them. It is essential to highlight the special sadism reserved for women during torture sessions; they were repeatedly raped by agents of the state, who, in addition to applying electric shocks to these women's genitals and breasts, took particular pleasure in shoving rats and cockroaches up their vaginas.

Back then, Dom Erwin Kräutler, the legendary bishop of the Xingu, was still a young priest, who had just arrived from his native Austria. By the time we met, he had already spent ten years accompanied by an around-the-clock police escort so he wouldn't be murdered. He told me about the day he had witnessed General Médici celebrating the Transamazonian Highway—a monumental road paved with Indigenous blood. "He [Médici] broke ground. People on stage went wild . . . they really went wild! Clapping! Listen, chopping down a tree like that! And saying it was the arrival of progress. It cut my heart. How could they applaud when the queen of the trees of Pará or the Amazon was felled, and with a tremendous crash? How is that possible?"

The sign marking this "historic moment" (a sign that would later be added) bore the following inscription. On these banks of the Xingu, in the middle of the Amazon jungle, the President of the Republic has set in motion the construction of the Transamazonian Highway, a historical kickoff toward the conquest of this gigantic green world." In Altamira, the place marking this event is known by a telltale name: *Pau do Presidente*—the President's Wood.

None of the governments that came in the wake of Brazil's late-1980s return to democracy ever abandoned this view of the forest as a body to be assaulted, exploited, and pillaged. But never was this perspective reinforced or intensified as much as when Bolsonaro ushered back in the militarization of the state, starting in 2019. The rainforest is now perilously close to the point of no return, the moment when forest will no longer be forest and cannot play its role in regulating the climate.

In opposition to this death project, archaeologists are looking toward the future when they investigate the Amazon's remote past. Terra do Meio—Middle Earth—is a front line in this century's great battle, the fight for the Amazon. This region is so named because it is a resistant enclave of forest conservation lying between two powerful forces that guide and protect it: the mighty Xingu River and its tributary, the Iriri, a river edged by gardens of stones and plants so exceedingly delicate it makes you cry. With mounting assaults on all flanks, Terra do Meio, like the entire Amazon, is under attack.

This is not a place we can simply check off like an item on some tourist itinerary: "There's the capitol." "Here's the monument to the pioneers . . ." No. The ecological station alone covers more than thirteen thousand square miles of forest that is formally protected by federal government decree but persistently invaded, sometimes by the president's supporters and even his friends. Terra do Meio—certainly the loveliest name in the entire Brazilian Amazon (or at least in Portuguese, because there are other marvelous names in Indigenous languages)—is a mosaic composed of some thirty-eight thousand square miles of protected areas. There is no consensus about what constitutes the territory called Terra do Meio. The definition I am using here encompasses all Indigenous lands that are tied to conservation units. Within this space, Terra do Meio includes three protected areas known as extractive reserves (Riozinho do Anfrísio, Rio Iriri, and Rio Xingu); an ecological station bearing its name; the Triunfo do Xingu Environmental Protection Area; Serra do Pardo National Park; and the lands of the Assurini, Araweté, Parakanã, Arara, Mebêngôkre Kayapó, Xipaya, Kuruaya, and Mebêngôkre Xikrin original peoples and also of isolated peoples. Some of these were among the most heavily deforested and invaded Indigenous lands of the 2010s, particularly Cachoeira Seca, of the Arara; Ituna-Itatá, where there are reports of isolated peoples; and Trincheira Bacajá, of the Xikrin. As of 2020, with the onset of the COVID-19 pandemic, land-grabbing and timber theft also advanced far into the extractive reserves inhabited by traditional beiradeiro communities.

It was quite the gringo idea to travel to this universe filled with so many worlds during the dry season, in October 2017. We left Altamira, the nearest city, and spent six taxing days on a *voadeira*—or "flyer," the fastest motor canoe on Amazonian waters. The rivers were so low that the boat kept running aground on the rocks and had to be pulled out by rope, bloodying unaccustomed hands. We set our feet down amid all sizes and species of rays, beautiful yet sinister. There is no living being I respect more in the water than a ray. I've seen many limbs pierced by their stingers, and they make me shiver when it's one hundred degrees out, just thinking about my poor, pasty-white feet.

When we reached the ecological station, we pitched camp on an island with a woman's name, Marisa. In the Amazon, pitching camp entails not only setting up a camp stove and protecting your provisions but also finding well-spaced trees where you can hang a hammock and some mosquito netting. Then you need to find a way to cover it all up with a tarp, because it will surely rain. In the tropical forest, rainfall means the gods open their huge mouths and vomit rivers over the land. When thunder and lightning hit, the forest writhes and what was hot goes cold.

After days of trails, excavations, and classifications, we devoted our nights to talking and eating hot food—fish or jerky, black beans, rice, and lots of cassava meal. Bill retired to his hammock early, protected by an impressive mosquito net evocative of a king's canopy. Inside his netting, he would open his Kindle to read Raymond Khoury's best-selling historical novel *The Last Templar.* Although Bill was born in Florida, he was reading it in French, one of his languages. He is fluent as well in Ka'apor, part of the Tupi-Guarani linguistic family. Bill lived with the Ka'apor for about a year.

I also retired early because I was the only woman in the group. The expedition's beiradeiros felt a bit bashful since they believed certain topics—"men's"—shouldn't be broached in my presence. I didn't have a princess hammock but a small synthetic structure with an attached mosquito net that, when closed, fit in the palm of my hand. Better to sleep in the fetal position for weeks than carry a lot of weight or have to display my alarming incompetence at manual tasks like hanging a hammock. I've always been a right-handed person with two left hands.

The best conversations took place after Bill and I disappeared from the center of the campsite—because he was the "boss" and I was a woman. To my good fortune, Márcio and Vinicius were always willing to fill me in on the evening's highlights the next day.

If you plan to accompany researchers into the rainforest, make sure you pick archaeologists. They're the best. They know how to walk in the woods, and they're fun, good-humored, and really enjoy what they do, even when they're exhausted, which is almost every day. It's curious how people who quite literally excavate the past, penetrating heavy layers of earth and stone, can be so light, as if the weight stayed there in the ground and not on their shoulders. I suspect that because they have to pick up a spade to do their work, it saves them from the arrogance peculiar to many academics. It may be that investigating the remote past imbues them with a more eloquent notion of the fleeting unimportance we all have, rendering any degree of vanity useless and even ridiculous.

What did these white researchers and forest dwellers talk about after a heavy workday? Women. Of course. But, since they were interesting men, they didn't boast crudely. To the contrary. They talked about how to give a woman pleasure.

One night Vinicius was trying to explain to the beiradeiros that there was a certain spot of the female anatomy that, if caressed, would make your partner very happy and appreciative of the attention. "Clitoris," he said to eyes bulging in amazement. How had the men of the forest lived all those centuries without knowing about this wonder?

The fog of misunderstanding gradually lifted. Before the brown howlers began crooning one of the loveliest songs in the Amazon, Zé Boi (Joe Steer, a beiradeiro who lives up to his name with his massive trunk of pure muscle—and also shows how cattle go far into the forest, where they shouldn't be) gave a shout, as if watching the machine of the world open up before his eyes: "Ooooh! The *castanhinha*—the little Brazil nut!"

They went off to sleep in their hammocks with a feeling of relief. It wasn't a lack of basic information, just a difference in nomenclature. In the life of forest dwellers, where Brazil nut groves are so important, something so treasured could only be known by a term worthy of its shape and flavor. The clitoris—such a scientifically sanitized name, where Portuguese speakers can't figure out where to put the phallic acute accent and many English speakers can't figure out whether to stress the first or second syllable—was replaced by a word that represented it. To honor the world, we need all languages.

15. the amazon is a woman

It isn't possible to cite the word *virgin* so many times and then move along as if I had been talking about the price of bread. *Virgin* isn't any old word, because it is flesh. In the Amazon, as in women's lives, the word is intimately bound up with destruction. Not just the destruction of a barrier, like the hymen, but the destruction wrought by controlling and dominating bodies. Using the word *virgin* to refer to the forest and other ecosystems not yet wholly dominated by men represents fascination with a "natural," "wild," and "untouched" body and also sheds light on the power relations now propelling the Amazon ever closer to the point of no return—a point that can also be understood as the moment when the forest will be entirely subjugated and its life-creating power thus destroyed.

Jair Bolsonaro's rise to power with the presidential elections of 2018 was also the rise to power, in Brazil, of a radical representative of all the values that have ruled what we call "humanity" and have brought us to the climate emergency: a white man who deems nonwhites only partly human; a macho who celebrates *machismo*; a misogynist who considers his fifth child, his only female offspring, the product of a "slip-up" on his part; a homophobe who says he would rather his son die in a car accident than be gay; a defender of the union of a man and a woman as the only legitimate family ordained by the Bible; an apologist for weapons as phallic objects of destruction; and a man obsessed with allegories involving the penis and anus.

Bolsonaro wasn't elected despite this collection of hegemonies, which have only more recently begun to bother liberal sensitivities, but *because* of it. In this sense, his election was a cry of resistance in the name of values that have kept a portion of humans at the top of the food chain, those same humans who are now feeling threatened. Bolsonaro's victory at the Brazilian ballot box was in step with the victories of other political specimens who are also exploiting growing insecurity in the face of a mutating human world. This evolution has been marked by two simultaneous phenomena: pressure from those who are considered representatives of society's peripheral humanities, like women, the LGBTQIA+ community, the Indigenous, and Black people, who want to occupy centers of power, and the pressure represented by profound, human-caused changes to the planet. Both phenomena presage a quaky present-future for some bases of support enjoyed by the despots elected in the 2010s.

The elections of Jair Bolsonaro, Donald Trump, and others like them can be interpreted as a desperate call for the return of a past that never existed, a past in which everything was in its place and everyone knew everything's place. Everyone knew their place in the racial, social, and gender hierarchy—and accepted it. In this past, whites and hetero males were ensconced in the patriarchal structure, while their alleged supremacy was neither contested nor threatened. Yet even a superficial glance at history, and histories, can show us how this peace for a few was constantly challenged and only sustained at the price of slavery, extermination, and erasures. These elected despots realized that selling false pasts with the guarantee that they would once again become the present was tantamount to hitting a mother lode of votes. For those who embrace them, a comfortable lie is worth more than a fistful of hard truths.

What does this have to do with the Amazon? Everything.

On July 6, 2019, Bolsonaro publicly declared: "Brazil [referring to the Amazon] is a virgin that every foreign pervert wants." In the vast bibliography of racist, misogynistic, homophobic, violence-inciting sentences uttered by this far-right career politician, none other has so effectively revealed how Bolsonaro views and treats the planet's largest tropical rainforest. For Bolsonaro, the Amazon is a woman whose body belongs to him, to do whatever he wants with. Not long before this, he had criticized "gay tourism" in Brazil, with the following caveat: "Whoever wants to come here to have sex with women, feel free."

Bolsonaro has shown that the assault of bodies doesn't bother him. To the contrary. Power lies in defining which bodies are available for assault. He proclaims himself an "upstanding citizen" because he doesn't accept the exploitation of one man's body by another. The way he interprets the Bible, in line with Brazil's ever more influential neo-Pentecostal Evangelicalism, only women's bodies can be exploited by men.

Once the place of bodies has been determined, the dispute is over which "perverts" can abuse both forest and women. As Bolsonaro sees it, for the foreign perverts who come to spend their dollars in Brazil, Brazilian women are for the taking. In the case of the forest, however, foreign perverts are using the excuse that the Amazon must be protected as a way of challenging Brazil's sovereignty over possession of a land rich in ore. So the problem is not abuse or rape, but an alleged threat to ownership of the forest's body. Like an avid pimp, Bolsonaro is open to any client, so long as said client doesn't question Bolsonaro's ownership of his profit source—and so long as his family and friends guarantee his share.

It is not possible for a man like Bolsonaro to understand the discussion about either the Amazon or women outside the logic of assault, ownership, and exploitation. As the president of the country that holds 60 percent of the planet's largest tropical rainforest within its territory, Bolsonaro embodies the logic of violent exploitation and dominion over bodies like no one else. The moral dogmas that form the pillars of white supremacy, the patriarchy, and gender binarism also sustain the capitalist model that has consumed nature and brought the planet to the climate emergency. These are not two different projects but one and the same. And nothing has left them as naked to the eye as the rulers of countries like Brazil and the United States at the close of the 2010s, at the very moment when only pathological liars can deny the climate crisis.

Trump and Bolsonaro did not become presidents despite their lies but because they lie. They are not climate emergency deniers—to the contrary, they know the crisis exists. They are one step beyond denial, because only denying—as the fossil fuel industry has for decades—no longer suffices. And when you can no longer deny, someone has to be willing to lie.

The scene that best illustrates this phenomenon is Bolsonaro addressing the seventy-fourth United Nations General Assembly in 2019. While he was busy avowing that there were no fires in the Amazon, the whole world watched the forest burn in real time. The disassociation between reality and his discourse did not bother the president. This episode will always serve as a symbolic image of this phenomenon of lying rulers, of an era when lying has become a strategic political asset for winning votes.

The fact that the mystification known as the "market" threw its support behind the candidacies of Bolsonaro and Trump likewise stems from the link between capitalism and destruction. Given the climate emergency fostered by big capitalist corporations—and also by their representatives within modern democracies' institutional system—uncouth barbarians had to be given a place at the table alongside refined murderers, so power would remain in the same hands. The lords of neoliberalism occasionally pretend to be scandalized and would in fact rather associate with more elegant, well-dressed people, but there is no capitalism without pragmatism. As stated by the British journalist Jonathan Watts, global environment editor for the *Guardian*, large transnational corporations have operated inside democracy for decades. When the climate crisis made denial impossible within democratic debate, they leveraged pathological liars into power with the mission of eroding democracy and imposing by force the interests of the great producers of destruction.

In the Amazon, this has also been a moment when women are playing a growing leadership role in struggles against annihilation. It is women who have responded to control over the forest's body by collectively placing their own bodies in the vanguard of the battle. And this is on all fronts, from the institutional level to physical skirmishes. Women know that this is about one and the same body, and assaulting one means assaulting the other.

Once again, this is no coincidence. For Davi Kopenawa's generation and, before him, the generation of Raoni—the Kayapó leader nominated for a Nobel Peace Prize—it was men who left their villages to confront the world of whites. During this century, and even more so in the second decade, a growing number of Indigenous women are on the front lines, along with quilombolas and beiradeiras. Not that there weren't any women leaders before, but they were the exception. Not anymore.

Women have pushed public discourse to be more radical. When they rise to speak today, they neither measure their words nor try to be diplomatic. In 2018, Sônia Guajajara, executive coordinator of APIB, Brazil's largest Indigenous organization, was the vice presidential candidate of PSol, the left-leaning Socialism and Liberty Party. The ticket had no chance of winning since the party was still small, but it was highly symbolic to have an Indigenous woman on the presidential ballot. Sônia Guajajara became the biggest political leader to stand up to Bolsonaro publicly.

Likewise in 2018, for the first time in history, Brazil elected an Indigenous woman, Joenia Wapichana, to the lower house. The Indigenous use their people's name as their surname, so whoever is listening to them knows who they are, to which people they belong, and how their life is. The Guajajara and Wapichana are both peoples of the Amazon, but from very different regions of the forest, thousands of miles away from each other. Yet they fight side by side.

The word *Indian* is a generic term invented by whites—and grounded in a monumental mistake. In the late fifteenth century, European invaders thought they had reached the Indies in their search for a route to spices. But they landed in the place they would call America. The name "Indian" stuck, because the invaders couldn't care less about people they deemed less than human. For the original peoples, however, "Indian" doesn't make any sense. A Wapichana's language and culture are different from a Guajajara's, for example, and neither is the same as the Yanomami's. But when they are up against their common enemy, these different peoples recognize each other as peoples of nature. So for the original peoples of Brazil, the word *índio* has acquired the sense of "kin."

While women like Sônia and Joenia confront the "forest eaters" in the halls of institutional power in Brasília, the federal capital, and in major cities of Brazil and around the world, today there are dozens of other women confronting wildcat miners, illegal loggers, and large companies on the ground. With their own bodies. Maria Leusa Munduruku is one of them. Her determination led her enemies to put a price on her head in 2019: one hundred grams of gold.

When this Munduruku leader speaks out at public events, she usually has a baby sucking on her breast or just snuggled up there to sleep close to its mother's heart. For journalists like me, it is tempting to compare her to a warrior Madonna. It's even right there in her name, Maria. But years ago, her people sent a letter to the white world's authorities to voice their rejection of hydropower plants in the forest. They made it a point to remind the *pariwats*, as the Munduruku call non-Indigenous people and also their enemies, "Our ancestors are more ancient than Jesus Christ."

Gold miners and deforesters want her dead. But Maria Leusa won't back down. And she doesn't miss a single public opportunity to reiterate: "Our inspiration is the ancient warrior Wakubaran, who fought for justice in the early times. He cut off his enemies' heads. We come from this line. If need be, we'll cut off some heads."

For the Munduruku leader, breastfeeding her baby is in no way incompatible with simultaneously threatening to cut off heads. The connection is obvious. The same love moves her to do the former and threaten the latter. The Munduruku women warriors built their own, much more radical, version of the #MeToo movement long ago. "We're on the front line because we've realized men trust authorities too much. And they take money easy too It's true that mining makes more money, but we're showing them that mining destroys our children's future." Maria Leusa goes on: "It's up to us to protect our people. We know we can't wait for the government or police to do it. We do it."

And they do. Side by side with the men, the women of the Munduruku people have destroyed the equipment of the gold miners who invade their lands or dig up riverbeds to wrest out gold. They also set fire to boats built from tree trunks stolen from the forest by loggers. Since public officials refused to recognize Indigenous rights, because they were planning—and still plan—to build a set of hydropower plants in this region of the state of Pará, the Munduruku community took it upon themselves to begin marking out the limits of their lands in 2014, in a process called auto-demarcation. In recent years, women have become the primary force resisting the ambitions of every government administration that has tried to dam up the rivers of the Tapajós basin—the Tapajós, a river so blue it burns your eyes.

In late 2019, Munduruku women warriors gave a show of strength that had an immensely symbolic meaning: they entered a museum in the city and took back what whites think of as archaeological objects but that, for the Indigenous, are their ancestors' spirits. They took them back because the imprisoned spirits were crying out. They wrote in a letter:

> We rescued the fish's mother, peccary's mother, turtle's mother, tortoise's mother, *tracajás*'s mother, and others that you pariwat don't understand. They are our ancestors' spirits. They have

been suffering ever since the Teles Pires and São Manoel hydro-electric power plants destroyed our holy places (Karobixexe and Dekoka'a) and left them imprisoned in a place they shouldn't be, making our people suffer the consequences. . . . Guided by our wise pajés [shamans], who hear the spirits' lamentations, we entered the Alta Floresta Museum of Natural History-MT to fulfill our obligation to visit them and take them food. When the pajés spoke to the spirits, they were very angry. The pajés heard a lot of crying and saw their suffering, and that's why it was urgent to free them. It wasn't only the pajés who felt it; everyone felt the spirits screaming *odaxijom* [help]. What the pariwat see as objects, our pajés know to be our ancestors.

The Munduruku women warriors walk together and take their children to what urban activists would call direct actions. It is from them, by example, that the children learn how to resist and act collectively. They are raised in community, cared for, fed, and educated with confidence in the collective. Milk and war.

The image of fighting women, babies hanging against their naked breasts, collided directly with the project of the far-right administration that took power in Brazil in 2019, both in terms of objective economic relations and in terms of the subjective view of women and maternity that aligns with the patriarchy and has been molded by neo-Pentecostal Evangelicalism. The link between conservatism in the realm of customs and the exploitation of the Amazon obeys the same logic and serves the same body-colonizing project. Unless we understand this intimate political relationship, it is not possible to understand the brutal destruction of the forest.

In 2019, Damares Alves, then recently appointed minister of women, the family, and human rights, released a video in which she proclaimed that Brazil was entering a new era, in which "boys wear blue, girls wear pink." Alves's prime credentials for holding office were her frenzied desire to control women's bodies and her fervor to evangelize Indigenous people, which is merely another way of using religion to control bodies, for economic purposes. A neo-Pentecostal pastor, Alves is the founder of an NGO suspected of trafficking and kidnapping Indigenous children and inciting hatred against the Indigenous. She also adopted an Indigenous girl through irregular channels.

If the minister of women, the family, and human rights is an opponent of the feminists who take to urban streets with their chests bared to say "my body, my rules," the power project she is pushing forward, hiding behind the mask of morality, also puts her in direct opposition to the female warriors of the forest, like Maria Leusa. "Because of the government, our forest is shedding tears. Tears that fall like milk from our breast," the Munduruku leader says, showing how the forest is flesh of her flesh and thus expresses itself literally from her body.

The Amazons of Greek myth have been portrayed with only one breast, because in one of the many versions of their story, they rip off their right one to make it easier to wield their bow and arrow. The real amazons of the climate collapse would never mutilate their bodies. They use their breasts to nourish future women warriors.

45. rape. and reforestation

It took me a while to understand that the violence of having a body always at risk is not just one more given in a person's life. It isn't some trauma or sad tale. Or several traumas or several sad tales. Violence is as much a constituent part of being a woman in what we call the world as are our bones, organs, and blood. Violence is structural to being and becoming in a woman's world, even as some of us can't help but exist violently as white women. We women comprehend what we are through the threats to our bodies.

Being a woman is being a body that doesn't feel safe anywhere.

If every woman thought about herself from a perspective of amazement rather than normalizing what is not normal, she would discover that her decisions involve where to put her body. How to put her body. How her body is viewed. And, mainly, how to protect her body. Protect it from eyes, hands, knives, and cocks she hasn't authorized to enter but that nevertheless do.

If the eye of the Other is what gives us our foundation, we discover we are women before we discover ourselves as women, even before we pronounce the word *woman*, through the eye that invades us. Not the eye that loves us, but the one that judges us. Not that recognizes us, but that turns us into an object. Not that asks our permission, but that assaults us. If the eye of the Other tells us who we are, even before we grasp the word *fear*, we are already afraid.

It is inside a body always on the verge of being assaulted that we walk down the street, defending ourselves from eyes and hands. That we board a bus or take the subway, defending ourselves from eyes and hands, and sometimes cocks. That we fear our male teachers, male doctors, male bosses. That we fear our uncles and male cousins, and sometimes our brothers. That we fear our stepfathers and sometimes our fathers. That we fear the man who sells candy, the man who sits down next to us in the cinema, our classmates in school and later at college. That we fear our male colleagues at work. That we fear.

We are the ones who must close our legs when we sit down because our vaginas must be hidden, even if they are much more of a mystery inside than out. A marvelous mystery we are taught to silence. We who have big and small labia and a tongue that grows erect in the middle of our sex—we are the ones they silence. And in silence we remain when our vaginas and anuses and mouths are assaulted. Being a woman is being a word that can't be pronounced; it's being a censured painting on Facebook.

Because they've taught us it is our responsibility to know where and how to place our body, to know what clothes to dress it in. Because they've taught us it is our responsibility to evade cocks and hands and knives. Because they've taught us it is our responsibility to evade the violence of the macho who can't resist his natural urge to invade, perforate, and pierce, we are blamed. For choosing the wrong place, wrong time, wrong clothes, wrong guy. We are blamed for bleeding and hurting and wanting to die so we will no longer be invaded, pierced, and perforated.

The conversion from girl to woman is a story that can be told by the hands on our cunts, the cocks they show us in the street (or at home), the disgusting jokes at school and work, the words hurled at our bodies when we try to pass, and by the words *bitch, slut, whore*. Bitch, slut, whore. Bitch slut whore. A thousand times. Bitchslutwhore. The conversion from girl to woman is a tale told by fear. It is knowing our growing chest will be assaulted even before it finishes growing and our maturing vagina will be touched without our permission. And looked at. Leered at.

When it is not our body of flesh they abuse, they cut and mutilate our expressions of ourselves with sharp-edged words. They cut and mutilate our written words with their pens and fingers. They cut and mutilate our performances with their shouts of "sexy." They call our literature and art "women's" because we can only exist inside labeled boxes. They interrupt our speech and finish our sentences, because we can't reach the end ourselves. And when we react, they call us bitches and crazy. Sluts and hysterical. Sexually frustrated because what we need is their cock. Being a woman is also being mutilated without blood or marks. Being a woman is being an absent word, a letter deleted with a click of the keyboard.

In Brazil, they say even violent criminals do not condone rape and so they rape the rapists, as if there were some justice in ramming a cock into the anus of someone who doesn't want to be fucked, perpetrating yet another act of violence and getting off on it. The truth is, many of the men who supposedly don't condone rape assault their own wives in bed, beat their daughters, and with a thousand eyes control the vaginas they consider theirs. And when they're arrested, they delegate this task to whoever is on the outside, while their mothers spend decades having their vaginas and anuses inspected at the prison gate. These criminals only see rape as a crime when it assaults bodies they consider their property, bodies only they can assault.

In the Brazil of blood, generations of men believed that to become men they had to assault their housemaids, as their fathers and grandfathers before them and as the slave masters and slave masters' sons and grandsons had done to enslaved women before them. They still believe it. And still do it. To terrified women, most of them Black, who have no chance of reporting it or crying out, women subjugated to the logic that their flesh is here to be used—and abused. This version of *The Masters and the Slaves* has never been considered rape, because housemaids are enslaved women who can never be freed. Being a woman is having your rape defined as a "cultural trait." It is screaming with a sheet stuffed in your mouth in the dungeon called the maid's room.

Being a woman is being the Xingu assaulted by Belo Monte. It is being a calcinated tree when smoke covers the Amazon sun to hide the horror of this crime.

I wrote these words a few months after moving to Altamira. Being in the Amazon is always an experience of the body. I only managed to (almost) fully unravel what it is to be a woman in a society like Brazil's when I connected with the forest and the women of the forest. Deforestation, the destruction of nature, the contamination of rivers with mercury and pesticides—this became a lived experience of violence within my own body as well, within me. This was the first sign I too was converting back into forest.

It has been an extreme experience, one that has forced me to travel my path backward and perceive my composition as a woman through a body carved from a long series of physical, psychological, and symbolic acts of violence. I am not someone unaccustomed to reflecting on herself, it must be said. I've been in psychoanalysis for over thirty years. My experience on the couch, however, takes place through a body that isn't ever touched during this connection with the unconscious. Words are mediators that both betray and protect us in their confrontation with the flesh. Even when European Western tradition (where psychoanalysis comes from) proposes to challenge taboos, it keeps the body static and under control, well-behaved and protected in the analyst's office, reinforcing the idea that what is most important takes place somewhere else in our complex geography.

Being in the Amazon thrust me into another type of unraveling. As I said earlier in this "image skin" called a book, not for one second will the forest let us forget we are body. The impossibility of escape is just that, an impossibility. There is no way to cover our skin when the heat index is one hundred degrees. There we are, nearly naked, always sweating, burning, making contact with other beings, wanting. Water, food, a shower, rest, other bodies. Our feet are on the ground and everything else is rubbing up against something living or being touched by something living. Our body and our mind, separated by the walls of Western philosophy, join up again, merge. Better put, they no longer exist as distinct categories. It's an event.

I only understood the forest as woman when I understood myself as woman in the forest, when I began what I might call my reforestation, meaning another way of comprehending myself in the world, with the world—*being* world. In November 2019, I gave an interview to an original program called *Córtex*, in which the interviewer, Bruno Torturra; the camera operator, Miguel Pinheiro; the director, Susana Jeha; and I traced my paths around Altamira while we chatted. It was only toward the end that I managed to articulate why I had moved to the Amazon—or made myself into Amazon. "Because I want to *unwhiten* myself," I said. I know I'll die failing at this task, but I went to the Amazon to become another experience of myself by decolonializing my body, understood here as the body of the forest as well—or a body in the forest.

For me, the destruction of the Amazon has become a personal matter, and I've come to understand the corrosion of the forest as the corrosion of my own body, and not just in an intellectual sense. Or rhetorical sense. I've come to understand myself as forest. Understanding myself as an expanded reality has led me to the realization that the fight for the forest is the fight against the patriarchy, against feminicide, against racism, and against gender binarism. And also against the centrality of the human person. In more than one sense, this book harbors the desire to make the Amazon a personal matter for those reading it.

It was the experience of being a woman, this experience of being a colonized body regardless of geography, color, or social class, that was my first point of contact with the forest and the women of the forest. What we had in common, despite all the differences between our worlds, was the colonization of our bodies.

I was no longer split apart in the struggle. I fought for the Amazon because without the world's biggest tropical rainforest, there is no way we can control global heating and thus, without the Amazon, we will have a hostile future. I still fight for this self-evident truth, which I never tire of repeating in my articles. But now I also fight for the Amazon because the Amazon is me and all who exist, people both human and nonhuman—all livingkind.

The notion of human centrality, as if we had won the perpetual right to be special, loses ballast when we start reforesting ourselves. This vertical, hierarchical perspective has guided the ruling humanity into the current climate crisis, pushing the very species that considers itself creation's masterpiece to the brink of extinction. It makes no sense. Except, of course, as a way of sustaining the supremacy of one specific human over genders, races, and species. Today, any dispute surrounding this model of humanity is immaterial because the model now threatens the very survival of the species.

The verb *Amazonize* goes well beyond the forest. It is a movement to return to being, and to being a part—rather than being apart, as we are when we place ourselves outside of nature, no longer part of the organic whole of a living planet. The more sensitive among us feel this uprooting in our guts. It is no accident that many feel "different" when they are "close" to nature.

What I want to say is that reforesting yourself—or Amazonizing yourself—is a radical movement. If it isn't radical, it will not be. The battle for the Amazon is not a fight for sustainable development. This is the term used by those who deem it possible to climb out of the abyss without relinquishing the capitalist system that threw us into it. Sustainable development is a palatable discourse that allows everything to proceed as is, with a few cosmetic changes but no radical transformations to structural inequality between genders, races, and species.

The great Indigenous thinker Ailton Krenak causes "cool" audiences and people who consider themselves green to gnash their teeth when he says "sustainability is personal vanity." Every single corporation today, including the most destructive, has a director, a manager, an entire department of sustainability. This is part of capitalism's ability to co-opt and adapt. Always something else asinine. In the words of Krenak:

> We've formed such an immense constellation of consumerism that, one day, Mother Nature said. "hold on, are you going to destroy ecological equilibrium, which sustains everyone and everything that can possibly exist here? Are you going to scrutinize the production of life and decide just how many life-sustaining resources each one of us can get? And from this position of egregious inequality, are you going to go around regulating access to water, oxygen, food, soil?" And so, acknowledging this began to put limits on our ambition.
>
> One way that humans have managed to regulate these ecologies was by creating methods of categorical control—for example, the idea that there's such a thing as "an environment" and that this universe is something you can regulate. And within this "environment," there's the notion that some natural resources and vital sources of life can also be measured, evaluated and certified, including with certificates of sustainability.
>
> If you draw water from the Guarani Aquifer, for example, it'll be very good quality water, and if you bottle it properly, then you are a "sustainable company." But who ever said that drawing water from the Guarani Aquifer is "sustainable"? Corporations incite violence at the source and receive a certificate of sustainability along the way. It's the same thing with wood. This is a dirty trick! There is no such thing as sustainable groundwater extraction, and there is no such thing as sustainable logging.
>
> We are an unsustainable civilization. We are unsustainable. How are we ever going to produce anything in equilibrium?

The battle for the Amazon, the reforestation of selves, and the Amazonization of the world is a movement to overthrow the hegemony of Western, patriarchal, white, masculine, and binary thought, which has ruled the planet in recent millennia—and exterminated, silenced, or driven to the margins all other forms of perceiving oneself in, for, and with the world. The battle for the Amazon is the battle to reforest worlds—outer ones and inner ones.

7. fierce life

It is time to tell you what a quilombola is—this other way of being in the world as a human person.

This particular quilombola body, the body of Maria do Socorro da Silva, holds the history of the ravaging of the Amazon. And it also holds what came before. It is likewise a record of fierce resistance made flesh. Socorro is fierce. She is one of those I call women of fierce life. When she tells her story, Socorro brings pain to her listener's body. It is as if the words, as they issue from her mouth, inscribe themselves on her listener's skin with a sharp point. After she falls silent and goes back to covering her fearsome jaguar eyes with the long black hair she says she never combs, her words still throb away inside the other's body. She, Socorro's body, persists. Skinny and shaky. Ravaged, like the forest, in all senses.

Socorro's story began long before she was born. Her ancestors were among the nearly five million enslaved Africans who arrived in Brazil from the sixteenth through nineteenth centuries. The ones who arrived alive. Hundreds of thousands died along the way and were eaten by fish—even their flesh was stolen, down to the bones, until their bones turned to salt.

In no other place was slavery practiced to such an extent as in the Portuguese Empire's portion of the Americas. This past was a present continuous even after the "independence" of Brazil, the last country in the Americas to formally abolish slavery, in 1888. Tens of thousands of enslaved Africans revolted against the horror of a life in chains and the swiftness of death that came even for those who resigned themselves to the yoke. They fled. And to avoid capture, they ventured deep into every forest, treading through regions only the Indigenous had reached.

These enclaves of rebels were called *quilombos* and the rebels, quilombolas. The only holiday honoring a Black hero in Brazil recognizes the importance of Zumbi, leader of Brazil's largest quilombo, Palmares, in Northeast Brazil, established at the height of the enslavement of Black Africans. In the seventeenth century, Palmares was home to twenty thousand rebels. In 1660, Rio de Janeiro, then the country's largest city, had a population of seven thousand, lending an idea of the size and strength of this resistance by those who refused to be slaves—and the fear it inspired.

Aquilombar-se—to become as a quilombo—is used as a reflexive verb in today's Brazil, conjugated in the plural by those who resist by coming together in enclaves of insurrection. A reference word for Black movements, it has also come to be invoked by everyone who fights against different forces of oppression and destruction. So to Amazonize yourself is also to quilombize yourself.

The Amazon wasn't the only destination for quilombolas. Northeast Brazil, epicenter of the enslavement of bodies to exploit sugar cane, had even more quilombos. For the slaves who rebelled in the Amazon, the forest was not fatherland but motherland, because it was a womb. The oral memory of the elders who settled the region of Barcarena, in the state of Pará, harbors echoes of life inside slave quarters on the region's sugar plantations and of life on the Jesuit mission of Gibirié, where priests began their efforts to convert the Indigenous in the early eighteenth century. In this patchwork of memories stitched together by ear, the priests forced everyone to be baptized, get married, and kneel down. But they never managed to thoroughly subjugate these people. Black people continued to quilombize, even when they could only do it inside themselves.

Socorro is the quilombola daughter of this story. And as a quilombola, she is part of the traditional communities of the forest. There are the *original peoples*, the ones called Indigenous, who were in the Amazon and all the other regions of Brazil before Brazil existed—and thus before the invaders arrived, before 1500. And then there are those called *traditional communities*, who came to the Amazon and other regions in the following centuries, a result of the colonizers' interventions. In the Amazon, almost every quilombola is also Indigenous. It is not possible to understand the Amazon without conjoining the identities of these peoples who have been beaten down for centuries but never vanquished.

Being discovered is the curse of all those who can only exist if they are forgotten. This is what Socorro discovered in the late 1970s, when she first heard the word *progress*. For the business-military dictatorship then ruling Brazil, the forest was the body they could rip everything from, especially ore. People like Socorro didn't exist for the white elites, except to be ravaged like the forest. Socorro made her own discovery at the age of thirteen, when the men from the mining company arrived, bringing progress to people they didn't consider people. "I'd never seen silk clothes before, I'd never seen leather shoes, or handsome men. That day I did. Pretty watches," she says. "And in they came. . . . They opened roads, tore everything up. That's how I saw this land butchered."

They were foreigners, speaking a language she still doesn't know where from. They were Brazilians from São Paulo and Rio de Janeiro, almost as gringo as the others. Her young girl's body was handed over to them, like the bodies of other dark-skinned children. Her uncle said that was how it was, and he benefited from it. And that was how it was. Then Socorro became a slave to an outsider who rammed himself between her legs. "When I went to school, he'd give me notebooks. When I went someplace, it was clothes. When he traveled to that big city and came back, he'd bring me a watch, a beautiful skirt. . . . That's when I saw I was becoming his property. I told my aunt, 'You changed me.'" When Socorro tells me of the rape, she says: "I don't know his name. I just remember he spoke Brazilian." So many decades later, Socorro still remembers and feels the rape. The rape is still raping her.

They put at least one child in her and forced her to rip it out; they put more in other girls. She remembers the cramping from the abortion. Those men sowed fetuses because they could ram their cocks into Black girls' vaginas, but they didn't want their whiteness sullied by DNA they didn't consider wholly human.

Then Socorro realized that what was happening to the forest was happening to her. Raped like her, bored into like her, its uterus grievously assaulted to rip out gold. Socorro saw herself melded with the forest, flesh of the same flesh. And she understood herself as forest. Not as forest poetically, as a turn of phrase. Not a metaphor. But literally: forest. Then she became Socorro do Burajuba, the name of her quilombo.

In March 2018, the Evandro Chagas Institute, part of the Brazilian Health Ministry, found that the Murucupi River is contaminated with high levels of aluminum, iron, copper, arsenic, mercury, and lead. Although the Brazilian courts shut down some of the production at Alunorte, which was suspected of leaking toxic waste, it has since resumed. Hydro companies have been repeatedly charged with environmental contamination over the years, but the battle is lopsided. It always has been. The company contests the institute's report, denies any contamination, and claims its practices are "environmentally sustainable."

The quilombolas of Barcarena have charged that no-stick pots and pans, beer barrels, and plane parts all contain a bit of their blood. But the wealthy portion of the world is hard of hearing. When Socorro hears the word *Norway*, her whole body stiffens up. When she is with climate activists, they find her horror puzzling. Like the mythological figure of Hydra, Norway has several heads, and one of them is an environmental defender. The Norwegian government has invested millions of dollars in protecting the Amazon rainforest. Socorro is a social movement leader, and when she traveled to the land of her demons to attend a climate crisis event, she says she took two bottles of water along and offered one to a Norsk Hydro director: "Do you want to drink my water or yours?" He didn't choose hers.

If Is w If Socorro were the forest's mirror. Like her, every year its body suffers a bit more devastation. Every year there's less of one and less of the other. Today, the once beautiful region of Barcarena is a devoured landscape where poisoned rivers die, and kill whoever drinks from them. Like Socorro, who has discovered a kidney cancer that eats a bit of her each day. "And you know how I got it? It came from heavy metals. Because I am forest people. I drink water from the river, I bathe in the river, I make food with river water. Many people in my family have cancer." Were Socorro not so fierce, she would be sad. "I'm the descendant of slaves and the granddaughter of Indians. I'm strange like that. I'm difficult."

At a gathering in Terra do Meio to discuss the centrality of the Amazon in the climate collapse, Socorro spoke to young climate activists who had come from Europe: "I want you to understand something well. Without us, the peoples of the forest, there is no river, there are no animals, there's nothing. If you want to normalize the planet's temperature, you have to take care of us. Because without us there is no future generation."

The youth who decry their parents' and grandparents' inaction in Europe listened as the quilombola recounted the horror of those who know they have been sacrificed, those who, like Socorro, know time is up. Like parts of the Amazon, they are beyond the point of no return. "Every day we drink water and every day we die a little. My generation eats and drinks contaminated food and water, so your generation won't have to eat or drink this water or this food."

The body of this now depleted forest is like Socorro's body, where nothing is born but tumors. Socorro knows that, like the forest where she lives, she is already dead. And because she is fierce, she sharpens her nails and fights so the next generation can live.

24. confession

I have no doubt that all women around the world can tell the story of their lives through the violence they have experienced. Some, it's true, have normalized things so much that they don't even realize what they experienced was violence. While the numbers are underestimated, because gender violence is still shrouded in silence, statistics indicate that Brazil is especially brutal for women. No surprise, given that Brazil is brutal for all the majorities who are treated like minorities and for all the minorities who are reduced to the category of subhumanity.

As I listened to the women of Altamira and the region, I saw that the intensity of this violence was unprecedented. I arrived there after more than thirty years of reporting, some of that time devoted to listening to women in different geographies across Brazil, as well as to a much smaller number of them in other countries. Sexual violence and physical and psychological abuse are common in their accounts, a horror that shouldn't surprise us given the number of denunciations spurred by movements like #MeToo in the United States, *Ni Una Menos* (Not one less) in Argentina and other Latin American countries, and *Meu Primeiro Assédio* (My first harassment) in Brazil.

In Altamira, however, I began encountering narratives of abuse or rape in almost all my interviews with women. Some took years to tell me about the violence they had suffered; others told me upon first contact. I wasn't interviewing these women to investigate sexual violence and I didn't ask a single question about it. I listened to them tell of their lives in the forest, their lives after they were expelled from the forest, or their pilgrimages before they reached the forest. For most of them, abuse or rape was their first so-called sexual experience, generally involving a family member or family acquaintance. This information shows there is so much more sexual violence than we realize, even today, when these denunciations have taken on a voice and a body—and taken to the streets as well.

This is what I have perceived in my experience from listening, not from a study conducted in accordance with statistical criteria. I don't actually think these women would answer this kind of survey candidly. My gauge here is built upon my entire lifetime of experience devoted to reporting, and it helps suggest pathways for further investigation and analysis. What I have heard is that sexual violence is not an exception in women's lives. It is the rule. And that changes everything, because abuse and rape have been treated as exceptions.

This discovery had a huge impact on me. It became a regular part of my life to listen to accounts of rape, even when I wanted to know about the healing power of plants or the contamination of fish in the river. As I went about organizing my life as a town resident, these testimonies began to go beyond my listenings as a reporter. If I was having my nails done at the salon, the manicurist would tell me she had been abused by her uncle. If I started talking to a clerk in a store, suddenly, standing there, I would hear an appalling first-person account. There was one day when I heard three accounts of rape, two of them outside the context of an interview. Sometimes I had to close myself up at home for a while to make space for the words they had entrusted to me, before I risked going out and listening to new testimonies about how being a woman and being raped are synonymous for many.

I should explain what "listening" means to me. In my opinion, it is the journalist's main tool. Before I can reach someone else, I try to empty myself out—of my worldview, my beliefs, my biases. Of course this emptying out is not complete, because it's impossible to completely abandon a cultural body. But the movement, the effort, is fundamental. It is what allows me to let someone else's narrative occupy my body *as* someone else's narrative and *not as* someone else's narrative distorted by what my beliefs or biases won't let me hear. Otherwise, I can't accomplish this other experience in existing.

When I listen, I "lend" my body to the other's words. It resembles the experience of possession, but it is not. My body, me, is an active mediator of the other voice. Of course, when I turn this voice into my written word, this delicate mediation will be present. It is the other's narrative, the other's experience, the other's words, after passing through my body. But my body is not an absolute vacuum, through which the other's narrative passes without being altered by the experience of passing through me.

I don't pretend to be empty packaging; I know how false that is. The movement of emptying myself out to reach another person and let the words produced by this other experience in being inhabit me, and only then making the trip back, requires a great deal of effort to accomplish, both the leaving and the returning. After reading one of my books, a psychoanalyst attending a book-signing event said, "You're an *escutadeira*—a listen-*eer*!" I consider this the best definition of my movement of listening as a reporter.

Of course, I too am altered by this experience. If that weren't the case, nothing would make sense. After all these years, I believe I can say that people sense the honesty of the intentions behind this movement, this language of the unsaid, this back-and-forth. People are in the habit of telling me things they tell few people, sometimes no one, and this has repeatedly put me in tough ethical positions. Sometimes I forget to "turn off" this movement inside me, and I go off to do something prosaic, like grocery shopping, with the button still on. Then I'm surprised to hear the confessions of strangers, who approach me with the pretext of talking about the price of potatoes but on their second sentence will vent about something intimate.

I must admit I don't like it when this happens, because at moments like this I'm not prepared, and I end up feeling what the other person feels. I try hard to remember to "close" this door when I'm not working. But it's different during interviews. I'm prepared. As I've already said, this doesn't mean that what I listen to from this position doesn't change me. It does, and a lot. You don't go into someone else's world with impunity.

When I read Davi Kopenawa's lengthy interview with Bruce Albert (their relationship itself is a delicate, deeply respectful web entwining narrator and listener), I noticed several times that Davi reiterated his fear of "becoming other" when he went into the white world, to big cities in Europe or the United States, where he traveled in the company of his stronger *xapiripë* so they could protect him from this conversion (as well). I imagine that when Davi talks about "becoming other" as he enters this world that he decodifies as dangerous and hostile—not out of bias but as someone who truly suffers the action of white people—it means something different to him than to me. I've witnessed many Indigenous people "becoming other" in their contact with whites, a contact often intended to corrupt well beyond a monetary sense alone.

For me, however, "becoming other" is inescapable. It is, at one and the same time, the grace and the risk of being a "listeneer." I've chosen a way of intervening in the world (what they call "work") that demands I become other without leaving myself completely at the same time. I have chosen to live in the *between-worlds*—or in the *between-bodies*. Often, this gives me a lot. Sometimes, however, it rips chunks right out of me. This is what happened when I began leading a daily life in which the raping of women was a fact of daily life itself. My body aches in Altamira. I ache.

In Altamira, the struggle against the destruction of the forest and the struggle against the destruction of women are one and the same. Once again, this is no coincidence. The logic of destruction does not distinguish between the body to be destroyed, forest or woman. This is a structural element of the system that conforms the world. More than needing to be changed, this system must be toppled, because violence is not just one more statistic but the very structure underpinning the entire edifice.

Altamira, for all that it is (something I explore in depth in a coming chapter), radicalizes what happens in other regions of Brazil and in our globalized world. It is an exception neither in Brazil nor in the rest of the world, but rather a kind of harbinger, in its rawness laying shamelessly bare what is still partially hidden elsewhere or what is still in the process of being uncovered. Even before I moved to this Amazonian city, I had learned to observe Altamira so I could comprehend what was underway in the world—and anticipate it.

0. resistance

This book can be understood as a narrative of massacres, in which the peoples of the forest often end up defeated, if not thoroughly destroyed. Violence and extermination weave the history of the white invasion of the Amazon with threads of blood. But this is only the most obvious interpretation, and since I don't like being interpreted superficially, I will joyfully commit the sin of guiding your reading. It's a fact that I am recounting a routine of violence that has left marks of brutality for centuries. But this is not my focus, or I would hardly be interested. When we read a narrative about acts of violence, our first perception is precisely this, that it is only about violence, injustice, and annihilation. That's easiest, because it's what everyone already knows; Brazil is a violent country, and the Amazon burns on screens around the world. Whatever is on the tip of our minds is what appears first, because it saves us time and effort. Over and done, understood.

But this isn't what I write about—or it is, but not primarily. I write about resistance. About how to make life possible despite all the many forms of death—or, in the case of the original peoples in Brazil, despite efforts to kill them in every way possible for more than five hundred years. This journey through the Amazon, far beyond geography, is also an investigation into acts of possible resistance at the moment we are experiencing the impossibilities created by the climate emergency and sixth mass extinction.

Just before the 2018 runoff elections in Brazil, a Portuguese journalist asked Ailton Krenak how the Indigenous would manage if Jair Bolsonaro was elected, since the then-candidate had declared he "wouldn't demarcate one more square centimeter" of Indigenous land. Krenak replied: "What I'm worried about is whether whites will resist. We, the Indigenous, have been resisting for five hundred years." He knows what he's talking about. In the nineteenth century, Prince Regent Dom João, future Dom João VI, king of Portugal, wrote a royal letter in which he placidly declared that the Botocudos (the branch to which the Krenak people belong) should be exterminated. "An offensive war" were the lovable sovereign's words.

This is how Ailton Krenak sums up more than five centuries of resistance:

> The Indigenous population in that region [Vale do Rio Doce, in Minas Gerais] was estimated at five thousand in the late nineteenth century. Only 140 individuals made it to the twentieth century. It was as if a bomb fell on Europe and only one hundred thousand people were left to tell the story. We were the victims of genocide and there is no way to tally this. The Krenak are back to a total of 120 families [today]. If we figure five people per family, there are a little over five hundred of us. We live inside a small reservation, segregated by the Brazilian government, in a little concentration camp the state made for the Krenak to survive in. During the dictatorship, it became a reeducation camp, which was actually a torture center. We've suffered so many outrages that one more now won't rattle us.

Brazil is a country founded atop human bodies, first of the Indigenous and then of enslaved Black Africans. And so too is the part of the Amazon that Brazil has (dis)placed inside its territory. But this is a limited way of seeing Brazil and the Amazon. I prefer looking at things inside out.

For many decades, the Brazilian elites enforced the myth of "racial democracy," an ideological fabrication with no basis in reality. Schoolchildren were taught—and shockingly still are—that what we call the Brazilian people comprises three races: white, Black, and Indigenous. And that they lived—and live—together in harmony. Facts prove there never was any harmony, or even any real living together; there were never any connections, just confrontations. Fifty-six percent of the Brazilian population is Black, but Black people occupy subaltern positions in society and are underrepresented in its parliament, its institutions, and throughout all areas. Black people are also the ones who die more from disease and violence, who have lower educational levels, are paid the lowest wages, more often live in homes lacking sanitation, and whose quality of life and life expectancy are the lowest. It is Black people who die more—and sooner.

In November 2020, when Bolsonaro was asked to comment on the murder of Beto Freitas by white security guards at a Carrefour supermarket in Porto Alegre, he once again invoked miscegenation as the generator of racial democracy. The presidential liar reaffirmed Brazil's favorite lie by denying that racism was involved when a Black man was killed while out buying groceries: "We're a miscegenated people. Whites, Blacks, mulattoes, and Indians make up the body and spirit of a rich, wonderful people." Bolsonarism is also a reaction to an extremely tardy attempt by part of Brazilian society to address racism.

The destruction of the Amazon can, and should, be understood as a moment when the colonial extermination project is proving stronger and more persistent. Admitting that the nation was built on at least two genocidal processes, against Indigenous peoples and against Black people, is progress—recent progress, and even so, limited to the most progressive slice of society. And while it is progress, it is a white perspective. We must subvert this perspective to see things better. What we call Brazil is a monumental example of resistance. Or, looking at it inside out to get back to the right side, Brazil was thrown at the Indigenous peoples—and Black people were thrown into Brazil. And even so,

Indigenous and Black people have resisted for centuries. Not only have they resisted, they've remolded Brazil.

During a brilliant talk, the anthropologist Marcio Goldman provided an accurate measure of their movement, covered up by many of his peers:

> While there is some dispute about the numbers, it is not at all unlikely that over the course of three hundred years, nearly ten million people were forced to board ships in Africa for the Americas, as part of the largest transoceanic migration in history. The point I would like to underscore here is that the four million–some people who may have reached what we now call Brazil encountered millions of Indigenous people here, victims of a genocide parallel to the African diaspora, processes that—it never hurts to remember—underpin the constitution of this world called modern. Within this history, which belongs to all of us, deadly powers of annihilation co-exist side by side with the vital powers of creativity. . . . The meeting of Africans and the Indigenous in the Americas is the result of the largest process of deterritorialization and reterritorialization in the history of humanity.

Today the Amazon is the frontier where the contemporary battle is being waged between the forces of destruction (represented by the extractivist, economic, political, and also intellectual elites; the religious and their churches, led by neo-Pentecostal Evangelicals; and large transnational corporations and the billionaires and supermillionaires with ties to them) and the forces of resistance, embodied by Indigenous peoples and traditional forest communities, such as quilombolas and beiradeiros.

This confrontation between destruction and resistance marked the onset of modernity, when Europeans invaded other worlds and divvied them up among themselves, like thieves splitting booty. Starting in the fifteenth century, various kingdoms destroyed nature—human peoples included—in what they called the New World, so they could expand and/or consolidate their power. In the process, they enslaved a portion of the original population and exported them like commodities to other colonies, where they became the labor forces used to exploit monetizable riches from territories taken by force. Body against body, nature against nature, perversely exhausting one in the effort to exhaust the other.

Using riches from other peoples' lands, which had been seized and converted into colonies, they achieved the Industrial Revolution and laid the foundations of capitalism, which centuries later would produce the climate emergency and the sixth mass extinction. For the first time ever, human action has triggered both a climate crisis and the annihilation of life by producing a globalized consumer society dependent on fossil fuels. We then became a species that eats its own home.

Since human life is moved by paradoxes, the same Northern world that in the past destroyed the Southern world is now the world where an awareness of the climate abyss has pushed the youngest generation into the streets, where it began holding school climate strikes in the second half of 2018. Today, Christopher Columbus's world is the world of Swedish environmental activist Greta Thunberg and Extinction Rebellion. The intellectual elites— just like the intellectualized middle classes in a Europe that grew rich off the blood of the nature they called America—are now the chief allies of the peoples who first resisted their forces of destruction. The banzeiro whirls round and round in what some insist on calling History, with a capital *H*.

What I am focused on here is the monumental resistance waged for more than five centuries by the original peoples of the forest—who also originated the forest, since they planted part of it—and by the people who converted themselves into forest, like the Black people who rebelled against slavery. Today, faced with a planet in climate anguish, scientists and climate activists, a large number of them teens, have joined this resistance. When the dominant minority of humans became a force of destruction capable of altering the planet's climate, they forged a hostile future for the whole of the species—and likewise for all the other species, who have contributed nothing whatsoever to global heating.

This book takes a side, in the sense that it proposes a broader perspective on the Amazon that can serve as an instrument in the dispute for a less brutal future for the majority of human and nonhuman peoples.

100. we are NOT all in the same boat

Ii Is Imperative that we delineate this century's confrontation precisely, a confrontation in which the Amazon is a leading protagonist. The matter is often presented as if the climate collapse had been caused by each and every single human. In turning the species into a generic category, the differences between the countless beings who make us up are erased, and so is the brutal inequality that has fashioned this tragedy.

The humans who have consumed the planet are a wealthy minority, mostly white, located in the global North, notably in Europe and the United States, and with ties to extractivist financial elites in countries of the South, the bulk of which were converted into nations by the colonial project. The humans who have consumed the planet are the same humans now erecting walls and redoubling legal barriers to keep the victims of their colonialism from entering their territories. The humans who have devoured Earth and today build ever more insurmountable walls are the ones who have produced climate refugees in the millions, a figure likely to multiply in the coming decades. Today, they use their power to transform their victims into threats, with the support of frightened, impoverished populations in their own countries. Once again, it is Black and Indigenous peoples, the poorest and women, who are hit first and much more violently by global heating and the loss of biodiversity. This is what the United Nations has called "climate apartheid"—and it assails the whole planet.

One of the biggest lies of the century is this commonplace sentiment: "With the climate crisis, we're all in the same boat." No, we're not. We're not at all. Just as we weren't during the COVID-19 pandemic, which killed more Black and poor people from the outset. And just as we won't be in the other, coming pandemics, a consequence of the destruction of nature and the capitalist processes by which people and commodities circulate.

The fact that must be affirmed loudly and clearly whenever possible is that when it comes to addressing and adapting to the climate crisis, most people have tiny paper boats whereas the minority, who provoked the crisis, have high-tech luxury yachts. While the number of climate refugees is growing, produced by droughts and floods as well as by the hunger and violence that follow in their wake, supermillionaires and billionaires are building bunkers in "paradises" like New Zealand to protect themselves from climate disruption and any violence on the part of the wretched it will produce. And, of course, to keep their privileges intact even to the end of the world. Apocalypse, yes, but in a climatized environment while imbibing the finest wine.

666. the end of the world isn't the end. it's the middle

In a public interview I once did with Eduardo Viveiros de Castro—
one of the most original voices in contemporary anthropology—he
said: "The Indigenous are experts in the end of the world, because
their world ended in 1500." These words resonated hard within
me, but they only became fully clear when I began my life in the
Amazon and was captured by the banzeiro.

While Viveiros de Castro's statement is acidly ironic, it is also
precise. When the Portuguese landed in what they would call Brazil,
it is estimated that millions of people were already living there, different people speaking different languages, part of a human occupation stretching back thousands of years. Researchers calculate
that 90 percent of the original population was exterminated in the
sixteenth and seventeenth centuries by the viruses and bacteria
that traversed the ocean aboard the invaders' bodies.

During the centuries that followed, under both the Portuguese
Empire and the republic established in Brazil in 1889—one year
after the formal abolition of slavery—the elites born of the colonial process believed in Indigenous assimilation and worked ar-
duously to achieve it. After genocide had wiped out most of them,
those who remained were supposed to vanish through ethnocide,
or cultural extermination—that is, when those who still are, quit
being what they are.

In everyday life and in Brazilian public policy, this alleged composition of the three races represented a project to "whiten" the
Brazilian population before it became too "dark." The nineteenth-
century immigration program that brought thousands of poor
Europeans to Brazil, with higher rates of Germans and Italians,

was part of the policy to "cleanse" the Brazilian people. Both Indigenous and Black peoples were supposed to be subjugated genetically (as well) by the superior race.

To the authorities, it seemed easier to eliminate the Indigenous through assimilation, since their numbers had already been over-whelmingly reduced through physical extermination. Black people represented a bigger "problem," since slavery had cast millions of them into Brazil, where they were bred as a labor force for four centuries, much like the cattle industry today, but with extra doses of explicit cruelty. Up through the mid-twentieth century, the elites remained thoroughly convinced that the blood of the surviving Indigenous would be diluted in the whitening process.

In 1934, Claude Lévi-Strauss—the Frenchman who would later be deemed the father of structuralism and the world's leading name in anthropology—had an enlightening conversation with the Brazilian ambassador in Paris, Luís Martins de Sousa Dantas. At a dinner on the eve of his departure for São Paulo, the young Lévi-Strauss asked the diplomat about the Indigenous in Brazil. Much to his astonishment and consternation, he received the following reply: "Indians? Alas, my dear sir, they all disappeared years ago. This is a very sad, very shameful episode in the history of my country. . . . As a sociologist, you will discover fascinating things in Brazil, but forget about the Indians. You won't come across a single one."

As we can ascertain from this parlor talk, the Brazilian in-tellectual elite believed the process of genocide had been com-pleted. Not the case. The Indigenous peoples resisted all forms of death, as they continue resisting today. Lévi-Strauss, as his fas-cinating life story tells us, did indeed meet Indigenous peoples in Brazil. Based on this experience, he wrote masterpieces like *Tristes Tropiques*.

In 1964, exactly thirty years after this conversation between the Brazilian diplomat and French anthropologist, a business-military coup ushered in a dictatorship that would kill over eight thousand Indigenous people. Their extermination came by bullet and also by epidemics unleashed in various regions of the country, because they were in the way of the project to exploit the Amazon and other ecosystems. According to some accounts, clothing contaminated with smallpox was airdropped into their villages.

And yet the Indigenous resisted. In recent decades, the original populations have once again begun growing in number in Brazil. But the attacks on Indigenous peoples never stopped, not even with the country's return to democracy. While it is not official, the policy of whitening remains in effect; it shapes both how authorities perceive color and what concrete actions they take. At least twice during the 2018 election campaign, four-star general Antônio Hamilton Mourão, then vice presidential candidate on the Bolsonaro ticket, proved how much this concern persists. On the first occasion, he associated Black people with *malandragem*—akin to hustling or deceitfulness—and the Indigenous with "indolence," while at the same time declaring himself "Indigenous." On another occasion, when introducing his grandson to the press, he said: "My grandson is a good-looking guy, y'know. The whitening of the race."

For General Mourão, this remark was so "natural," and also so obvious, that he didn't even realize he was committing a racist act. The coup-mongering skill of the generals in Bolsonaro's administration was a surprise only to those who hadn't seen them in the Amazon, where, even after democracy was restored in Brazil, their commanders continued to behave like they were the country's top authorities, and they were treated as such by the civilian authorities. Never entirely abandoned by subsequent democratic governments, the dictatorship's policy for the Amazon was renewed under Bolsonaro's militarized administration.

When COVID-19 hit, Indigenous lands were left vulnerable to the virus. The government not only refused to draw up an immediate plan to protect the original peoples; it also vetoed proposals involving basic rights, like providing them access to emergency hospital beds and drinking water. It even rejected an information campaign that was to be released in various Indigenous languages. Several requests were lodged with the International Criminal Court calling for Bolsonaro, Mourão, and other Brazilian government officials to be investigated for genocide and other crimes against humanity because of their deliberate negligence during the pandemic.

Viveiros de Castro's memorable statement shows that attacks against original peoples never ceased, from 1500 to today. And so Indigenous worlds have ended more than once. For some ethnic groups, the most recent apocalypse was triggered when they were deliberately left exposed to the disease. Because Bolsonaro used the virus as an unexpected biological weapon in his plan to destroy original peoples, in the future he will likely be considered the author of one of the deadliest attacks on Indigenous populations in the past five hundred years. Many of the elders who taught their people to resist, who safeguarded their culture, and who were in some cases the last to speak their language, died of COVID-19. People like Aritana Yawalapiti, Paulinho Paiakan, and Aruká Juma fell like the forest's great trees.

I only grasped the full depth of this idea that the Indigenous know how to live beyond the end of the world when I began to live in the Amazon and share life with the peoples of the forest, when the banzeiro sucked me in and I had to decide if I would reject the vortex and return to my illusory safety zone of hyperurban life in São Paulo. Brazil's biggest city is a monstrosity where more than twelve million inhabitants walk or drive over rivers that have been buried and cemented over—as well as along rivers that still reach the surface but only in the form of sewage. It is also Brazil's only cosmopolitan city and a laboratory where resistance is bred in its violent yet fascinating peripheries. I always loved São Paulo, which welcomed me into its concrete arms when I, at the age of thirty-three, arrived there from far southern Brazil. I always loved it, and I still do.

I realized, however, that I no longer had any choice. There was no way I could return, either to a life that no longer existed or to the woman I no longer was. My decision had been made much earlier, when I started traveling to Altamira more and more, drawn by forces I couldn't yet name. The banzeiro was already dragging me in, even when I lived thousands of miles from the Xingu. The day I set foot in Altamira to stay, I didn't know it, but I had unconsciously flung myself into its swirling.

To summon the courage to consummate my transition in physical terms too, I convinced myself the move would be temporary, just for a year. I'd be like someone who travels to Europe or the United States to do their doctorate at a major university and then returns with a diploma that lends them a "first world" shine and fluency in a more influential language than Portuguese. I would be doing the exact opposite by venturing deep into Brazil, but I was labeling my move as temporary and leaving myself the chance to go back to my home and established life in my own more-than-comfy apartment and back to a marriage that had given me immense joy, intense intellectual exchange, and total companionship for fifteen years. I would return to São Paulo and continue down my path, but with one more experience amassed.

That's not how things went. My entire life was transfigured and not even my marriage survived the disruption. Altamira, the Xingu, and the Amazon haven't given me a home. My move didn't mean I'd reached the place where I really belonged. To the contrary. Altamira, the Xingu, and the Amazon have made me understand that there is no home for me so long as the entire planet is writhing, parts of it agonizing. I used to feel at home everywhere. I would easily set up a little house for myself at the hotel when I traveled as a reporter, and if the trip lasted a bit longer, I'd even make a circle of friends in temporary places, with a right to Sunday brunches with the family. That's over. Never again have I felt at home anywhere. And this has been one of the most challenging side effects of my plunge into the banzeiro. Clarity is a permanent state.

I can say that Altamira is the only part of the world that seems real to me. And in that sense, it is the only part of the world where I feel whole, even though I'm fully aware both of my fragmentation and of the fact that there are parts of myself where fractures will never heal. Everywhere else, be it a big city in Brazil, Europe, or the United States, I feel like I'm inside some kind of mockup, or at a resort or a Disney theme park. Reality is a planet undergoing an accelerated process of destruction. Sometimes, when I'm somewhere like London, Boston, San Francisco, or Berlin—a few of the cities I've visited in recent years—I want to yell at the "cool" people in the cafés and parks. A scene from the blockbuster movie *Titanic* flashes through my mind: the orchestra keeps playing for first-class passengers dressed in gala attire while the ship sinks.

Altamira is ruins. Like Brazil, Altamira is a constant building of ruins atop the most monumental of all ruins: the forest that once was there. Like all symbolic frontiers, Altamira is the world's vanguard. It was there that I finally understood, with my whole body, that the end of the world is not the end, but a middle where we might find a means.

I've learned to live in the midst of catastrophe, and this has made me a much more dangerous human. I've accelerated my process of adapting to the years and decades that will come, that are already coming, that arrived with the COVID-19 pandemic. Like the peoples of the forest—and like the peoples who were forest and today are forest in ruins—I don't want this catastrophe, and I fight against it. Yet I know I can survive it. Perhaps not as an individual, but in the way that matters most, collectively. I too am becoming fierce life.

13. in-betweens of the forest

It took me a while to get here, to this whorl of the whirling world where my love lies. As a journalist, I tell stories about the Indigenous and quilombolas. I listen to them. As an inhabitant of this planet, I often fight forest destruction alongside them. In 2004, however, I was captured by another way of being-and-becoming in the world: the traditional communities of the Amazon rainforest comprising the people known as beiradeiros. And I've made them not my object of study but the flesh and blood I've been examining in fascination, longer and closer up than other topics.

I've published a few reports about beiradeiros in English, and no matter how much I explain who this population is, readers and book reviewers alike end up referring to them as Indigenous. As if everything that is not us, whites, were therefore native. Even Brazilians have trouble grasping that neither the word *beiradeiro* (from *beira*, or edge) nor its synonym *ribeirinho* (from *ribeiro*, or stream) do not simply mean "one who lives on the edge of a river." So I realize I have to do a better job explaining things when I introduce this human forest existence that is an entire universe, a transmutation of people, the very birth of a way of being, an explosion of creativity, and a complex form of resistance.

To tell you about this third people of the forest, who are neither Indigenous nor quilombolas, I will start backward. In 2010, the government headed by Luiz Inácio Lula da Silva, of the Workers' Party, opened a public tender for the Belo Monte hydroelectric power plant, to be built on the Xingu River. The project had first been conceived by the business-military dictatorship (1964–1985), but no administration had ever managed to implement it, given resistance both by the Indigenous, especially the Kayapó people, and by social movements in the Altamira region. The resumption and execution of this project by the most leftist experience in government in the history of Brazilian democracy stands as eloquent proof that every ideological hue views the Amazon as a body to be dominated and exploited. Lula's idea of the Amazon, later shared by his successor, Dilma Rousseff, proved to differ little from that of the dictatorship's generals.

During the thirteen years that the Workers' Party remained in power, at least three large Amazon rivers—the Xingu, Madeira, and Teles Pires—were dammed up, and with tragic consequences. The Tapajós would have been next, had it not been for the monumental resistance both of the Indigenous Munduruku people (which shaped leaders like Maria Leusa) and of the beiradeiros in Montanha-Mangabal. In part, the hydro dam projects planned for the Tapajós basin were delayed as a result of the 2008 world economic crisis, which hit Brazil harder in the early 2010s, and also of Operation Carwash, an in-depth investigation of the connections between government sectors and large contractors, conducted jointly by the Federal Police and Public Prosecutor's Office. Pharaonic public works projects, rife with evidence of corruption and denunciations of Indigenous ethnocide, form a long chain of destruction that is far from ending.

Since 2011, beiradeiro families hit by Belo Monte have been my main subject in investigative journalism. I have been following some of them for almost ten years. Their battles, their suffering, their resistance. Their advances and retreats, their disputes and weaknesses. Births, disease, deaths. I have aged along with the adults, and with them have witnessed the crucial moment when children once of the forest become teens on the periphery of the city, taking a turn in the road from which there is no going back. The banzeiro teaches us that turns are never returns.

Belo Monte, dammer of lives, assaulted the forest and those who are forest, and continues to assault them more every day.

These people include the beiradeiros, who would like to destroy the dam and free the river so their lives can flow again. I am going to tell you about this third people of the Amazon rainforest through the story of this confrontation, which is likewise a story of annihilation and resistance, the two forces at work in the various Brazils. The beiradeiros are not "beings of the forest," like the original peoples who have had less contact with whites or have managed to better protect themselves from contact with whites. After observing beiradeiros for so many years, I came to the conclusion that they are the "in-betweens of the forest." "In-betweens" is the name, and the concept, I have woven as a way to better grasp these people who are the most invisible in the Amazon. When I write about them, my prose immediately turns poetic. I'm not asking permission, just letting you know.

When I write about the beiradeiros, I tell stories of lives dammed up by an ideology that was imposed by force. This ideology turned into thousands of tons of steel, concrete, and cement on the Xingu, one of the great rivers of the Amazon. They named this human monstrosity Belo Monte, Beautiful Mountain, because the act of naming things also contains violence. The sadism of calling a weapon of destruction "beautiful" also contains pleasure. So the people crushed by this dam have also resisted through words, renaming the jailer of the Xingu Belo Monstro— Beautiful Monster.

Beautiful Monster is a hydropower plant that produces energy only part of the year, because the rest of the year the water in the Xingu shrinks.

It dries up. Hides.

Beautiful Monster is built of ruins.

Brazil is a great builder of ruins.

Brazil builds ruins of continental proportions.

A while back, someone asked me what the river would say if it could talk. But when the river does talk, we don't understand. You have to inhabit the river's skin to hear it. But the whites who inhabit it are only microbes, sometimes fungi, a trifling thing living in the river's pores. We walk atop the river's flesh but don't truly inhabit it. Because we cannot grasp the language of the river. For us, everything is indistinguishable noise.

And then the river is dynamited.

This language, we whites can identify.

And there is a far-off aching.

And everything falls silent.

The river is not completely dead. But it sounds like death. Because we can't even hear its murmur. The silence of the Xingu makes a terrible noise. It leaves us in suspense, suspended. The silence of the Xingu is the immanence of something. On the edge of—

This is the point we are at.

The threshold.

The Xingu today is a threshold.

The Indigenous know it. Beiradeiros know it. Whites do not.

I tell the stories of dammed-up lives because I don't understand the river. My stories are born out of this impossibility of grasping the language of the Xingu. For nearly twenty years I have laid my body down in this river's language, rubbed my skin on its skin, tried to scratch it with my nails, and I know the Xingu is a woman.

But there is no language there for me. And so I listen to the people who have come closest to inhabiting the river. I listen to human peoples, the ones who have vocal cords like mine.

The first to show me that two words can have the same sequence of vowels and consonants and yet not be the same was a man named Otávio das Chagas—Otávio of the Stigmata. I would soon realize his name was a prophecy.

Otávio das Chagas was born on Ilha de Serra, one of the Xingu's hundreds of islands. And his body was defined by this experience, the experience of living on land, between waters.

Otávio was made small, four feet, nine inches, to camouflage into the forest and not weigh heavy on the belly of the river when slipping along in his canoe. Whenever Otávio returned to land, he knew the river had fewer fish tickling its body of water. And he thanked it for the generosity of the food.

I met the man after Beautiful Monster had wrenched him away. I don't know if you've ever seen a man who's been wrenched. It's terrible. The horror doesn't lie in his image but in the feelings he stirs, because his body is wholly there yet he's missing parts.

Otávio was already living with his family on the poor periphery of Altamira, in a rented house. It was 2014 and Otávio, then over sixty, was discovering his first hunger. Belo Monte had converted him into a fisher with no river and no fish.

Otávio spoke but couldn't find language. So he vanished down the tight hallway of his house and returned with a plastic binder, where he kept the white people's words. Trapped in papers he couldn't decipher, these words were tearing chunks from his life. Otávio was there, on the margins, penned in between violence and trash, because he had signed a paper he couldn't read. Spots on the paper, spots he couldn't decipher, had stolen everything from him.

The binder held Otávio das Chagas's stray bullets. Bullets on target. Written words fired at the bodies of the unlettered by the owners of pens.

Otávio showed these to me because he believed I could decipher the documents and explain how it was possible for sheets of paper to rob him of everything, even what life knew of him. But I'm not a good reader of death sentences perpetrated in an attorney's hand. Not knowing how to explain the impossible, I asked about life. Otávio wanted to tell me something, but the words reached me crisscrossed. They fell on my ears but said nothing. They were words riddled with holes.

We had lost each other in that house of despair.

All around us, Altamira roared. It was already the most violent city in Brazil. But we didn't know that yet.

His son Francisco gestured, pointing to his own body. Here. This scar is from when an axe fell on my foot there on the island. I was two.

Then I began traversing the terrain of their bodies with my ears, listening to Otávio das Chagas's scars.

I finally began to understand.

It was Otávio's stigmata that told me, because stigmata were all he had left.

His body was his name.

Otávio das Chagas, Otávio of the Stigmata, was a refugee from his own country. A refugee in his own country.

Please understand what I was slow to understand.

When someone is forced to leave their country, their fatherland or motherland, their soil, driven out by hunger, war, or epidemic, when the geopolitics of those who enjoy power and privileges on this planet wrench someone from their country, something remains.

Something is left.

There is a materiality that says this person lived. Even if it is ruins, even if it is their dead.

But when someone's island is drowned, as was Otávio das Chagas's case, memory becomes water.

There is nothing to lend materiality to their existence.

Everything that said Otávio had a life, loved Maria, fathered nine children, had been happy and sad, was almost violent but grew tame, all of that liquifies. Even his father's bones were lost, buried in the exact spot where they would erect the Belo Monte dam wall decades later. And then Otávio discovered that a body, his father's body, could be lost, crushed, and drowned, all at the same time. And so his dead father also had neither place nor matter anymore.

Back to his house that will never be a home, the one where we first met in Altamira: Otávio and his son Francisco were pointing to their own geography. They drew a map in their bones, their flesh, their skin. They told me each scar's story.

I understood, at that moment, that the horror of the Belo Monte refugees is the horror of being reduced to the territory of one's own body.

Otávio, already so fragile, so small, a man shrinking on the outside, would also have to make his body a tomb for his father. And with the immense space taken up by a father, Otávio's own territory was even further compressed.

The fisher with no river could count on nothing but the scars from his stigmata to say he existed. He was a man adrift in the dryness of the city, anchored only to himself.

What is the name of this act of violence?

Then I understood that these were word-scars. And ever since, I too have also listened to word-scars, my fingers touching letters of flesh.

A while back, I accompanied Otávio das Chagas and his family to Ilha de Serra, where he was born, a two-hour trip in a small motorboat. Today, the island lies beneath the Belo Monte dam wall. Only a tip of it is left. We navigated there after crossing the barrier by foot. But the security guards expelled us from the island because now they are the sentinels posted at every door.

They expelled Otávio das Chagas from the place they had previously taken from him by force and by fraud. They inflicted this further violence and declared they were doing it for the safety of Otávio das Chagas's body. The security guards hiding behind the company lanyards guaranteed they would wrench him from there once again, in order to—guess what—protect Otávio das Chagas. The monster that swallowed Otávio das Chagas's island then vomited him up. It didn't even want him in its belly, there where Otávio's life, like his father's bones, had already been shredded and dissolved into steel and concrete.

The dam wall literally crushed Otávio's existence, along with his father's bones. And when he was returned to the river in agony, he no longer knew if he was an undead or an unalive.

Now the river has a banzeiro.

Ever since they built ruins on the Xingu's body, there are times of the day when it rises up, twists its arms and legs in the arms and legs of the wind, there are butts and breasts too—this furious dance is almost erotic. The banzeiro doesn't let anyone by.

It is a whirlpool, a vortex.

The river expels everyone from its dammed body.

At these times, the river wants to be angry alone.

Otávio das Chagas's word-scars cast me into a banzeiro of inner waters, and that is where I am today. Writing—the writing that leaves marks on paper, that is found in Otávio's binder and the binders of so many other Belo Monte refugees, that wrenches everything away, that is a murderer—this type of writing has been one of the main weapons of the elites throughout the history of what we call Brazil.

Writing is so much of so much. It is also a weapon to oppress, subjugate, enslave, and destroy all the other people who narrate life orally, through the bodies of the river, of the trees, of rocks, of maps made from other matter.

I know those who have died because of this type of writing. I've seen their blood. I've smelled their corpses. Heard the painful cries of those they loved.

I was at their burial.

In Brazil, writing is this kind that writes to leave out—and writes to expel. This writing erases while it writes, erasing those it doesn't want to exist. This writing is also the writing of the powers of law and medicine, which assault listeners in order to preserve walls, crafting a language whose code is known only to the initiated but that affects all lives.

So how could I, who have made writing my being and my becoming in the world, use this violent instrument to denounce violence? In doing so, was I not also legitimizing the supremacy of one narrative over another and thus consummating a violent act?

I had fallen silent, horrified.

But I have learned as a reporter that we can only move through the world carrying our contradictions with us. Trying to circumvent them usually just causes more erasure. Otávio das Chagas taught me I must continue my gesture of writing, but without denying the violence of this gesture.

Writing leaves marks on my body as well. I too have word-scars.

From this position, I witnessed Otávio das Chagas pilgrimage through three different houses.

And none of them is his home. The men from Norte Energia S.A., the consortium that won the concession for Belo Monte, had this to say about his house on the island and those of so many other beiradeiros: "This is not a house." For them, the concept refers to a house in Leblon or Vila Madalena, upscale neighborhoods in big cities in Southern Brazil. "House," we discovered there, was also a concept defined by whoever had the power to define it. If the company has the power to declare a house not a house, it can also declare that no building exists, no people reside there, and, therefore, no compensation is due those who are not in the house that also isn't. Those who exist but aren't recognized are condemned to hunger. And hunger exists.

For Otávio das Chagas, a house is a babassu roof and also the air coming through the never-locked door. It's fruit trees in the forest and fish in the river. It's fields, and the freedom not to go into the fields. It's agouti and paca in the woods, the call of the howlers in the middle of the night. A house is also neighbors and laughter at sunset, boys and girls playing soccer. It's where you hang a hammock for whoever shows up.

But this house wasn't registered on the papers of the company men.

Who says what a house is?

Who says what is?

They say: "This is not a house."

So where did Otávio live, where did Otávio's befores live, where had Otávio loved Maria, where had Otávio's children been born?

Expelled from their house and from words as well, expelled from a whole world, Otávio das Chagas and his family went from paying rent to a resettlement, from a resettlement to a house donated by a group of Austrians who were horrified by the violence produced in the tropics.

They never got home.

They won't get there as long as there is no river.

Beiradeiros like him refer to the city as "the street." I'm going to the street. I came from the street. Some of them had a second house "in the street," where they would stay when they went to sell fish or needed to deal with some bureaucracy. It was a backup house, the one in the city, where they would arrive ready to depart, because the river didn't like them to be far away and its call distressed their legs and heart. The city gave them a bellyache. They suspected it was the water, the overly salty food that disguised the fact that it wasn't fresh, the hubbub.

Otávio never had this second house. He was a man averse to all streets.

Yet Belo Monte stuck Otávio das Chagas out in the street. It put him on the outside.

Otávio das Chagas is an inhabitant of outsides. The outside of himself as well.

It is because he is outside inside that Otávio das Chagas and so many others are refugees in their own country.

Beiradeiros like him hold a long saga within their very bodies, one that began in drought and was then inundated. In the late nineteenth century, their forebears were taken from Northeast Brazil's arid sertão region to the Amazon rainforest to collect latex and make rubber. They were fleeing the dryness of the land, hunger, and centuries of servitude at the bejeweled hands of rural barons. In the jungle, bosses subjected them to labor relations akin to those of slavery.

During World War II, another army of poor Northeasterners was taken to the forest to make rubber, this time for the Allies. Every single time people of the drought were dumped into the humid forest, the bosses abandoned the workers in the woods as soon as profits plummeted. There they created a way of life that made the margin—of the river and of the official country—an experience not of exclusion but of freedom. This experience, of subverting the margin, is the way of life we call beiradeiro, the people of the between-worlds.

Navigating between worlds with your only border the body of the river has become a survival strategy. On the river, boundaries are pure movement. They don't dam up, don't limit, don't injure. They are fluid. The beiradeiros fish and hunt, crack Brazil nuts, pick açaí, plant fields, make flour, sometimes raise chickens. They might tap rubber if the price is good, prospect a little when there's a new gold strike. They hunted a lot of jaguars and oncillas in the past because whites wanted the hides. They live between forest and street, in the between of worlds.

There is no "or" in the beiradeiro life, just "and." It is all about sum totals. Being a beiradeiro is being here and being there. It's being this and also that. Being Indigenous and also not. Being quilombola and also not. It is and it isn't—and in those cases where it isn't, even subtraction is an addition, because whatever isn't *also* is added in; it too becomes part of the body.

Being beiradeiro, an inhabitant of edges and margins, is being multiple.

They were poor, and when their bosses abandoned them in the forest like cheap, thoroughly expended flesh, they reappropriated their own bodies.

You will often hear the descendants of these first rubber tappers proudly proclaim: "Nobody has ever bossed me around."

Or: "I've never had a job."

Freedom lies in moving.

Along the course of the river, of toils, of desires.

But how can you move along a dammed river?

When land pressure increased in the Amazon, and white invaders advanced to the margins with their gunmen, many beiradeiros migrated from the edge of the continent to the islands of the Xingu.

It was their last stronghold of resistance.

Not of a single life, but of an entire saga. From the dryness of the Northeast sertão to the excesses of the Amazon's rivers.

Then Belo Monte drowned the islands.

And the beiradeiros were reconverted into poor, now urban.

I asked some of them: "What does it mean to be poor?"

"Being poor means having no choice. About what to eat, where to come and where to go, what to do or not do."

Being poor is having no choice about your desires.

I asked what it means to be rich.

"Being rich means not needing money."

We need to understand this as well.

Beiradeiros are not just the victims of a notion of development that kills.

That would be a reductive way of viewing the enormity of what they are.

The beiradeiros of the Xingu and other Amazon rivers carry insurrection in their bodies.

They are an uprising incarnate.

While Brazil was living through different periods of its official history—two dictatorships (the Estado Novo, from 1937 to 1945, and the business-military dictatorship initiated with the 1964 coup and lasting to 1985) and two redemocratizations as well—the beiradeiros forgotten in the forest made a revolution literally *on* the margins, and also *outside* the margins of the state.

They became a unique experience.

Not beings of the forest. But in-betweens.

And then the state, the same one that more than one hundred years earlier cast their ancestors into the forest, came back to expel them from there.

The state came back not to guarantee rights but to build ruins. And the island-quilombos became water. Dead trees stretch gaunt arms toward the sky, turned to statues of despair. And the skin of the river rots. The water now smells like a corpse.

I listen to the dammed lives of the Xingu. And fail at my attempt to convert them into words. Failure is a condition for those who write. Life always escapes. Life spills over, life is bigger. Life flows in words but refuses to be dammed up by them. Life is a river that doesn't submit to hydropower plants.

The one who taught me that writing is an act *of* and *in* the body was the Xingu River. Since then, I've known. All I have to offer is myself, this body made of word-scars that I've tattooed on myself while writing about others. Like a transmutation, this is the inescapable lot of the storyteller who, when she writes on paper or screen, also writes on her own body, in blood-ink. It is this body riddled by letters, tragically insufficient, that I inscribe here.

This is my body present.

5. forestpeoples: the alliance of the beings and in-betweens

I've chosen to tell you about the beiradeiros through the catastrophe called Belo Monte, the most recent chapter in the long act of building ruins in the Amazon, because the genesis of this unique population lies in a confrontation. Beiradeiros were born as a wondrously creative response to the violence of the state, in its classic association with predatory elites. When all this happened in the late nineteenth century, men (because generally only men were taken to tap rubber) were torn away from another landscape, that of Brazil's semiarid Northeast, and cast into the forest, against the forest. There, at the same time that they killed the Indigenous, some of them learned with the Indigenous. At the same time that they raped Indigenous women, they loved Indigenous women and had children and families with them. By the time Belo Monte reached them, in the 2010s, the dam encountered another people.

The construction of the Belo Monte dam project on one of the Amazon's giant rivers continues to represent this relationship from the past, the relationship between the state and predatory elites. This time, however, they encountered not transitory inhabitants but a population that had converted into forest from the shock between worlds—a population that is recognized today as a traditional community, even in law. The drought their ancestors left behind is memory, but—very importantly—not origin.

The people who call themselves beiradeiros were born there, out of this encounter with the forest. What they are is a victory of the forest that made them part of itself, absorbing them into its body and blending them with its fluids. The beiradeiros—literally, the river-edge dwellers—made the edge of worlds, the between-worlds, into a place of resistance and insurrection. In this birthing they resemble the quilombolas, who forged themselves in the forest and across different geographies as other beings, children not of slavery but of uprising. Africa—in a much broader sense than the one ascribed by colonialist geopolitics—is memory for the quilombolas, but not origin.

With multiple reasons for mistrusting each other and much blood spilled in their pasts, beiradeiros and the Indigenous, and in some regions quilombolas too, joined forces for the first time to combat the forest destruction brought by the resumption of the colonialist-inspired project to erect huge dams in the Amazon. Recommenced in the 2010s, this project was no longer driven by the twentieth-century business-military dictatorship, but by the most left-leaning administration to come out of the redemocratization of Brazil.

This unprecedented alliance emerged on all fronts in the battle against the dams. The symbol of this alliance was the auto-demarcation of the Munduruku Sawré Muybu land, a monumental endeavor that began in 2014 and was undertaken by the Indigenous and beiradeiros side by side. This was followed by the auto-demarcation of the beiradeiro territory of Montanha-Mangabal, likewise a joint accomplishment of beiradeiros and the Indigenous. Theirs was an alliance of peoples of the forest against the white world intent on destroying them; it was their refusal to be converted into the generic "poor" of the peripheries of Amazon cities. They fought like forest—and called whites *Others*. Beings and in-betweens against Others, this has been the great war of recent years. But most Brazilians, including much of the press, have preferred to ignore it, indulging instead in hit series like *Game of Thrones*, without sensing or assigning true significance to something fantastic that has been happening in their own time and, geographically at least, much nearer to them.

Now that quilombolas and beiradeiros have been introduced, standing alongside the various Indigenous groups that form the forest's human composition, I'm going to stop calling them "forest peoples" or "peoples of the forest" and start referring to them as "forestpeoples." I believe one of the premises of this book is now obvious: the forest doesn't belong to them (or to anyone), and so I've never said "peoples' forest" or "forest of the peoples." In fact, this is a logical and conceptual impossibility that finds expression in language as well: when the forest begins to belong to human peoples, as a form of property, it's no longer forest. Ownership presumes annihilation of the body. So what can belong to humans is no longer forest but its ruins. What can belong to humans are soybean fields, cattle pastures, hydropower plants, railroads, and highways. By definition, the forest is constant exchange. It is planted by human and nonhuman peoples as much as it plants them. The concept of property is as strange to the forest as it is incompatible with it. When subjected to it, the forest becomes a nonbeing.

I began this book and reached this point using the expressions "forest peoples" and "peoples of the forest," the concepts I usually employ in my articles, where I have neither the time nor the space to elaborate more deeply. "Peoples of the forest" implies that these people belong to the forest, not that the forest belongs to them. To be considered a people of the forest and recognized as such, these people must embody two transgressions against the capitalist system. First, their being "of the forest" has nothing to do with property, but with belonging, two radically different things. Second, human peoples are the ones who belong to the earth, not the other way around.

When we grasp something about the hundreds of different Indigenous peoples, the something that ties them together, and when we grasp the origin of beiradeiros and quilombolas, we reach another layer of knowledge. These peoples do not own the forest—this much has been made clear. Yet merely saying they belong to the forest is still not precise enough. They don't belong to it; they *are* it, because being beiradeiro and quilombola and Indigenous, far beyond any category, means understanding yourself as nature. So they aren't forest peoples, but forestpeoples, one inseparable from the other.

This modification of language wrought by our real world—and that is also wrought in the real world by language—is a political operation fundamental to defining the future. It goes to the very root of the dispute over the Amazon. The COVID-19 pandemic has fully evinced what the climate collapse had already made explicit: we will not overcome the greatest challenge in the human history of this planet without altering our very way of thinking. We will not escape the abyss by relying on the same thinking that brought us to it: white, patriarchal, male, and binary. We must listen to those who have been silenced and who, even though silenced, have resisted as a collective, despite constant genocide— those Ailton Krenak has defined as "a subhumanity, a people who clings to the land."

In Krenak's sardonic words:

> How have we, over two or three thousand years, built the idea of humanity? . . . The idea that white Europeans could set about colonizing the rest of the world was grounded in the premise that an enlightened humanity needed to reach out to a benighted humanity and bring its members into their incredible light. . . . How can we call ourselves a humanity when over 70 percent of us are completely alienated from even the minimal exercise of being? They are called "savages" so they can be civilized and made members of the Humanity Club. But humanity is a blender. If it survives, it will have to fight for the slivers of the planet it didn't eat up. This civilizing abstraction suppresses diversity, denies the plurality of life forms, existence, and habits. It serves up the same menu, the same dress code, and, if possible, the same language.

Amazonizing yourself thus means modifying language and with it the structure of thought. The Indigenous warned of the climate collapse when the general population was still unaware of the issue. No one listened to them. In 1989, the British pop star Sting went on a seventeen-country tour with Raoni Metuktire to help amplify the Kayapó leader's voice. Raoni had long repeated the same trenchant message: "If you continue the burn-offs, the wind will increase, the Sun will grow very hot, the Earth too. All of us, not just the Indigenous, will be unable to breathe. If you destroy the forest, we will all be silenced."

The Indigenous have sensed the deformation of the planet in their very bones, literally, since understanding oneself as nature is not a matter of rhetoric but of existence. It isn't just the planet's morphology that has been changing but the morphology of the Indigenous body itself as an expansion of nature. The problem is that whites can't comprehend the language of nonwhites. This goes well beyond the inability to understand their tongues—for this, we have the possibility of translation. What whites do not comprehend is the language of nonwhites, something much broader. And since they don't comprehend it, they mock it. Many Brazilian intellectuals, as well as many intellectuals in the countries where Raoni toured with Sting, ridiculed them simply because they didn't understand language that was other and thought it was all just smoke signals.

When the Indigenous say the river is their grandfather, they really mean it's their grandfather. They are not speaking naively, unwittingly, like some people from the so-called prehistory of civilization, as certain luminaries of ignorance believe. To the contrary. This way of comprehending life and each one's place within it is much more complex. It is another form of relating to all other beings and engaging in exchange with them—and not monetary or monetizable exchange, it should be emphasized.

The climate collapse stems from this enormous misunderstanding: a dominant minority that perceives rivers, mountains, and land as resources and commodities, meaning it can do whatever it pleases with them, removing them from one place and putting them elsewhere, killing one part over here to increase GDP over there, and so on, while the voices of a kaleidoscope of other peoples are often silenced by bullet, because these peoples insist that so-called resources and commodities are actually other beings, neither more nor less important than human peoples, and that collective existence on this planet can only be ensured through this interweaving of dynamic exchanges.

When I talk about listening to those who have always been treated as subalterns, it's not only about opening our ears but also about sharing power. What we call civilization has been the protagonist at only one moment in time: the moment when the species that has always feared catastrophe became the catastrophe it feared. What we call humanity is a dominant minority that has converted the species into a destructive force capable of altering the planet's climate and, through this change, altering the very morphology of the only house we all share.

This isn't rhetoric, or the talk of dreamers oblivious to reality, as "realists" like to claim—they are the ones out of touch with the real world, walking in shoes of arrogance into the abyss they have dug with their own feet. I don't know how we could have more eloquent proof—proof, not evidence—that if we continue to rely on the way of thinking that has brought us to the climate collapse, we will do nothing but augment, in the present, the hostility of the near future. The time has come for us to be led by those who have resisted humanity's destructive force, by those who know how to live with all livingkind, both human and nonhuman.

There is an explicit purpose to the weave of this book, which is also a summons to Amazonize the world, well beyond the geographical territory of the Amazon: it is time—and perhaps the last time we'll have—to listen to the people who have been called barbarians, people relegated to the condition of subhumanities throughout the colonizing process, which over the centuries has modified its aesthetics but not its ethos. And listen neither condescendingly nor out of pity but moved by an ultimate survival instinct. Perhaps, if we are fortunate, those whose lives have so often been destroyed by those who label themselves civilized will agree to teach us to live after the end of the world, despite everything we have done to their bodies.

87. between-worlds

In her book *Handeln statt Hoffen* (Act, don't hope), the German-born activist Carola Rackete quite rightly states:

> This is an unprecedented challenge, and we need all democratically minded people to meet it. We only have two options: we can either throw our planet's ecosystems off balance—which simply isn't a solution!—or we push for a global transformation, a radical reorientation of our system that will fundamentally reshape society.

Carola became known around the globe in 2019 when she stood up to the far-rightist Matteo Salvini, then Italy's minister of the interior, and landed the boat she was captaining at the port of Lampedusa, with forty-two rescued refugees from Libya aboard. She was arrested and later released.

We met on a Greenpeace ship in the Antarctic in January 2020, both of us taking part in a scientific expedition to research the impact of the climate crisis on penguin populations and also to chart whales, those beings who don't fit into something as precarious as words. Carola believes we have to confront the capitalist system directly because our only chance is to create another kind of society. Fast. Yesterday.

Carola approaches the climate emergency from a human rights perspective and also counters the hegemonic viewpoint in arguing that the social sciences have a central role to play in addressing global heating and mass extinction.

We don't need to discuss scientific information. We already know it: 99 percent of scientists affirm that the climate crisis was caused by our species. We have to discuss how we can quickly create a society better than this one, which has brought the planet to exhaustion. Our future might be very difficult from a climate perspective, but we have an opportunity to create a more just society.

We talked for more than two hours in the ship's infirmary, the only place we managed to find a little privacy, and I asked Carola how to create a new kind of human. She was categorical: "The problem isn't civil disobedience but obedience." It's time to act— and acting means disobeying. Disobedience, however, is harder than it seems. Shaped and conformed to the capitalist system, which has structured our language and thought, we have to confront our own selves every single day. Carola is one of these new humans forged by the climate urgency—her house is where she rests her backpack; she doesn't kill a single animal to feed and clothe herself; and she wears what she's given on the ships where she works, on scientific missions or for social-environmental and humanitarian causes, most often as a volunteer. German by birth, she has become a human with many limits and no borders.

Carola is a member of a global community of people who consume only the minimum possible, whose acts of resistance have led to their arrest by the world's despots in various countries, and whose family is the population of the entire planet. I'm telling you about Carola so you can understand the type of disobedience I'm referring to. Not everyone can or wants to be Carola, but disobedience, at whatever level, is a profound, and profoundly difficult, act. It's also an inescapable one if we want to have a future where it's possible to live.

Sharing life with new people on the frontier of climate resistance for fifteen days aboard an ecological combat ship was one of the most important experiences in joy I've ever had. Joy in the sharing, joy in being released from having to constantly explain that we can't destroy the only house we have, joy in finding a place in the placelessness of the world. Joy in belonging—I who am always unbelonging. It also expanded my awareness of my footprint on the planet.

We know about carbon footprints—how much each of us devours our shared house because we live in a capitalist system where, whenever a child is born, so too is a consumer. Some, like myself, make an effort to reduce this footprint, decreasing the trail of destruction we will bequeath to future generations. Yet no matter how hard we try, we fail, because the capitalist system pens us in from all sides. For example, to reach the Antarctic I had to take a plane, and the ship on which we did combat used fossil fuel. Activists like Carola Rackete radically change their way of life to break out of the system's prison as much as possible, but they know we'll only manage to achieve a society that quits eating up its own house by ending capitalism.

I had just engaged in an experience to fight explicit destruction—the destruction of chain saws toppling centuries-old trees, of fires incinerating the forest, of Belo Monte drying up Volta Grande do Xingu, of big rivers smelling like corpses, of gunshots piercing the bodies of Amazon defenders. Then I was cast into a blue world, because the Antarctic is not a white continent but a blue one, like Earth seen by Yuri Gagarin, when he was the first to view us from space. Ice has so many shades of blue and so many nuances our eyes don't have room for. In this world, just the act of taking a single step demands a delicacy; it's a hard decision to make, because you must have a very good reason for setting your feet in the Antarctic.

Every time we left the ship to land on islands or the continent, we had to thoroughly disinfect ourselves, our entire bodies, each centimeter of clothing and the soles of our boots most of all. Any alien microorganism could alter the entire ecosystem. It took me days to be really sure I had the right to set foot in the most beautiful landscape my senses had ever experienced, and whenever

I did, I studied the ground, step by step, before moving my foot forward. The Antarctic is the closest experience we can have of a planet without humans, an experience of beauty at a level I didn't even imagine could exist.

Each step weighed much more than my own body because I was fully aware of what it meant. Migrating from the anguished land of an Amazon ever closer to the point of no return, I was stepping on the least-touched place on Earth. The least touched and, even so, melting day after day because of the actions of the dominant minority of humans. From the beginning to the end of this passage, my steps were accompanied by the rumble of glaciers turning to water. A sound that freezes you from the inside.

In my process of Amazonization—or dewhitening—I believe we need to be even more radical than Carola Rackete has proposed in her very powerful book. We must defend the rights not only of human peoples but of nonhuman peoples as well. Or expand the concept of humanity to include all other peoples who inhabit this planet. The famous crisis of Western democracies, discussed so much in the 2010s, is a crisis of selective democracy, since democracy has never been fully realized even in countries where a larger number of people now have a considerable collection of rights.

Selective democracy has encompassed only a small slice of human populations, leaving all others on the outside. In Brazil, this paradox is more than evident. Yet it is not enough to expand democracy to the human peoples now excluded from it. Democracy must also be taken to nonhuman peoples. Not only the ones we call animals, but rivers and oceans, mountains and forests as well. These beings cannot vote, but we must create legal instruments and mechanisms that can represent them in all democratic forums and institutions. Just as attorneys defend humans who are very different from themselves, and prosecutors bring suit against corporations in the name of communities to which they do not belong, so too can attorneys and prosecutors act in the name of a nonhuman person or a forest or river or mountain, or even the oceans.

This humanization of justice, which can only be achieved by pushing beyond the borders of our definition of "human," is visible in the concept of ecocide. At the urging of society, a growing number of jurists are pressing the International Criminal Court to include this in its Rome Statute as the fifth crime against humanity. Ecocide as the death of our planet-house.

On September 10, 2021, I sat on the panel of the Permanent Peoples' Tribunal, which began judging ecocide against the Cerrado and the cultural genocide of peoples of the Cerrado, a vast savanna biome that may vanish in the coming years. There I defended a new interpretation, that is, that all ecocide is an act of genocide—and all genocide is ecocide. Since humans are a part of nature—and not something outside it, as capitalism has indoctrinated us to believe—there is no way to separate these two crimes, nor to separate their consequences on a planet where everything is interdependent. In this regard, the concept of genocide must also be expanded to all peoples, not just human ones. Ecocide is a concept that responds to the challenges of climate justice, but I believe we must be bold enough to rethink it through new language.

To address the climate emergency, we must complete the decentralization of human peoples that Galileo began when he removed Earth from the center around which the sun was supposedly spinning and put it in its proper place; followed by Darwin, who proved we are not the center of a god's creation, but the result of natural selection, adaptation, and evolution, just as much as amoebas, flies, and mice; and continued by Freud, who showed that our unconscious is determinant in our existence, and so our celebrated conscious doesn't even control its own decisions.

We only exist in relation to all others, those outside us and those inside us. Inside us, we should remember, our decisions and actions are influenced not just by our drives but also by bacteria. To ensure a less hostile future, humans need to relinquish their reliance on centrality and hierarchization, which have condemned life on this planet. In a short space of time, we must become capable of creating an egalitarian, horizontal society. The experience of many Indigenous peoples, who recognize and position themselves as part of an intricate web of relations and exchanges with all other beings, visible and invisible, is a rich source of inspiration and knowledge.

With this in mind, I will return to the most difficult formulation, which generally stirs unease even among ecoconscious audiences: The forest belongs to no one. It doesn't belong to a country or countries, nor does it belong to what we call humanity. The forest doesn't even belong to the peoples of the forest since, if a people of the forest believes it owns the forest, it is no longer a forestpeople: either it has become white, or it has become poor.

The Amazon, in its broadest sense, belongs to itself, and we are all part of it. For generations who have been trained and indoctrinated to see themselves as consumers, customers, and owners, this sounds like an idea conceived by some lunatic. But believe me: what we call world was born neither with fences nor with shelves. And not even with humans.

Carola Rackete told me about solastalgia while she was steering the ship between Antarctic ice blocks. I wasn't familiar with this term that describes the melancholy I've felt for so long in the Amazon, and that deepened in a world literally melting before our eyes. This concept, proposed by Australian philosopher Glenn Albrecht, has helped me decipher my own nagging question about what a house is. Solastalgia is nostalgia for a world we know will soon be another. It is the homesickness we feel not because we are far from home but because we're at home and know this home will soon cease to exist. It made us tremble every time the glaciers rumbled into the sea, and it has made me shiver at one hundred degrees Fahrenheit every time smoke announces the incineration of another piece of rainforest.

12. the conversion of the forestpeoples into the poor

The concept "poor" is strategic to understanding the Amazon and the system that caused the climate crisis. All ideologies, from far right to far left, divide the world into poor and rich, since this is an important concept in the thought tradition embraced by the European West. In capitalism, being poor or being rich relates directly to the quantity and quality of one's material assets. This has the immediate effect of converting poor people into a homogeneous category, a generic entity called "the poor," a figure everyone thinks they're familiar with, knowing who they are and what they desire. The poor, all of them, would supposedly like to consume and, of course, get rich.

Ensuring that the false generic category of "poor" is applied to this heterogeneous multitude of people, who constitute the majority of the world's human population, is essential to the workings of capitalism. Even the more radical left doesn't question the concept of poverty. To the contrary, poverty is seen as a condition that needs to be overcome solely from a material standpoint, as a concept, as an ethos, but one that is rarely questioned.

The populist center-left that occupied governments in Latin American countries in the first decade of this century, like the Workers' Party in Brazil, believed they represented the poor and, at least formally, they defended the idea of government for the poor. The West's most powerful religion, Catholicism, is grounded in a discourse about the poor, "for theirs is the kingdom of heaven." A good number of neo-Pentecostal Evangelicals—the portion I prefer to call "market Evangelicals," the portion that has won worldly souls and filled pastors' pockets since the latter half of the twentieth century—has adopted prosperity theology, in which wealth is a blessing from God and giving money to the church can enrich a poor man here and now, right in our earthly kingdom.

Notwithstanding differences between the actors who wage the debate about wealth and poverty in various spheres—in religion and culture, in economics and politics—this ideological discussion revolves almost exclusively around how to overcome poverty. While interpretations about the causes of poverty and solutions to it may diverge, there is scant disagreement about the concept itself, beyond the amount in dollars per day that defines poverty lines.

The forestpeoples, the ones who "cling to the land," defy this interpretation of the world head-on. They defy it with their way of life, with their very existence. They do not fit within the binomial equation of poor-rich. When asked to do so, they make things messy, saying, as I mentioned earlier, that being rich means not needing money (which in their case means they have everything they need in the forest) and that being poor means being alienated from your own desires (for example, having a boss and being required to work when the boss wants). They would, for example, classify as extremely poor the CEO of a transnational corporation who remains in work mode 24/7 in a climatized environment, surrounded by luxury furniture and dressed in international designer labels, and who travels by helicopter and private jet, all while hooked up to the latest technology.

The beiradeiros can wake up in the morning with the urge to fish and then go fishing. They can change their mind and, instead of going for one day's fishing, go for ten. They can head out to their subsistence fields, or decide to do something else, or even nothing else, or leave it for the next day. They can live in some crook of the river for years, and then, for some reason or just because they want to, choose to make their home on the other bank. They can even opt to rent out their body's labor to a *fazendeiro*—a large rancher or farmer—if they need money for some specific purpose, but they'll quit as soon as their set goal is reached. Life is living, not accumulating. As nature within nature, they lack nothing essential.

To expel them from the forest, the persistent partnership between various government administrations and predatory elites from the white world needs to de-forest them, making them poor This is the most efficacious way to uproot them from lands that are coveted for speculation and raw material production, from soy and beef to ore. Prospecting often figures in here as well—not only for gold but also for bribes, a routine component of major infrastructure projects. Corruption is a hugely popular extractivist activity in the Amazon and within relations between Brazil's various government administrations and the business community. The culture of bribery pervades private initiative, particularly but not solely among large construction companies. That's how it went under the dictatorship and has continued under democracy.

Since classic genocide—the extermination of bodies—has encountered a greater number of moral obstacles in this century, the machinery of converting forestpeoples into the poor has been refined. In a globalized world connected by the internet, if you kill more than eight thousand Indigenous people, as the dictatorship did just a few decades prior, it can hamper trade relations and lead to charges before the International Criminal Court. It has become harder to cover up state crimes. This hasn't ended the extermination of those who get in the way of big corporations and the predatory elites, but it does mean their agents have to find ways that don't extract blood and don't produce large numbers of corpses—especially images of corpses. Subtler processes are required by the more delicate sensitivities of this era (and by a hypocrisy dependent on props such as the sustainability departments at unsustainable businesses and corporations).

The process of building Belo Monte, forced on the peoples of the Xingu, was perversely planned. To expel a forestpeople from the forest is to kill them—and no reparations can ever atone for cultural death, which is in some cases followed by illness and demise. Even so, the compensation paid to some of them was not even enough to guarantee minimally decent housing by urban standards, near the river and downtown, where they might find a job and have access to the scarce public services available in Altamira, the region's largest city.

Literally overnight, hundreds of families found themselves poor. Like Antonio and Dulcineia, whom I met in 2017. This beiradeiro couple was living on an island in the Xingu. Expelled by Belo Monte, they went to living in a rented house with four rooms but only one window. One single window for the whole house. And this one single window had bars, because they lived on the marginalized periphery of Altamira.

When they begin feeling crushed between the walls, Antonio and Dulcineia discover hunger. They can't find words to describe it. When I ask them to, Antonio, this sixty-something man who knew nothing of city life before, tears up. And Dulcineia Dias, who tells me she's fifty-two, cowers in a corner of the room, her back pressed hard against a cracked cement wall. *Hunger* is a word that only has meaning for someone who doesn't live it. For anyone who does, it's a word that isn't said. I recall Carolina Maria de Jesus, the first female favela dweller to become a writer in Brazil, in the 1960s. She wrote that hunger is yellow. Only then, pierced by Carolina's words, did I come closer to understanding what wasn't understandable to me. The ages provided by Antonio and Dulcineia coincide with the information on their ID cards, now always at hand, because they have become poor, and the poor need papers to prove who they are.

When he became poor, Antonio, who had never thought of filing for retirement, because he "didn't need to," went on Brazil's universal old-age pension so he could feed his wife, youngest daughter, and grandson. He had entered the world of papers, first by signing his own eviction without knowing what he was signing and then by becoming the recipient of a public pension he only needed once he became poor, a pension that would later force him to risk going to the bank during the COVID-19 pandemic, when he was malnourished and ailing. The family's rent and electric bill swallow up more than 70 percent of his pension, leaving around fifty cents a day per person to live on. And, unlike in the forest, "in the street" you have to pay for everything.

In the summer, the heat index tops one hundred degrees in Altamira. And in winter, the rainy season, it can still approach ninety. Antonio and Dulcineia live in their single-window home with no refrigerator and no fan, which means they don't even have cold water or any way to store their food. The main decoration in their living room is a photomontage of their youngest daughter and two grandsons, with her as a princess and the boys as two armed soldiers against a fake Disney backdrop. Portraits— and also delusions.

When the dam's reservoir began filling up, Antonio witnessed forest creatures drowning. Monkeys, agoutis, armadillos, and sloths threw themselves into the water in search of terra firma. "We managed to save a few by pulling them into the canoe, but we saw a lot die," he says. As part of the forest, which he also is, Antonio feels this pain piercing his body. Like the nonhumans, he has yet to find terra firma. When he wakes each day, he feels he's drowning in the loneliness of the city. If hunger is yellow, loneliness is dry, and Antonio has discovered it's possible to drown in dryness. When I met him, he had just adopted two puppies, because he didn't know how to "live without animals." He borrowed money so he could buy powdered milk to feed them. Two more displaced creatures in the family, finding a place with each other.

"My life was even better than anyone's in São Paulo," says Antonio, referring to the country's model city of wealth and progress. "If I wanted to work my land, I did, and if I didn't, the land would be there the next day. If I wanted to fish, I did, but if I'd rather pick açaí instead, I did. I had a river, I had woods,

I had tranquility. On the island, I didn't have any doors. And I had a place." Dulcineia takes a step forward. She wants to talk too: "And on the island, we didn't get sick. Here the heat makes us sick."

Antonio and Dulcineia's is a life of firsts: first light bill, first rented house, first time they needed to buy what they eat, first time they didn't have money to buy what they eat, first hunger. "I never worked for anybody. I was always free," he says over and over. "On the river I know everything, in the street I'm nothing."

Early every morning, before four o'clock, Antonio wakes up feeling suffocated and escapes to the backyard, which is a tiny, cemented square, barren of plants but where you can glimpse a piece of sky. Antonio doesn't sit because he doesn't own a chair. Standing, he clings to this scrap of freedom, sometimes crying. And he says: "Being poor is living in hell."

Dozens of other expelled beiradeiro families were pushed into neighborhoods labeled with bureaucratic acronyms, as corporations like to do: RUC, for Reassentamento Urbano Coletivo, or Collective Urban Resettlement. The impersonality of these letters is yet another trick they use in an effort to cleanse their actions of filth that is brutally personal, because it always targets the same people. Built miles from downtown by Norte Energia, these neighborhoods consist of houses constructed from second-rate material, following an architectural design that has nothing even remotely to do with the local way of life. The neighborhoods had barely been born when they started falling apart, from crumbling walls to a daily life ruled by criminal factions.

The centuries go by, and the colonial project continues to reproduce itself. Inside an office, technocrats drew up a map that suited the interests of Norte Energia and the government. Architects and engineers dedicated themselves to planning cheap housing that would last as long as companies' contractual responsibilities. Social workers distributed families as if they had no lives, as if there were no ties between relatives, or friends, or neighbors, nor any desires or rights. The construction of these RUCs was an evocation in miniature of what big European powers did during their fashioning of the phantasmagoria called Africa. And thus began yet another catastrophe.

Uprooted from nature, uprooted from themselves, separated from their neighbors, community ties torn asunder, the beiradeiros found themselves lost from everything and from themselves. "On the river, I was king," said Raimundo Berro Grosso. "Living on the riverbanks," he explained to me, means "walking on riches."

> I didn't need money to live happy. My whole house was nature. Lumber, straw, didn't need any nails. I had my patch of land where I planted a bit of everything, all sorts of fruit trees. I'd catch my fish, make manioc flour to eat with my fish. If I wanted to eat something else, I'd grab a hen I was raising. If I wanted meat, I'd hunt in the forest. And to make money, I'd fish some more and sell it in the street. I raised my three daughters, proud of what I was. I was a rich man.

One day in 2012, which he didn't write down because he'd never needed to write down dates, Berro Grosso was startled to see some strangers arrive in a motorboat. Men "from the company." They said his island was going to be "removed." It's always curious to observe the lexicon used by bloodless killers. How can an island, a living organism, be "removed"?

Berro Grosso responded, "I'm not leaving here." Then they told him his island was going to be left under water—either sign, or go down with it. "I signed a document. But I can't read. I only know how to draw my name."

Berro Grosso was tossed into one of the tract homes in one of the RUCs. The company named this neighborhood Blue Water. There's no water, since the shortest path to the river is over three miles. Oftentimes there isn't even any water in the taps. The beiradeiro converted into poor man watched the walls of his home cracking in the first few years after they went up.

> Now I'm poor. I don't have abundance, I don't have leisure. Now I have to buy everything I need. Since I don't have money to buy what I want, I buy what I can. I like manioc flour, but I can only afford rice. I used to harvest four hundred good watermelons, but today I can't afford a bad one. I used to harvest the chicken I wanted to eat, today I can't afford to buy one. I used to have a living river, today I have a dead lake, and I have to pay for transportation to get there.

Berro Grosso then practiced his first desperate gesture of resistance. He disrupted the monotony of lookalike houses. He built lean-tos in front and out back, à la beiradeiro, packaging his tract house in the aesthetics of the forest. He painted them bright yellow, clashing with the whole street and with the company as well. Right at the front of the house, where every passerby could see it, he put his canoe, navigating dryness. That enormous object on the veranda of an urban home is like himself, a displaced life, a misplaced life, a hallucination. It was Berro Grosso who told me, looking at his riverless canoe, that being poor means having no choice.

87. joão da silva and the return of the poor

None of the heiradeiros I have known and followed have hurt more than João da Silva. When I met him, in 2015, he had already tried to commit murder and now he wanted to commit suicide. I had spent days sailing down the Xingu in a canoe, seated next to his wife, Raimunda. Much to the irritation of our traveling companions, the two of us talked instead of rowing. Or rather, she talked, and I listened and wrote it all down in my notebook.

I couldn't row properly because my back is now deformed as the result of two other expeditions. On the first of these, in 2006, I had accompanied an adventurer on his solitary walk across the Sahara Desert in Mauritania, a journey without GPS but with us dragging water, food, tents, and sleeping bags along in a kind of pull cart. The second was a journey into vipassana meditation, in 2007, during which I delved so deep into my inner reality that, after spending ten days in a row, twelve hours a day, in the same lotus position, I found I was in horrendous pain and had no fine motor movement when I returned to normal reality. I left the meditation center floating, the pain duly separated from me as I observed it from elsewhere, but in practical terms I was unable to type on my cell phone or tie my shoelaces.

Raimunda, on the other hand, the woman I listened to while sitting side by side in the canoe, is a good rower, but she had dislocated her shoulder. So we were two deadweights amid half a dozen very pissed off men, most of whom thought we had suddenly decided to play the "weaker sex." I understood their frustration. Rowing all day long beneath that sun was indeed for the hardy. Raimunda and I, however, were very much alive and rowing down a river of stories.

Raimunda is a woman but also a force. A force of nature itself. She is one of the most powerful creators of meaning I've ever met during my wanderings and navigations. As I write this book, years after we first met, I've been watching Raimunda turn into a thinker of the forest who reaches increasingly larger, more distant audiences. She sees herself as a pindoba, a palm tree that is reborn even after they set fire to it. When we met on this canoe journey, Raimunda had just seen her house on the island burned down by the company that the Belo Monte consortium hired to "clean up" nature so men could create their version of how the world should be.

She was still in the middle of the river road, trying to get to the island so she could at least collect her furniture and tools and rescue her smaller plants, when they set it ablaze. There was nothing left, and she sang to the trees and flowers she couldn't save, producing a scene in which a very skinny Black woman sang alone on a murdered island. A human sculpture entrapped by the ashes of her life and all the life that existed there, in the middle of the immense, convulsing Xingu. Raimunda sang to ask forgiveness of everything that had been living and went dead, forgiveness because she couldn't save them.

Like Socorro do Burajuba, Raimunda is also of fierce life. And so she knew she was being reborn when she told me a story that began when, at ten years old, she worked as a maid in the home of a white family, a contemporary slave. She was still in the Northeast state of Maranhão, where Brazil's social indexes are the worst and where she had been born in less than a stable. And where her father had taught her to step without making any noise so she wouldn't bother the white people. Before embarking on our canoe journey, Raimunda showed me on land how she still walks with feet as light as cotton, because the shackles they put on your soul in early childhood are the hardest to rip off.

Becoming forest was how this woman alone, in search of a place, space, and freedom, rose up.

Raimunda still walks literally without making a sound, but she has raised a racket in Brazil and abroad in her fight for justice for the Belo Monte refugees, a fight that bothers very powerful people a great deal. She makes speeches, sings, poetizes, as stunning as a palm tree reborn into the eternal newness of the world. Raimunda is also the daughter of several apocalypses, and she knew this was simply one more—the worst of them, the most perverse, but as long as Raimunda had her imagination, the end of the world would not be an end but a middle, and a means. Raimunda is a ray in the world, and she gave me my first clue that the best political instrument for freeing the future is imagination. Imagin-action.

Raimunda had left her husband João in their house on the poor periphery of Altamira, where they had been shoved as if they were things. I visited them when our trip was over. Impaled by João's voice, I ached all over as I listened to him, standing there in the middle of the room in the house he didn't recognize, with his eyes I see as blue and Raimunda as green frozen in horror at an image only he could make out: "I just see darkness. The hole . . . the hole in my life." João suffered from too much clarity. I listened to João's voice and gestures, hearing more from them than from the words of that man standing there—destroyed but standing—in the middle of the room. Around us, Altamira roared away, and the wood of the nonhouse cracked in the sun. João didn't have time to weave a net around himself like we do when we mourn someone vital we've lost. Instead, his brain collapsed and so he remained trapped in the horror.

Some weeks earlier, he had been called to "negotiate" with Norte Energia. There's no negotiating when you've been expelled from your home, there's no negotiating when they set fire to your home, there's no negotiating when they drown your island. But this was yet another one of those words from the lexicon of bloodless assassins that makes up the world's biggest dictionary in every language.

João knew they were transforming him into a poor man. And João knew exactly what it was to be poor. He was a recent bei-radeiro, one who had been scaling the map of Brazil from public works project to public works project, including hydro dams, until he settled on the island with Raimunda to become forest. And then, once again, he was expelled. After the island, there was nowhere else to go, because the island was the last stronghold. Then João knew they had condemned him to being poor again. And João knew what hunger was, because it had left a broad scar on him.

João entered the company office determined to kill Norte Energia's agent. As he explained to me, he was going to sacrifice his own life but, by calling the attention of Brazil and the world to his gesture of despair, he would save the lives of all the others who had been uprooted. But João is not an assassin. All the violence they did to and against him and the forest did not turn into an act of self-defense. Instead, his body locked up, his voice went mute, and he was carried out of what they called an office but was a gallows. To keep from killing someone else, João almost killed himself. We would later learn he had suffered a stroke.

When I met that convulsed man—a man whom Raimunda called undead, whose legs were locked up by a stroke, condemning him to unbearable clarity—João still had a plan. He would refuse to end his life as a poor man. He tried to convince the whole family to immolate themselves on the burned island to draw the world's attention. João desperately needed to be heard, to the point that he was once again willing to die. So Raimunda hid the canoe and began keeping watch over every step taken by the dead man who, to live, needed to die. One year later, in 2016, days before then-president Dilma Rousseff cut the ribbon on Belo Monte, João had a second stroke. And once again, he neither died nor lost his clarity.

33. flying rivers

Belo Monte is a monstrous mountain of horrors. It's also an assembly line for the explicit conversion of forestpeoples into the poor. And a paradigm. There are, however, many other ways to achieve this conversion, some much more sophisticated and harder to combat. It is vital to understand that this conversion is strategic to destroying the Amazon. The forces of destruction know this and are working at an accelerated pace to produce poor people. Blocking this perverse process is imperative to keeping the Amazon from reaching the point of no return.

Yet many of those who support the protection of the forestpeoples do not understand this unavoidable issue. The only effective way to reforest the Amazon is to reforest the forestpeoples who were or are in the process of being converted into the poor. If not for humanitarian reasons, then because they are the front line in the great battle of our time, that of the climate emergency and mass extinction. Unless the forestpeoples *are* forest, there is no possible way the world's largest tropical forest can play its role in regulating the climate through its continuous gesture of launching "flying rivers" into the world's skies.

In 2014, the Brazilian researcher Antonio Nobre, one of the most inspiring earth scientists on this planet, released a report in which he synthesized more than two hundred scientific papers: "The Future Climate of Amazonia." Translated into various languages, it was a landmark study. Antonio is the fifth of six siblings, four of whom are well-known scientists working to defend the Amazon, but with different approaches and ideas about how to protect the world's biggest tropical rainforest.

Among Brazilian scientists, Antonio has gone the farthest in absorbing an understanding of the forestpeoples, and this is one reason the language of his scientific texts is interlaced with the poetry he feels in nature. Because of this, those who espouse the hegemonic, obtuse view of what a scientific text should be—generally boring, poorly written, and inaccessible to nonscientists—have tried to hamper his work. Scientists who produce readable, fluent, appealing texts are only tolerated in so-called science communication books, which are thought of as science for "regular people." Academia, as we know, is a bloody battlefield that could inspire thrillers as entangled as a Cold War spy novel.

In his poetic-scientific report, Antonio Nobre stated that the Amazon needs a "war effort." The scientist denounced the economic forces that were then gestating Jair Bolsonaro and the era looming around the corner. But few were willing to listen to him. Given the many catastrophes triggered in more recent years, especially the fireworks sponsored by Bolsonarism in 2019—when his supporters set the forest aflame—what Nobre was saying seems obvious today, even a given. But that wasn't the world in 2014, nor Brazil in 2014, when the construction of hydro dams in the Amazon was a project not only used by the Workers' Party (PT) to leverage the reelection of Dilma Rousseff for a second term but also used by Brazil's historically extractivist and colonialist elites and also by the liberal press, who did not hide its opinion that Belo Monte was—as it is so often called—a "magnificent engineering project" and that agribusiness was an example of national "might." The "free market" was still the oracle, not science, much less forestpeoples.

At that time, critics of agribusiness expansion in the Amazon and in the Cerrado, another hard-hit ecosystem, were scarce, other than social-environmental organizations, and there were almost no barriers to it. Dissonant voices were cowardly attacked by the right, center, and also the left with ties to the PT. Belo Monte, like the Jirau, Santo Antônio, and Teles Pires dams, was built by violating nature and the rights of local populations, making them part of a thorny chapter in the dispute for power. These dams are a crime perpetrated by the alliance in power, led by the PT in alignment with large contractors and various other segments of the country's political and economic elites. Since the message was inconvenient, the outcry had to be silenced.

For much of the press, Belo Monte only became something to be denounced once Operation Car wash had shown what the forest-peoples, social movement leaders, and scientists had said well before the power plant dammed up the Xingu: that Belo Monte had been designed to generate more bribes than energy. At that point, given the newfound interest in removing the PT from power, Belo Monte no longer represented a magnificent engineering project but instead more proof of the incumbent party's corruption. While the violation of people's rights and the rights of nature had been denounced in more than twenty suits filed with the Public Prosecutor's Office, neither the right nor the majority portion of the left had ever assigned this any importance. It was only after the first rumblings about Dilma Rousseff's possible impeachment that the press made it a regular practice—one that was both stimulated and stimulating—to blast Belo Monte. The same press that had said nothing about the project, failed to investigate it, or even defended it now began denouncing what everybody already knew, as if it had never done precisely the opposite.

As a paradigmatic example of an Amazon-destroying project—the serpent's egg where an entire organic structure decries the corrupt, predatory colonialist worldview—Belo Monte expresses the context of those thirteen years of the PT in power, from the perspective of the forest. The Amazon was treated like a periphery, a source of raw materials for export, and, at that moment, also as a source of hydroelectric power. The extractivist perspective was embraced by a left that had been built around unions, with urban roots and embedded in industrialization, the left that deems the factory a symbol of progress. The extractivist perspective was also shared by those who belonged to what is conventionally (and, in my opinion, erroneously) called Brazil's "new middle class."

When Antonio Nobre released his report in 2014, only limited groups of society were interested in the Amazon and climate, topics that were only tangentially a part of national debate back then. The scientist was attacked by part of the Brazilian news media, who distorted what he wrote. It is reasonable to assume that some were driven by pressure from advertisers, who saw their interests in the Amazon taken to task. Antonio was also targeted by his peers, although generally behind the scenes. There were few frontal attacks on a report that valorized the best of science produced on the climate and the Amazon by the best of scientists, but there was much backstage whispering into opinion makers' ears with the goal of undermining his credibility. Nor was Antonio defended by his peers, many of whom had seen their work generously cited, analyzed, and popularized in his report. Envy and cowardice are entwined sentiments. It is never easy to deliver bad news that powerful sectors don't want announced to the public. Antonio ended up alone. Over the years, his active role, grounded in his understanding of himself as a scientist with public responsibility, has literally cost him pieces of his heart.

As for me, someone who had been traveling to the Amazon as a journalist since 1998 and closely following the wreckage caused by Belo Monte, the report woke me to the fact that it wasn't enough to denounce violence against the Xingu. I had to engage in the "war effort." It was through Antonio Nobre's words and his exhaustive endeavor to investigate everything of relevance that had been produced on the Amazon both inside and outside Brazil that I came to understand this as the great battle of my time.

Shortly after the report was released, Jan Rocha, the most Brazilian Brit I know, summoned me to her home. Jan was already a veteran of this war, having covered the Amazon ever since the destruction wrought by the business-military dictatorship's various government administrations in the 1970s, when she had realized that fighting for the Amazon and its peoples also obliged her to fight for those who had been disappeared, tortured, and imprisoned for political reasons by South American dictatorships. Jan was seventy-something but still had more energy than most of the young reporters I knew. A pair of probing eyes, a razor tongue, and seemingly perpetual bangs—these were the features an artist would use to draw her caricature. With Antonio Nobre's report ringing in her mind and her pupils lit with a spark, Jan received me in her home in São Paulo so we could sketch out a plan to awaken different spheres of Brazilian society and convince them to join the fight for the Amazon.

Jan and I knocked on a number of doors, sometimes with moderate success, mostly with none. Blatantly naive, we presented our "case" in a letter entitled "Carta para viver" (Letter for living). We opened with a quote from the US philosopher Donna Haraway. I had heard Haraway speak at "The Thousand Names of Gaia: From the Anthropocene to the Age of the Earth," a colloquium held in Rio de Janeiro in 2014, organized by the French philosopher Bruno Latour and the Brazilian thinkers Eduardo Viveiros de Castro and Déborah Danowski. When the seminar ended, I did a two-day-long interview with Eduardo and Déborah. Published in my column for *El País*, the piece resonated with intellectuals, who seemed to be waking up to the topic right then.

"The Thousand Names of Gaia" had my head swirling. At that time, I was unfamiliar with the Gaia hypothesis proposed by James Lovelock, one of the most famous British scientists alive and the closest to an inventor of fiction that we can find in the real world. In the late 1970s, Lovelock ignited passions and hatred, a cult following and mockery, when he introduced the idea that the planet is a dynamic, self-regulating community of intensely interacting organisms, a theory he baptized with a name borrowed from Greek mythology. For a more multicultural reader, it is quite evident that his thesis echoes centuries-old knowledge found in the cosmogony of most Indigenous peoples, but Lovelock acquired this knowledge along the course of a very specific journey and in his own terms. Language, after all, is not clothing but a way of inhabiting your own body. In an interview with the *Guardian*, philosopher Bruno Latour said that the electron capture detector, one of Lovelock's creations, revealed truths about life on the planet much as Galileo's telescope revealed truths about the universe.

At the historic seminar in Rio de Janeiro in 2014, the reference to Lovelock's Gaia theory was meant to evoke Earth's potential for creation and destruction. The event was both a warning and an irresistible invitation to ponder human experience through the effects caused by a species that had converted itself into a force of destruction capable of altering the planet's morphology.

Years later, in 2020, the banzeiro once again flung me into its implacable whirling, and I found myself having lunch at a typical British cottage on the banks of the Channel. Seated far enough away to comply with pandemic-imposed physical distancing requirements, I was talking with James Lovelock, who became Jim, and his wife, Sandy, an adorable American from Florida. At one hundred and one years old, Jim was almost as active as ever, working on a book, walking two kilometers a day, and with a mind as sharp as his tongue. My companion had indoctrinated me exhaustively about controlling my equally sharp tongue so I wouldn't set off any political discussion that might rouse tensions and sour the delicious fish pie, since Jim is politically conservative.

Minutes before, with the generosity of someone looking for a common topic to discuss with a stranger, Sandy had asked me why poor women in Brazil had so many children. She had read a few chapters of the book I'd published one year earlier in the United States and Great Britain, a collection of news stories, and it had left her depressed, frankly. Jim and Sandy are a charming couple, brimming with the savory stories of those who witnessed the twentieth century from the front row, and I believe that after the age of one hundred, you've won the right to say whatever you want.

In 2014, however, another thinker had captured my attention. A quotation from a video interview with Donna Haraway became my mantra. She lent words to the way I'd been living in recent years, the way, I suspect, I'll live forever. Here is how I remember her words: "We must live in terror and joy." Nothing about the experience of living at the intersection of the climate collapse and the sixth mass extinction seems more exact to me. This perception was to prepare me for life in the time of pandemics.

Here is Jan's and my "Letter for Living," dated February 2015:

"We must live in terror and joy."

This quotation is from the US philosopher Donna Haraway. It is a fitting quote at this moment in history, in which humankind has stopped fearing catastrophe to become the catastrophe it feared, in this era in which the climate crisis is possibly the greatest challenge in human history on Earth, at this point in time when all our efforts will be driven by the difference— and not a small one—between a worse planet and a planet hostile for our and other species, the latter of whom are innocent.

It was likewise with terror and joy that we read the report by the scientist Antonio Nobre, based on his analysis of two hundred scientific papers, entitled "The Future Climate of Amazonia." Joy, because Nobre describes forest processes that rival the beauty of a Beethoven symphony, a painting by Picasso, or a poem by Fernando Pessoa. Terror, because he shows us that 47 percent of the Amazon rainforest has been impacted by human activity in the last forty years. If this pace of destruction keeps up, children born at this moment, now, may reach adulthood with the forest converted into a cemetery. Joy because of the beauty, terror because of the brutality.

Antonio Nobre writes:

The forest has survived volcanism, glaciation, meteors, and continental drift for over fifty million years. But now, in less than fifty years, it is under threat from the actions of mere human beings.

As if all the extraordinary, surprising power of life in the Amazon did not suffice, the region is strategic to regulating the climate in Brazil and on the planet. It is possible that the current collapse in Brazil's water supply, especially in the Southeast, which has transformed São Paulo into a futurist dystopia, is also related to forest destruction.

A single large tree releases one thousand liters of water a day into the atmosphere through transpiration. The entire forest releases twenty trillion liters of water every twenty-four hours. By way of comparison, it should be remembered that the Amazon River releases less than this into the Atlantic Ocean. You don't have to be an expert to imagine what will happen to the planet without the forest. . . .

Earth will continue to exist despite the destruction of the forest and the impacts of climate collapse, but our life on it will be much less interesting. As always in such unequal societies, this will happen earlier for some than for others, but it will be worse for everyone the next instant. Not only will the life of human peoples be affected, so will the life of the many nonhuman species who can only sense we are finishing off their world. . . .

We have turned ourselves into a force of destruction and self-destruction capable of ending the possibility of living in the only home we have. And nothing seems to indicate that our fantasy about having other planets to immigrate to—and again set down the path to destruction there—is remotely close to anything but that, a fantasy. . . .

What terrifies us most, however, is that the majority of people, even when faced with such elegant proof, and with the immensity of this threat, have continued to deny the reality they too built. . . . We suffer disconnection from the world right at the most connected era in human history, when most people spend almost every waking hour of their lives online. It seems we are still the inhabitants of a modernity where humans believed themselves capable of overcoming even death, when the future was nothing but potential and progress, as pathetic in their illusions as in their arrogance. Confronted by tragedy, we call for government works projects, convinced that some paternal (or maternal) figure will save us from calamity. Or we label our disastrous actions "fate."

For many, too many, it makes more sense to mobilize for an end to a fictitious world, like the one in Mayan prophecy, precisely because it is fictitious, than to mobilize to address the many real epilogues represented by the climate emergency, where the Amazon rainforest plays a crucial role. In the interview "Dialogues on the End of the World," the anthropologist Eduardo Viveiros de Castro proposed using a concept by the German thinker Günther Anders to explain why most people—and not just in Brazil but all around the planet—are disconnected from the challenges of the climate crisis.

We are all familiar with the notion of subliminal phenomena, so tiny and invisible we simply can't perceive them. Anders talked about the "supraliminal," phenomena so large we can't perceive them either, this time because of their immensity. In his era, he used the word to refer to the atomic bomb, to the moment when humans created something whose effects they were incapable of imagining. Eduardo Viveiros de Castro has suggested that the climate crisis will be one of these supraliminal phenomena, which we can't see precisely because its impact is so huge.

It seems we can sense life corroding, but we are unable to name it. Or we give it other names. We are experiencing a kind of alienated stupor, which might partly explain the success of zombie movies and television series. The tragedy is that there is no time to shape a new generation, one capable of comprehending the world it lives in and reacting to what is already here, assuming its responsibility. As Antonio Nobre says in his report, it is not enough to reduce the deforestation of the Amazon to zero now, immediately, something nowhere near happening. We must restore the forest. Now, immediately. The Brazilian scientist urges us to engage in a campaign as efficacious as the one against tobacco: once a symbol of glamour between the lips of a Rita Hayworth in the role of Gilda, cigarettes are now a symbol of decadence that triggers revulsion rather than seduction.

Nobre talks about a "war effort" for the Amazon, if we don't want to reach the point of no return, already so close at hand. If the Amazon is destroyed, neither the big soybean planters nor the big cattle ranchers who are cutting down the forest today will be spared; their businesses are already feeling the effects of climate collapse. . . . The challenge of reforesting the Amazon demands an alliance among all of society's forces, all areas and all fields of knowledge, an alliance against ignorance. The Amazon can no longer be seen as a body to be exploited, as an imagination at the service of opportunistic nationalisms.

The Amazon is a world to which one belongs but which belongs to no one. Everything we do from this point on will not be to save the forest but to save ourselves. The ones who will have to take up this task are the imperfect generations now here, consumerist men and women, inconsequential and arrogant, generations of which we too are part. The only human matter we have is ourselves. The time to wake up has passed. Now it is time to wake up in a panic.

This is where we come in, filled with terror and joy. Terror because of the urgency and monumental size of the task. Joy because we have snapped out of our paralysis and stupor and are beginning to move.

This text is an invitation for you to move with us.

The image that inspired this letter, that of the rainforest transpiring and saving the planet, moves me every day. Its flying rivers are masses of air filled with water vapor, formed largely when the forest transpires. Propelled by winds, these invisible air streams leave the Amazon laden with moisture and are transported to Southeastern, Central-Western, and Southern Brazil, where they fall as rain under certain atmospheric conditions. It is as if the forest were a kind of sump pump, pulling evaporated moisture from the Atlantic Ocean to the continent, where it turns into rainfall and drenches the Amazon. The forest then transpires, releasing moisture back into the atmosphere in the form of water vapor, which flies through the sky to become rain in other regions, in a chain of interconnected events.

The flying rivers irrigating the world above our heads, rivers that once were the sweat of oceans, have expanded my concept of beauty. When my body is fixed in the Xingu or the Iriri or the Riozinho and I look up to the sky, I connect with the feeling of how tremendous it is to have one river flowing through me on Earth and another in the air. I remember a certain evening in 2001, in Yanomami territory, when I dove into a river of stars merging into a sky of stars. High atop the hills, the village was having a ritual party and the rhythm of dancing feet pounded in my ears like drums. It was the first time in my life I felt myself nature. I was complete. I think it was there that the Amazon captured me. That's when I began belonging to her.

But the road would be long until I finally got there. Antonio Nobre's scientific-poetic report was an important chapter in my quest. This is also what a scientist does, after all. Antonio Nobre was the first scientist I met who had learned from the original peoples and traditional communities that science and poetry share the same root; they are not two trees but one. And he was the one who taught me the forest is not only the world's lungs (and its kidneys and liver) but, along with the oceans and other ecosystems, is also its heart. While I write, the forest is moving a complex hydrography above our heads, pumping water through the body-planet.

In our response to Antonio's summons, Jan and I seemed like two rather eccentric figures, knocking on doors to proclaim the end of the world as if we were some bizarre Amazonian sect born in São Paulo. At five foot five (and shrinking), I'm not exactly tall but I look like a basketball player next to Jan. We went to visit a filmmaker we both admired, at his production company; he even offered us coffee, though he didn't have the slightest idea what to do with the exotic duo sitting across from him. When we left, Jan remarked that we looked like Don Quixote and Sancho Panza. The truth is, we knew who we were fighting against, but we didn't yet know who might fight with us—or how.

Early one morning not long after that, I was checking my Twitter account and came across a report about the first climate initiative against the state to be taken by civil society, a representative group in Holland that also included thirty children. My heart did vaults like the gymnast Rebeca Andrade. That's it, I thought. Jan and I contacted Conrado Hübner Mendes, a constitutionalist and professor at the University of São Paulo Law School; I'd just met him because I had needed to bother him about another topic, I don't remember now what. Our idea was to file a class action suit on behalf of the Amazon, in the name of children, mainly as a political-educational movement to awaken an awareness of the climate emergency, a movement capable of crossing the various Brazils and uniting them around this bigger cause. Other people and organizations joined us and the first idea evolved into another, as it should be, and the group grew and multiplied. The movement was launched at a closed seminar in August 2016 at the University of São Paulo Law School, where I read the Letter for Living. When the strategic lawsuit was finally filed, in November 2020, these roots had already been forgotten. The best thing that can happen is for an idea to be embraced by various protagonists, to the point that those who started down the path are superseded—which is different, of course, from being erased. This is the best way for a movement to not have an owner, although this might also mean that what you thought up turns into something else, sometimes much better, sometimes much worse. But this is how movement transpires when it involves all peoples.

On this pilgrimage with Jan, I came to understand that it isn't enough to do what we know how to do during this era we've been given to live in. We must also do what we don't know how to do. With Jan and the Letter for Living, I started doing what I didn't know how to do. And that's where I still am today, doing what I know how to do and what I don't. The letter and subsequent gestures were my first acts beyond journalism and literature. Some call this activism but imbue this generous word with a pejorative connotation. I feel honored when I'm called an activist, because I take action and try to do so swiftly, never alone and always in the name of the commons. But I prefer to call it "collective responsibility." We're defined by what we choose to be at extreme moments in life, moments that are inflection points and that require us to take stances that imply concrete and symbolic losses. By doing what I know how to do and what I don't, I assure myself every day of my right to look the next generation in the eyes, the generation that will inherit the world we leave behind. In the words of the Uruguayan writer Eduardo Galeano, addressing the young people who occupied Barcelona in 2011 as part of the 15-M movement: "This shitty world is pregnant with another."

I want to be fully alive and I want my life to go on, and so I've joined with those who are birthing a world where we can live. As an individual, my existence is limited, but as a collective, we can continue to live and create life, enduring not only as a human collective but well beyond. I am aligning myself with Indigenous peoples when I let my life be guided by the conviction that the collective is more important than the individual. The collective is the forest, this organic planet where I am—and I only am because I am in an intense relationship with all livingkind.

In 2020, Jonathan Watts wrote a seminal article about the struggle for the Amazon as the great battle of the twenty-first century. It was also a letter, although it didn't announce itself as such. Watts recalled how people from different parts of the world, different classes, and different professions joined in the Spanish Civil War (1936–39), people who intuited that they were hearing the call of a generation, that it was the moment to engage in a fight against totalitarianism before it took root in Europe. And then he compared this active intuition with the need to engage in planet-wide solidarity with the planet's largest tropical forest.

For nearly two decades, Watts had been a correspondent for the *Guardian* in Japan and then in China, where he had followed the fascinating and frightening supergrowth of the Asian giant, which had a big impact on Brazil. In 2012, he became the *Guardian*'s correspondent in Brazil. He thought he'd find a country where social equity and environmental conservation could be reconciled, but soon discovered that wasn't the case. In 2017, he knocked at the door of the collective space I shared in downtown São Paulo and invited me to help create a fund to finance reporting on the Amazon. By following other paths, Watts had also realized that the accelerated destruction of the rainforest demanded that we enable ourselves to do more than report. Not because it's easy to report, much less because reporting does little. But because we also had to do what we didn't know how to do in order to answer the summons of our era.

In Watts's case, soon after arriving in Brazil he'd figured out that both the Brazilian and foreign press told the story of the

forest much less than it should, considering its strategic importance. This is partly because reporting in the Amazon is expensive and the business model practiced in newsrooms was in deep
crisis. In my opinion, the international media and part of the
Brazilian press, based in the South-Central region, especially in
São Paulo and Rio de Janeiro, was—and still is—woefully ignorant of the Amazon. Much later, in 2019, by which time I was living in Altamira and Bolsonarism was setting the forest afire, this
ignorance produced scenes that would have been comical were
the situation not so serious. Journalists from all over Brazil and
from abroad called me to ask where the fire was. Not looking for
satellite information, but almost as if they wanted to know the
fire's address, something along the lines of "Turn on Waze and
off you go."

The reporters thought they could disembark at the Altamira
airport and there would be the fire, surrounding the city. Since it
wasn't, and they needed to meet the deadline set by their bosses,
who also had no idea how the forest works, they ended up taking
their chances. One journalist arrived in Altamira without talking
to anyone, rented a car at Localiza, the local rental agency, and
asked if it would be okay to take the Transamazonian Highway.
Of course, the airport staff said. And off she went, alone, venturing down side roads along the Transamazonian, looking for
smoke. She ran into gunmen and returned unscathed to tell the
story only because they must have realized she really had no clue
where she was. Another journalist tried to get to Altamira but
ended up confusing the Amazon, the region, with Amazonas,
the state. She bought a ticket to Manaus, and from there spent
days on a boat before she finally reached southwest Pará. Others
thought they could take care of it all in two days—and by taxi.

I bring up these examples simply to illustrate how crucial it
was right then to find a way to expand and enhance coverage of
the Amazon. As a journalist enthralled with his profession and
rooted in the idealistic model of the *Guardian*, an independent

newspaper that directs its earnings back into itself, Watts wanted to figure out how to multiply investments in news reporting on the Amazon. His goal was to foster both international and local reporting in Amazonian cities and states, with particular interest in encouraging journalism by forestpeoples, in the forest.

By the time he knocked on my door to extend his invitation, this Brit, who had spent twenty-one years far from London, the city where he was born and raised, had already asked Norway's International Climate and Forest Initiative (NICFI) for $1.5 million. It was a bold move with little chance of working. But not only did it work, the program with ties to the Norwegian government pledged $5.5 million over the course of five years. The project was also expanded to include tropical rainforests in Asia and Africa. Thus the Rainforest Journalism Fund (RJF) was born, an idea of Watts's, with the help of five other journalists he had recruited: Daniela Chiaretti, Thomas Fischermann, Simon Romero, Fabiano Maisonnave, and me.

Once the project had been set up and financing guaranteed, fund management was assigned to the Pulitzer Center in Washington, DC. Those of us who founded the RJF were limited to sitting on the committee that defines priorities for coverage in the Amazon and selects the projects to be funded. Great achievements usually begin with idealistic gestures that should inspire other movements but instead are often swallowed up by larger structures. Making memory and impeding erasure is one of the noblest missions of the journalism that merits this name.

When Jon Watts framed his six feet, two inches, in my doorway that day, we had never met. We only knew of each other from reading each other's articles, and I had an atavistic mistrust of gringo journalists. I imagined I would listen to him with a Mona Lisa smile and send him out the same door he had come in. Jon, however, is a people whisperer. I'm famed for making the worst coffee in the world, but when I gave him a cup, he thought it was great. He had several servings of my cold coffee and dug into the cookies I'd bought at the bakery. We chatted on the balcony, in Portuglish, while downtown São Paulo snarled around us. It was mid-2017 and I was preparing my move to Altamira, scheduled for August of that year. We would only meet again much later.

On November 3, 2020, on the eve of England's second COVID-19 lockdown, we were married on the banks of the Thames. We had already begun building our home in Altamira on the banks of the Xingu. Our pact is one of love, of journalism, of caring—for each other and for others. Of life and struggle. Our only unbreakable agreement is to have a living life together. Rivers were also flying above our heads.

10. the soccer ball

Xingu, the word that designates the Amazon River's colossal branch, means "dwelling of the gods." Antonia Melo, the most notable grassroots leader in the Middle Xingu, interpreted my move to Altamira as a matter of destiny, decided by the goddesses and gods who have made the Xingu their home. They had taken me there, Antonia believed, so I could fulfill my mission with the forestpeoples. It always does me good to hear this kind of prophecy repeated by the kapok tree in the form of a woman called Antonia Melo, whose powerful roots nourish other women in a gesture of might within Altamira's social movement.

I'm generally not driven by certainties. I'm more a creature carried along by uncertainty and a sense of intuition that grows ever fiercer as I age. Since I feel lost all the time, off-balance and off-track, I'm grateful when someone believes there's something determined and predestined in the erratic path of my life. This certainty coming from the outside grants me an ephemeral moment of peacefulness. And then I start questioning everything all over again.

I remember looking at myself from the outside, seated in my favorite armchair in my apartment in São Paulo a few weeks before I moved to Altamira, feeling so deliciously cozy and at home. At the same time, sitting there with a book in my hand and a glass of wine on the end table, soft light falling from an old lamp, I sensed the banzeiro that was already spinning away inside me. I guessed that nothing would be like it was before, that I would never return to that armchair with the feeling life might finally become welcoming and soft.

I realized this was my last chance to stay rather than leave and dedicate myself to my eternal plan to write nothing but fiction about the excessively real stories I've witnessed or experienced. It was my very last opportunity to interrupt the flow of the waters pulling me to the Xingu. The *buiúna*, a creature half anaconda, half woman, had cast her hair over me like a web, reaching me even in the giant city where rivers lie buried and cemented over, reaching me even in my middle-class São Paulo life. She invaded the scene of this woman drinking wine, book in hand, seated in an antique armchair in the dim light. I looked at the man who had been by my side for fifteen years and said: "I'm afraid of what's going to happen. I'm so afraid I feel almost paralyzed."

I didn't have the strength to resist, and I didn't want to. All of the intimate, personal life I'd woven up until then, with deep love and some skill, was now splintered by this choice, including a marriage that had given me the best that a loving partnership between two people who respect and admire each other can give. It had also given me a much more generous view of myself, sewing me up inside with threads spun of utmost delicacy over the years. But only the following year would I know how much I'd need to destroy to recreate myself as a Xinguan. And not because being Xinguan was my destiny, but because I only know how to be by recreating myself from time to time, and what is comfortable discomforts me. I don't think things were better or worse; they were better and also worse. They were. And here I am. And from here I go on.

When I reached the Xingu in 2017 to place my body in the Amazon in a different way, I carried with me the experience of a series of comings and goings. I'd made my first foray into the beiradeiro world and the Xingu thirteen years earlier, in 2004, when I became the first journalist to travel to Terra do Meio, back then much more isolated and harder to reach than it is today. I traveled in the company of a small man with the slight body of a bird and the eyes of an oncilla. Herculano Porto's eyes spent every second stalking his own body.

Herculano had undertaken his long passage—via river, rocks, and rapids—from Altamira to the territory known as Riozinho do Anfrísio clutching a soccer ball. He'd caught a bad cold during his spell in the city, where he'd had to reach so far outside his world that it cowed him. The ball was a kind of anchor; without it he'd be flung untethered into the air. I think it was only then that I understood what soccer is about in Brazil, this game that federation officials, team presidents, and transnational corporations have devoted themselves to destroying.

In 2014, I was to cover the World Cup from the angle of life around the Brazilian national team. But I never saw this kind of soccer at the team's headquarters in Granja Comary, neither inside nor outside the gates. When the German national team annihilated Brazil—with a 7 to 1 score that didn't traumatize anyone, because most everyone knew the Brazilian national team was the portrait of a corrupt country—I was stunned like everyone else in the stadium, but only by the insane speed of the balls that wouldn't stop entering Brazil's goal. I wasn't saddened. A soccer ball was the ball Herculano held as if he had the whole world in his hands, and he did. The ball on the turf in Mineirão stadium was something else, billions of dollars spinning around it, with damaged boys balancing on their sponsored cleats.

Herculano Porto, the man with the ball, was the only person in the beiradeiro community of some two hundred adults and children who had an ID card. So he was the only person who existed officially. That's why he'd been chosen to undertake a journey to the country called Brazil to tell them the beiradeiros existed—and that they were in danger of existing no longer. Herculano had traveled five days on a speedy voadeira motorboat to the nearest city, Altamira, where he delivered a petition that asked for protection. It was signed by every head of family in his region with their thumbprint, since no one in Riozinho do Anfrísio was literate except him. This had been Herculano's first mission in the city, and he accomplished it. The second, just as important, was to get a soccer ball. Herculano accomplished this as well.

Herculano, like all the other beiradeiros, had descended from the first Northeasterners dispatched to the forest to tap rubber. And he was literate because his father had once been the boss of a small rubber plantation. Herculano was born a beiradeiro, married a beiradeira, and raised a family of beiradeiro children on the banks of the river they call Riozinho—Little River—but that, like almost everything in the Amazon, is small in name only. The forest has no room for diminutives; in it, even the invisible is great. And the Riozinho is possibly the biggest little river in the world. It is called Anfrísio's Riozinho because a man named Anfrísio Nunes was once the region's greatest rubber baron. In the logic of the day, the Riozinho was therefore his, because if there was a white man, there had to be property.

Forgotten by the official Brazil, the community had lived almost a century without being endangered. And then the *grileiros* arrived with their gunmen. This figure, the grileiro—or land grabber, to put it simply—is key to understanding the destruction of the rainforest, yesterday, today, always. Most of the big grileiros are men from South-Central Brazil, many from São Paulo, Goiás, Minas Gerais, Paraná, Rio Grande do Sul, and the Federal District. They don't live in the Amazon or get their hands dirty. They are members of the elites, who pass themselves off as "clean" and "civilized." Some move in sophisticated circles and, right now, while I'm writing and you're reading, they might be playing polo or listening to the São Paulo Symphony Orchestra. Others are coarser, and there are even some grileiros who head up churches that espouse market neo-Pentecostalism. In 2017, I met—and the photographer Lilo Clareto photographed—an example of one of these Christians fishing in the Terra do Meio Ecological Station in holy illegality. Known in the region as "the Apostle," he arrived in his own plane and landed on a clandestine airstrip. That night,

Lilo and I were subtly locked in by the bodies of two of his collaborators, who also had "property" in a formally protected area. They tied a hammock to the door of the house where we were staying so we couldn't get out. A lovely night.

Most grileiros have front men in the region, and the front men command the gunmen. Others, lesser by comparison, live in Amazon cities like Altamira, are explicitly truculent, and often run for local office or put forward right-hand men as candidates— and often win local elections, one way or another. When Jair Bolsonaro came onto the scene touting the torturer Carlos Alberto Brilhante Ustra and displaying chances of winning the presidency in 2018, grileiros in Altamira and throughout the region went nuts. Members of a broad array of parties, they joined forces to plaster Amazon cities with billboards in support of "Bolsolegend."

Grileiros are people who take thousands and sometimes millions of hectares of public land illegally and generally by force, in a scheme known as *grilagem*. To solidify their dominion, grileiros in the Amazon rely on militias of hired guns who drive out forestpeoples—the Indigenous, beiradeiros, and quilombolas. Forestpeoples are murdered in the process, placing Brazil on the podium of countries where the greatest number of environmental defenders die, year after year. Grileiros chop down trees for their hardwood—known as "noble" wood in Brazil because of its value on domestic and foreign markets—and set the rest of life ablaze, igniting the fires that horrorstruck the world in 2019. Then they bring in cattle mainly to guarantee possession. The illegal work is often done by enslaved men. If they rebel, they're buried right there, in graves never to be found.

In 2005, Lilo Clareto and I spent a few days in Castelo de Sonhos—Castle of Dreams—one of the most insane, violent places in insane, violent Altamira. The madness begins with the fact that Castelo de Sonhos lies nearly seven hundred miles from Altamira, the city, and even so it is part of Altamira, the municipality (roughly akin to a parish or county). Given the scarcity or even nonexistence of public policy implementation at the level of the municipal seat, it's easy to imagine how fast and often these policies make themselves felt in the outlying district of Castelo de Sonhos. When I interviewed the town's hospitable founder, he told me about journalists who had been tossed out of planes midair. Nice.

Amid this insanity, one must go insane as well, and so at one point, Lilo and I rode around Castelo de Sonhos in a pickup truck with a gunman under the bed cover. I interviewed the fellow in the hotel room while Lilo somehow managed to calmly take a shower in the room next door. The gunman was on the run from other gunmen. As he sat there, he told me one of his job duties was "settling" labor issues for grileiros, and then he gave me an account of the places where the bodies of rebellious workers lay buried.

Part of my news story was told in graphic terms through the cemetery in Castelo de Sonhos, where the tombs are related to each other, since some victims are buried quite close to their executioners, who were subsequently killed by someone more dangerous. Here is an excerpt from my report:

> Castelo de Sonhos is Amazonian madness. These half dozen streets wrapped in clouds of dust are part of the municipality of Altamira. . . . Altamira is the size of Belgium and Greece combined and . . . larger than twelve of Brazil's states. As is so often the case in a new land, those who move to Castelo want to leave their past behind and build a new identity. So there are few last names and lots of nicknames there. Nicknames are more common in the cemetery—no cross, no name, no family to follow up on the death. The only people known by their full names are the ones who have fenced in their landholdings and thus ensured a fixed place in the new world. . . .
>
> The people who lie buried in Castelo de Sonhos cemetery believed the town's name was a sign of good luck. The people still alive have stayed because there's no way to go back, or be-

cause they've gone too far. Located along Interstate BR-163, Castelo de Sonhos is a dusty snapshot of the state of Pará, national champion in land conflicts, murders in the countryside, and the enslavement of laborers. The cemetery, with its unequal division between victims and gunmen, is a synthesis of the region's geopolitics. No instigators are buried there; natural deaths are a rarity; to die after the age of fifty is to earn immunity. In Castelo de Sonhos, you can watch a replay of the brutal colonization of Brazil in present time, portrait of a country that inhabits various historical eras simultaneously. Brazilians who see the Far West as folklore from some distant world are wrong. The fate of the Amazon is decided in the most ancient way possible in Pará. At gunpoint.

Using their connections in Congress and also in the executive branch, grileiros push through laws that legalize the stolen land with the pretext of "land tenure regulation," which regulates nothing but large tracts of land taken from the state. These are what part of society calls "Grilagem Provisional Measures," which later turn into Grilagem laws. In this century alone, Lula, of the center-left Workers' Party (PT), sanctioned one such law; Michel Temer, of PMDB, a right-wing party that portrays itself as centrist, sanctioned another; and, at the time of this writing, Bolsonaro is trying to pass the most outrageous of them all.

Legalization washes the blood from both land and language. Through this alchemy, criminals are converted into "fazendeiros," "ruralists," and "rural producers." Many of them sell the land. Speculating with what used to be forest but is now a commodity in the country's land bank is the best deal on the planet, since the land is stolen and the only investments required are the hired gunmen's low pay and the cheap (and scant) food that just barely keeps the enslaved alive—that is, when the laborers themselves aren't forced to pay dearly for it, accruing unpayable debts, in another form of contemporary slavery. When they aren't enslaved, the laborers receive a disgraceful sum in the form of day wages.

Land speculation is the prime objective for some of these grileiros, a word that literally means "cricketers" in Portuguese, from the insect. The name was acquired because the men used to consummate their fraud by placing new sheets of paper and live crickets in boxes where the insects—so lovable in Disney productions but known in the Amazon for other talents—produced excrement that yellowed the documents and made them look more believably like old land titles. Of course, none of this would have been possible without the well-paid collaboration of deed registrars. This particular type of criminal earned the title *grileiro*, or "cricketer" and the act of stealing public land and converting it into private property through this form of counterfeiting eventually became known as grilagem, or "cricketing." INCRA, Brazil's land and agrarian reform agency, offers the following definition of *grilagem*: "In generic terms, any illegal action aimed at transferring public lands to third-party assets constitutes [an act of] grilagem or *grilo*, which commences in office rooms and is consolidated in the field through the issuance of land ownership."

In the Amazon, the looting of public lands finds an ally in agrarian and environmental legislation, where abundant loopholes facilitate obtaining deeds to illegally appropriated land. In practice, grilagem occurs on two planes, one on the ground, the other on paper. The physical appropriation of land often takes place by expropriating it from other occupants, even legitimate ones such as beiradeiro and quilombola communities. At least part of the area also has to be deforested, since toppled forest is the verifiable "proof" of occupation. Violence is the main instrument of control over this stolen land. On paper, the land is withdrawn from public assets and transferred into the grileiro's private assets. This process is repeated time and again, historically and circularly. After the land has been appropriated and deforested, lobbies push for amnesties that will make the crime a fait accompli and transform illegality into legality. And then the cycle starts anew: illegality produces laws that in turn create repeated circles of illegality.

Nobody taught me more about grilagem than Maurício Torres, an academic, journalist, and top-level researcher who moves through the deep forest with uncommon adroitness, always in the state of Pará, where he blends consistent theoretical knowledge with thousands of hours of fieldwork. Maurício possesses a caustic sense of humor that spares no one and a pair of eyes that take in everything. Whenever I go on an expedition with him, I try to stay out of his line of fire so I don't become a character in one of the mind-boggling stories he so often tells to thoroughly rapt audiences. I always fail.

In one of his studies, Maurício Torres showed that the municipality of São Félix do Xingu would have to be three stories high to account for all the titles registered at land deed offices in 2009. While the municipality covered an area of 32,500 square miles—roughly the size of South Carolina—registered deeds tallied more than 110,000 square miles. "A modest building," remarked Maurício, "if we bear in mind much worse cases, like Vitória do Xingu, also in Pará, where registered land deeds totaled hundreds of times the municipality's area." These figures help explain both the voracity of grilagem as well as the corruption on the part of public and private agents who allow public land to be registered in private names. It also shows why land conflict is common even among grileiros, since there are too many "owners" for these lands that, according to the Constitution, actually belong to the entire population.

The Amazon is first destroyed for speculation, and then later, maybe, somebody will contemplate producing soybeans to feed cattle or cattle to feed humans. Duly laundered and legalized, the theft then becomes "agribusiness," while the criminals become "upstanding citizens," sometimes mayors, recognized by local society as "pioneers." And when they die, with a little effort they might merit a street name or a statue in a park.

At the time of my first foray into the Xingu, in 2004, Brazil's biggest grileiro was Cecílio do Rego Almeida. One Brazilian magazine labeled him "the world's biggest grileiro," but I have found no evidence to back up this affirmation. Don Ciccillo, as he was known, lived in Curitiba, capital of the Southern state of Paraná. He was the owner of the construction firm CR Almeida and also claimed ownership of over 23,000 square miles of Amazon rainforest, comprising Indigenous lands, public lands, and INCRA settlements. The country that Cecílio stole from Brazil became known as Ceciliolândia—Cecil Land. It was as big as Holland and Belgium combined and was embedded in Terra do Meio. Riozinho, the extractive reserve where Herculano Porto and his beiradeiro community lived, was part of this kingdom illegally ruled by one of the most illustrious members of Paraná society.

Cecílio became Don Ciccillo during the business-military dictatorship, when CR Almeida chomped up thirty-seven major federal works projects and became a powerhouse. Until his death in 2008, Cecílio was never held accountable for his evil deeds, and he used to refer to Brazil's regime of exception as "the mildest of dictatorships." Certain of his impunity, with all due reason, Don Ciccillo never minced words. When Marina Silva was Lula's environmental minister from 2003 to 2008, he once called her "that totally sick, illiterate little Indian." Olívio Dutra, ex-governor of Rio Grande do Sul and ex-minister under Lula, earned the epithet "fag." And he referred to Chico Mendes in these terms: "The rubber tapper who got fucked."

That's the person, and personage, he was. None of these credentials kept André Vargas, federal congressman with the PT and then assistant speaker of the house, from drafting a bill to honor Don Ciccillo in 2009. By March 2013, the bill had passed through three house committees and been praised on social media by members of the PT. Under the proposal, a stretch of

Interstate BR-277 (one of Southern Brazil's main highways), between the cities of Paranaguá and Curitiba, would be christened Cecílio do Rego Almeida Highway. I decided to check out the rationale offered by this lawmaker, who would later be arrested for corruption as a result of the Carwash investigation. Vargas defended his tribute to "Brazil's greatest grileiro" with these words:

> The designation intended to be conferred on the cited stretch of highway is a just tribute to Mr. Cecílio do Rego Almeida, the founding entrepreneur and chair of the Administrative Council of the Grupo CR Almeida, which encompasses more than thirty companies working in the areas of heavy construction, highway concessions, transportation logistics, chemicals, and explosives.

The lawmaker closed with: "He persevered in his work goals and now, after his death . . . this charitable citizen shall receive a well-deserved tribute."

It was against this type of power—wielding this much might and maintaining a presence throughout public institutions and across the whole ideological palette—that Herculano Porto and two hundred beiradeiros whose existence in Brazil had not been officially recognized were fighting on the forest ground. When I reached them in 2004, motorboats were passing by their houses loaded with armed gunmen, who would first set their Brazil nut groves ablaze and then their homes. And if the beiradeiros didn't then abandon the region, it would be time for bullets to find their bodies. The fight was led by the beiradeiros Herculano Porto, Raimundo Belmiro, and Luiz Augusto Conrado (known as Manchinha), armed only with the courage to dig their feet into the land and resist like forest.

I wasn't ignorant about the Amazon when I got to the house-forest, mother-forest, and people-forest of Herculano and his beiradeiro community. I had already traveled the Transamazonian

Highway, accompanied midwives of the forest in the state of Amapá, journeyed through Yanomami territory. Terra do Meio, however, carried my senses to another level of experience. It was like reaching the beginning of the world, one day before the forest was hit by the destructive power of whites. And it was like reaching me, an unknown part of me, silenced and shoved to the bottomless bottom. I wasn't able to ascribe words to it then, but Riozinho made a home inside me. From that moment on, I have never stopped wanting to return time and time again to Terra do Meio and the rivers of the Xingu basin.

We traveled five days by voadeira with no awning and no seats, exposed to sun and rain, hauling the boat through rapids by rope, hanging our hammocks on the riverbanks to cook our only daily meal, sometimes fish, sometimes a river turtle called a *tracajá*, food we brought with us or food the bowman caught along the way or bartered with the few Indigenous whose canoes crossed with ours. And then on the fifth day, when we reached the mouth of the Riozinho do Anfrísio, thousands of yellow butterflies flew up and away at the sound of the motor. It was like being sucked through a door and cast into an even more wonderfully wild world. For me, Riozinho will always be the land of yellow butterflies. And will always be my inner place in the outer world. Years later I would leave instructions to my family that when I die, my body should be cremated. Half the ashes will be buried in the tomb I bought in the cemetery in the rural village where my father was born, in far Southern Brazil, and half will be spread at the mouth of the Riozinho, there where it kisses the Iriri.

Before I go on, I have to tell you a little bit more about this passage from the official country to the invisible country, from buried rivers to wild rivers, from outside to inside me. Since I was still quite white in my reading back then, the first reference that popped into my head to name my amazement was Joseph Conrad's *Heart of Darkness*: "The best way I can explain it to you is by saying that, for a second or two, I felt as though, instead of going to the centre of a continent, I were about to set off for the centre of the earth."

Its gentle christening aside, the little river of Riozinho is wild. Tree trunks formed caves atop the water, a pair of giant otters dove about right in front of us, and thousands, perhaps millions, of yellow butterflies kept us company on our labyrinthine course. It seemed we had been swallowed up into some unknown dimension in a distracted blink of the eye. I felt like I was diving deeper and deeper into Earth. A certainty burned between my breasts the whole time, a certainty that no matter how well I might write, I would be unable to capture the dimension of what I saw and lived.

Any journalist who makes themself out to be a great adventurer is simply foolish. Just live alongside the pilots and bowmen of Amazonian motor canoes and you'll retreat into your inescapable insignificance. They can spot *tracajá* eggs where I see only sand, pointy rocks where I see only water, rain where I see only blue. I could barely manage to hang my hammock in a tree at bedtime.

The pilot who took us to Terra do Meio, Bené, was a legitimate Amazonian. He had been it all and done it all. In his toils and travels as a rubber tapper, woodsman, cat hunter, pimp, and gold miner, Bené had gazed deeper inside the human beast than sanity allows. On the last day of our trip, we had to spend the night in the middle of thick woods because the motor on the voadeira died before we reached our intended place of rest. While we waited for the fish to roast, Bené told us one of his mining tales. A plane had crashed on a clandestine airstrip and Bené had helped pull the dead and living from the wreckage. I actually thought the story a little ho-hum, with just two lousy dead men—the night before he had dispatched some forty of them off to hell. But I was naive. Without a pause, as natural and fluid as an eel, Bené declaimed his vexing punchline: "The mechanic was all burned up—the only distinguishable thing left was his bottom half. And then my buddy goes over and has himself a quick little piece of ass!" We all assumed he meant this in the biblical sense (which would in itself, if you will, be absurd). But Bené cleared it up: "He sliced off a chunk and ate it. And said it was yummy. The fellow had a stomach you wouldn't believe."

The first two days were the most complicated for me. It was like leaving one world and entering another, no layovers. It was a lot of everything: a lot of sun, a lot of one-hundred-degree heat, a lot of mosquitoes, caimans, rays, a lot of spiders, a lot of jungle. And it was the first day of my period, and there were five men with me and no privacy. By the third day I was overcome by the spirit of Saint Teresa of Ávila and from then on remained in a state of constant ecstasy, something that generally happens on my travels. I had taken *On the Road* to read at night in my hammock before sleep, using my fashionable headlamp. Sorry, Jack Kerouac. In my situation, on the river, your adventures made me yawn, which was great for falling asleep in a forest populated by jaguars and very quiet anacondas.

The middle people—as I call the beiradeiro community from Terra do Meio, or Middle Earth—were extremely shy around strangers like me. White, a woman, from the world out there. They blended into the forest, moving as sinuously as jaguars and snakes, regarding me with watchful eyes. Though we seemed to speak the same language, we actually didn't. For them I was an alien. And that's precisely what I was. I was traveling with a representative of the Pastoral Land Commission, who was taking them their first two-way radio, donated by a Dutch organization; the equipment would be used to denounce death threats, fires, attacks. I knew this would be the most important news story of my life, because never again would I be able to leave that world that wasn't me but reminded me of me. I went back to São Paulo, but never again have I left Riozinho or Terra do Meio.

The story I wrote had a big impact. Marina Silva was then minister of the environment and, as she was to tell me over the phone, people like Herculano, Raimundo, and Manchinha, the three Riozinho leaders who were suffering death threats from the grileiros, were her family. Marina had once been a rubber tapper like them, so she was no stranger to that world, even though it was an Amazon different from hers. What followed was a rather epic story, in which the three men were swooped out of the forest by helicopter and taken to Brasília to tell cabinet ministers what they were going through. Hoisted away as he was heading out to the fields, Raimundo had malaria in his body and no shoes on his feet when he confronted the official Brazil. The three of them paid their first visit to the planet of necktied aliens, starting with Brasília no less, the modernist capital designed by Oscar Niemeyer. Elevators and escalators would later take the shape of starships in the bulging eyes of small children on the nights when Herculano illuminated the forest with stories of an unknown world known only to the three heroes.

In November of that same year, 2004, the Riozinho do Anfrísio Extractive Reserve was born under a presidential decree signed by Lula, and since then it has been a protected territory in the form of a federal conservation area. It was a victory for the resistance: first, that of the beiradeiro community, the ones most responsible for this outcome, since it was their bodies facing the bullets; next, that of organizations fighting for the forest, like the Pastoral Land Commission and the Socioenvironmental Institute (Instituto Socioambiental, or ISA); and, further, that of a power project that respected the forest and its peoples, as was the case with Marina Silva and her group, then under heavy attack from developmentalist sectors within Lula's government, whose most visible representative was Dilma Rousseff, mines and energy minister.

It was also a victory for me and Lilo Clareto as reporters, fulfilling our role as a bridge between worlds, traversing many Brazils to reach the voices of the beiradeiro community and carry them to the ears of authorities at a volume too loud to be ignored. It was one of the few victories I had achieved in more than thirty years denouncing assaults on life. Since I'm a regular visitor to the psychoanalytic couch, I believe this rare victory within an existence of defeats was determinant in my decision to live on the edges of the Xingu more than ten years later, when I came to understand that the Amazon was my generation's struggle and Belo Monte was the project that told of an entire country. I could have gone to any other river in the Amazon, but it was Riozinho that called me like a mythical creature, from inside, where it had long washed across my depths, birthing yellow butterflies.

It was several years before I saw any of the three leaders again. Then, in 2011, when I was in and around Altamira investigating Belo Monte, Antonia Melo told me Raimundo Belmiro was in town and she called him up. Raimundo had a price on his head at that time because he continued to denounce the attacks on the forest in Terra do Meio. The creation of the extractive reserve had left the grileiros more cautious but hadn't driven them completely away. They knew of what material government administrations were made, much better than we, beiradeiros, journalists, and activists did.

When Belo Monte was forced on the Xingu, against the forest-peoples, against social movements, against environmental organizations, and against scientists, the grileiros were the first to understand that federal policy had simply changed its route and that having the PT in the government wouldn't make that much difference in protecting the forest. The grileiros then resumed their attacks on conservation units too, like the Riozinho do Anfrísio Extractive Reserve and all the rest. I denounced this danger, and Raimundo Belmiro began receiving federal protection as an environmental defender targeted by death threats.

Years later, in 2014, I would return to Riozinho and Terra do Meio for the extractive reserve's tenth anniversary, at the invitation of the community. Herculano Porto, the little bird with cat eyes; Raimundo Belmiro; and Manchinha all had patches of gray in their hair, potbellies straining against their party shirts, and, to my greatest amazement, had become very talkative indeed. They were them, but they were also others.

It was the first time I had witnessed the effects that could be exerted by a public policy guaranteeing permanence in a territory. The beiradeiros of Riozinho had even changed their way of walking and their tone of voice, now that their existence and way of life had been recognized. Riozinho was no longer Anfrísio's, much less the grileiros. Riozinho was forest and didn't belong to anyone. It was with them, and it was in them.

Watching those three men—men who ten years earlier hadn't known if they would wake up alive the next day—as they ate the first three slices of commemorative cake, heads high and chests puffed out, treated like the community heroes they are, this was a scene that healed me. I'd been sickened by the horror of watching as the political project embraced by at least two generations of Brazilians had been betrayed by (among other things) the decision to build mammoth hydropower plants in the Amazon, and this scene showed me the way home. There I realized that for me, home is where the front line of resistance is.

When the guests left and the reserve's main office emptied out, I stayed on to pay another visit to the beiradeiros from ten years earlier, taking a journey along the river. They were much younger than a decade before. I don't mean this rhetorically; I could swear they were years younger than when I met them the first time. Once again, I was witnessing the effects of a public policy that recognized their existence, the effect of the state when it does what it should. Even though the grileiros were still harassing them, they couldn't do it as readily as before, when they had been the only law. Even if the authorities were few and flawed, the beiradeiros had authorities to listen to them. Official law was with the community, and this feeling—later to be crushed when Michel Temer assumed the presidency after Dilma Rousseff's impeachment and, still later, with Jair Bolsonaro in power— also seemed to renew the cells in these people's bodies. The new generations, which had grown up on an extractive reserve, displayed a different level of self-esteem and new desires.

At the same time, I was also witnessing the effects of another public policy, the Bolsa Família antipoverty program. A world that had previously revolved without any money, through bartering alone, or with very little money, was now driven by the desire to consume. Most families in Riozinho had begun receiving the Bolsa Família, which was good for the women, enabling them to frequent the stores in Altamira. When these people entered the official country, it launched them into the world of federal programs, since they had no regular source of money whatsoever, which automatically assigned them to being "poor." So people who had lived on other terms, existing in and through the forest, came to experience a monthly income.

Programs like the Bolsa Família were planned for another kind of population; they were thought up precisely for the poor. Government staff who were ignorant of life in the Amazon didn't consider any alternatives that might not require constant forays into the city. Pilgrimages to banks and government agencies took beiradeiros into the city (almost) every month and took goods from the city to the beiradeiros. You can't go into the city and the capitalist world of the city without this experience deeply altering your way of life, food, diseases, leisure, and also your desires, which became desires to consume. Suddenly the beiradeiro children of the Riozinho also became teenagers, a word and an experience that hadn't existed before.

I remember how I was dazed to see hundreds of castoff cans and PET bottles lining the banks of the Riozinho when the party was over. It was a little big scene with more meanings than I was able to decipher right then. I also remember missing the sound of couples dancing at the *forró* at Herculano's home, in 2004. It was the sound of bare feet on bare ground, and I'll never know how to reproduce it, but it was so lovely. And then came the noise of the amplifiers and musicians hired for the party in 2014. I know life changes and the community probably prefers it like this today, but I felt grief, nostalgia, and also fear.

Something from a white person's head, I suspect. This fear has stayed with me ever since I visited Raimundo Nonato da Silva. In 2004, he didn't know who Luiz Inácio da Silva, then president of Brazil, was. But there was a soccer field across from his wattle-and-daub house, roofed with palm fronds. On Sundays his boys swapped their tapping knives for the ball. Raimundo, son of a rubber soldier who dropped dead in the rubber groves, only knew that a place called "city" lay beyond the river, a place he imagined as "a kind of movement." "It'd be nice to know the name of the president of Brazil just to know it, but it doesn't make any difference," he had told me then.

Ten years later, Raimundo knew very well who Lula was, his wife was enrolled in Bolsa Família, and he was very familiar with the city. He didn't want to tell me about the forest but about the stereo occupying his living room almost like an altar. He explained he had first purchased a smaller one but didn't like it because it wasn't powerful enough. Then he bought the one to which he introduced me with so much pride that if I had reached out my hand, I could have touched it. He turned the creature on, and the walls of the house, still waddle-and-daub, literally shook. I shook too. That tremor stays with me as I observe the lives of the middle people unfold.

While government programs designed to fight poverty do benefit the forestpeoples, it became quite clear to me that they are just that: designed for the "poor." To repeat: when programs tailored to the poor are applied to forestpeoples, there is the risk the forestpeoples will likewise be converted into poor. The marks of poverty—manifested in new diseases like obesity, diabetes, and hypertension—made victims in the forest, and they are only one link in a long chain of low-income consumption habits. Even time began to be gauged differently, since you now have to plan a trip to the bank every month, and age heralds your right to a pension.

This isn't an easy or simple analysis. Public policies are fundamental, but they can't be generic in a country like Brazil, which
isn't one but many, where people have extremely diverse ways of
existing. Applied generically, as these policies were, without considering differences in how people live, vital programs became
new instruments for converting forestpeoples into poor. And
thus one more instrument for deforesting the Amazon and deforesting Amazon peoples.

I want this chapter to end in a party mood. And in the Amazon,
every party is also an occasion for baptism. In the Xingu and
throughout most of the Amazon, the Catholic Church stands
alongside the forestpeoples and, unlike other regions where it
works, doesn't try to corrupt their souls. It took some centuries
and some carnage for them to learn, let us never forget, but progressive Catholics have indeed learned, as demonstrated by the
Amazon Synod, led by Pope Francis. Since the bodies of beiradeiros harbor the memory of the Catholic devotion that their
grandparents brought with them when they arrived here as fervent believers, the beiradeiros like to have priests at their cele-
brations. People who have experienced shortage always welcome
a little something extra and generally don't refuse anything offered them. There is also a consensus that it doesn't hurt to bap-
tize your children when a cleric shows up, without this implying
any commitment to religious rites after the day of festivities.

The cleric presiding over the ten-year anniversary of the extractive reserve was Patrick Francis Brennan, Irish by birth,
Amazonian by all the rest. He lost the name of the international
movie star in the Xingu and was rechristened Father Patrício. No
more like a movie star than a piranha is like a pirarucu, Father
Patrício is an omnipresent figure on the stage of the toughest
battles, his huge feet always shod in flip-flops. His face seems
poorly etched out but conveys an intransigent goodness, topped
off by a pair of X-ray eyes. I met this Xinguan priest at the community festival and my soul immediately did a little skip, de-
lighted to find a brother.

I don't know if he felt the same thing, but at the end of the mass, Father Patrício converted me into his assistant. Since I'd been caught with a pen and notebook in hand, it was the general opinion that I was qualified for the job. I shed the journalist in me and spent hours registering the baptisms of children of all shapes and sizes, feeling an importance journalism had never given me.

That same night, Father Patrício and I discovered further affinities when we both suffered cases of diarrhea, which were to dehydrate us for several days while we shared the woods and one lone bathroom with hundreds of other people, and the community continued to hold dances every night thirty feet from my hammock. Day would break and the footwork continued. Every time the musicians tried to quit, someone would show up: "I've got ten bucks for another half hour!" The *brega* music twisted my bowels, and off I would stagger to the bathroom, disrupting a few teenage kisses along the way and praying the priest hadn't reached the lean-to first. Whenever I felt glorious in the Amazon, the forest immediately put me back in my place.

Father Patrício was particularly illuminated during that party. In his sermon, he recalled the entire history of resistance by the Terra do Meio community and mercilessly excommunicated the grileiro Cecílio do Rego Almeida. A beiradeiro in the back brought the pious clergyman up to date by shouting: "He's dead, Father!" And Father Patrício bellowed back, his hands raised to the heavens in divine jubilation: "Praise be to God!"

121. overlords, vassals, and serfs

The structure of grilagem recalls feudalism. Between the over-
lord and the humblest serf lies an intricate web of vassalage relations. To date, the Brazilian legal system has rarely managed (or
ever wanted) to reach the top overlords, the ones engaged in politics at court, with soft hands and well-chosen words. Or the men
in command, who work in the field. The individuals who are generally arrested during government operations—if someone is arrested at all—are the lower-ranking serfs or vassals. In 2011, I
traced this intricate genealogical tree to tell the stories of João
Chupel Primo, who was murdered, and of his friend, who was
forced to flee the settlement where he lived after both men contacted public authorities to denounce a vast criminal operation
to steal timber from forest conservation units.

The entire operation was controlled from a single street in
Areia, an INCRA settlement lying between the municipalities of
Trairão and Itaituba. But it unfolded on various fronts, including
conservation units in the region of Interstate BR-163 and Terra
do Meio, in western Pará. The denunciation that ended Chupel's
life and condemned his friend to life as a fugitive brought together people who are usually called "barbarians" and people
who are regarded as "civilized." The complex genealogy of grilagem helps us see what routinely transpires in the Amazon. In the
past and present.

The life stories of João Chupel Primo, murdered on October 22,
2011, at the age of fifty-five, and his friend, forced to flee at thirty-
eight, raise two intriguing questions that traverse decades and the
forest. How could immense quantities of *ipê* timber have been

removed from conservation units protected by federal decree? How was it that Chupel and his friend had reported a criminal operation to authorities at various offices and then, despite that, been murdered in the former case and forced to flee in the latter?

The answer can be found in the denunciations made by both men. The state established a set of conservation areas in Terra do Meio but never fully occupied them. So at that point, rather than abandoning the region, the grileiros just switched to a new line of work. Instead of razing forests to make pastureland, they started harvesting hardwood from inside the protected areas. Exit livestock raising, enter logging. In practice, since the state never provided the necessary oversight, this change in their business model made crime more efficacious.

Grilagem is structural in Brazil, a part of the country's very foundation. Since the days of Brazil's hereditary captaincies, the concepts of grilagem and private property have been intimately bound up. In his paper "Grilagem for beginners: guide to basic procedures for stealing public lands" (in Portuguese), Maurício Torres writes:

> Until not long ago, Brazil was an immense overseas *latifúndio* [a large, privately owned estate] for the Portuguese. Thus it was invented, and here the latifúndio prospered. "Make me fruitful and multiply, says the latifúndio," even before Brazil had put its hands on this Iberian inheritance. . . . At the roots of the latifúndio—and thus of the dominial structure of land ownership in rural Brazil—is grilagem, born from colonial capitalism and kept going by the slave traffickers who were migrating to a new activity. If illicit appropriation is centuries old on the coast and the South-Central, the looting of public lands is happening now in the Amazon.

I denounced this extensive timber-theft scheme in 2011, the first year of the first term of Dilma Rousseff, who lent continuity to Lula's two terms as president. Later, under Michel Temer (2016–18), and later still, under Jair Bolsonaro (2019–present), it all got much worse. The state was placed explicitly at the service of grilagem and the legalization of stolen public lands. The escalade continued with Bolsonaro's declarations incentivizing grileiros and gold miners, accompanied by deliberately weakened oversight and assaults on protective legislation. This official encouragement of public land invasion was heard, and it brought an immediate reaction: burn-offs and deforestation exploded under the Bolsonaro administration. The most emblematic response, now historical, was Fire Day, August 10, 2019, when grileiros set fire to the forest as part of a direct action organized via the messaging app WhatsApp, in a show of strength and support for the president.

In 2011, this shift in how public land was exploited illegally, from cattle to timber, obeyed clear logic. Raising beef demands a bigger, more permanent structure than logging. Cattle have brands on them, logs don't. Felled forest shows up easily in deforestation measurements. But detecting the selective harvesting of timber like *ipê* requires fieldwork and elaborate technology. It's the difference between imploding a building—something everybody sees—and ransacking it. You look at it on the outside and think everything's fine. But once you're inside, you realize it's just a shell. When you take a single-engine plane ride over the Amazon rainforest, it's easy—and horrendous—to spot the clearings in the woodlands where every tree has been chopped down, in technical language called clear-cutting. But much of the forest you see from above and that appears to be conserved is no longer forest, just the shell of one. Underneath, it has all been ripped out or razed.

In practice, even in protected areas of agrarian resettlements, the grileiros continued to act as if they were the legitimate owners, their territory marked off and secured by force. The "landowner" generally received 25 to 30 percent of the value of the timber when it was removed from his "property." It fell to him to guarantee security and eliminate any resistance on the part of the beiradeiros, Indigenous, and settlers, so "work" could proceed without any mishaps. To this end, the so-called landowner maintained a militia, with a commanding officer. The *gato* (cat), or "extractor," paid a commission to the "landowner" and was responsible for the logging itself. This extractor was in charge of several logging crews, but he was merely an employee within this criminal setup. Anyone who opposed the operation and reported it suffered death threats. If even this failed to shut the person up, there were only two ways to go: the person was either included in an institutional protection program, or marked for an unnatural death.

Known in the region of Itaituba as João da Gaita (Accordion John), João Chupel Primo was a *gaúcho*, born in the far Southern state of Rio Grande do Sul. He migrated through various states before reaching the Amazon and Pará. At parties, he always found a way to rip a few gaúcho-esque tunes from his accordion. Before João became a whistleblower, the leaders of the fight against grilagem generally viewed him with suspicion. Chupel owned an automotive repair shop in Itaituba and had "purchased" an area of land in the Riozinho extractive reserve. To close the deal, he partnered with a group of people from the town of Sorriso, in the state of Mato Grosso. The so-called Grupo Sorriso—Smile Group—was then one of four that were parceling out conservation units, drawing up their own maps that registered land deeds in a public area.

Chupel had two strong reasons—since he's dead, we can't know which held greater sway—for reporting a scheme in which he himself was once an active participant:

(1) In 2011, *ipê* wood grew scarcer within the territory of Carlos Augusto da Silva's group. Augustinho, as he is known, was feared throughout the region as the most violent organized crime boss. He began invading the Grupo Sorriso's area to steal timber from those who were in turn stealing timber from the protected area. Chupel went to call them out on it. He ended up taking a beating. He would later hand authorities a bloodstained note-

book from that day. Jotted down in its pages were the GPS coordinates where timber had been felled on his "property." Cornered, Chupel knew he couldn't count on the local police. He contacted the state Public Prosecutor's Office in Itaituba. And then he gave a statement to both the Federal Police and the Chico Mendes Institute for Biodiversity Conservation (ICMBio). He submitted a recording to authorities that included this dialogue:

AUGUSTINHO: *The police have helped me out a lot!*
CHUPEL: *Yeah, if they hadn't shown up here yesterday, it*
   would've been tough. . . . It was good they came, right?
AUGUSTINHO: *. . . The chief has always got our backs!*
CHUPEL: *That's right.*
AUGUSTINHO: *I've got to give them some money, five hundred,*
   a thousand bucks.

(2) In early 2011, Chupel lost his only son, electrocuted when he stepped in a puddle of water near the repair shop. Then his wife left him. According to his friends, on the one hand, Chupel concluded he didn't have anyone to leave his estate to now; on the other, he started thinking about where he stood with God. Chupel was described as a fervent Catholic, with "deep knowledge of the Bible." After losing his son, he saw a star in the puddle and believed it was the dead boy. In the recordings, he alternated his accusations with phrases about God. Chupel was in search of meaning, as happens with so many people after a loss. And this diminished him in the eyes of men like Augustinho. There's no time for grieving in hired-gun land. João Chupel Primo started to record compromising conversations and gather documentation. Next, he reported the criminal operation to the authorities. And then he died with a bullet to his head, thirteen feet from where his son lost his life.

Chupel's friend, whom I will call the fugitive, shares the same history as so many migrants who heard the promise of a piece of land in the Amazon. Born in the interior of Paraná, he lived a life in the fields, employed as a farmhand and working his own small plot as well. In the early 2000s, he suffered his third case of pesticide poisoning. The doctor warned him he wouldn't survive a fourth. The farmer migrated alone to the region of Trairão, along Interstate BR-163. Months later, he moved his wife and three kids there. Later on, he purchased a lot in PA Areia—Settlement Project Areia. And for a few years he was also a logger in the Trairão National Forest.

When he and Chupel began whistleblowing, the authorities were a little leery, since the two men had themselves committed environmental infractions. If you live in the Amazon—as in any conflict area, where it is all still being written—you know that between black and white, reality displays an entire rainbow of nuances. Chupel and his friend epitomize the importance of understanding the complexity of life in that geography. With no state presence, a portion of those residing in PA Areia and the community of Trairão lived outside the law. "Until the government implements a forest management plan, everything will stay the same," the fugitive told me back then. "People need to eat. And the only way to do that there, today, is cutting down timber. That's what needs to change."

The man who would become a fugitive soon collided with local logic. He discovered that although he lived in a government housing project, his every move was under the control of crime bosses. He had to pay a "toll" to enter and exit the settlement. So strong was the grileiros' sense of ownership that they actually issued receipts.

In 2007, the fugitive started challenging some leaders of the region's logging sector. That year, the PA Areia Community Association partnered with Amexport Indústria e Comércio de Madeiras Ltda., a logging company based in Itaituba, to establish a community forest management plan, the only legal way to log inside a settlement. According to the fugitive, who took part in the agreement as an association representative, the proposal was submitted by Luiz Carlos Tremonte, of Amexport, and Marcos Sato, of the firm Amazônia Florestal. But relations between the parties soon grew tense.

When I reached out to Luiz Carlos Tremonte, he stated that the fugitive was "crazy, a complete idiot, who really made a mess of things." As to Chupel, Tremonte said that after the man's son died, "he started seeing his son in the moon." "Other companies participated too; they signed a contract with the settlement. Marcos Sato's Amazônia Florestal was one of them. Write that down, talk to him," he suggested. Marcos Sato told me he had quit buying lumber from the association because it was "too much of a hassle." He also used the same expression as Tremonte in referring to the fugitive: "crazy." And he said: "This guy has denounced everybody around here. You can't imagine how crazy this guy is, he even denounced Jader Barbalho, a senator!"

As part of the community management plan, the association had received a permit to remove 11,546 cubic meters of timber from inside the settlement. To make this more understandable, this meant the association had a credit of 11,546 cubic meters. When logs are taken out, the credits have to be deducted online to legalize the timber so it can then be sold. It is a proven fact that almost all the credits had been used up by 2008. The problem: not a single tree had been logged off inside the settlement. The timber had been pulled out elsewhere, where there were more hardwood species.

The fugitive claimed the credits had been used to launder wood removed from conservation units, thereby legalizing it, in a process known as credit trafficking. But who did this? The fugitive accused Tremonte and Sato. They denied it. "I'm IBAMA's [Brazil's environmental protection agency] dream come true," said Tremonte, a figure who would be comical were he not so tied up with tragedy. "I was a big mahogany producer, before it was banned. Today I only use soft wood [the cheapest], which you can find all over." Sato said: "I export hardwood [the finest, like *jatoba* and *ipê*], but I've never done anything illegal. Where's the proof? There's no proof to this nutcase's claims."

When he complained about the fraud, the fugitive started receiving threats. His twelve-year-old daughter came home crying one day. The family thought that "since she is already 'developed,' someone might have done something to her." The girl refused to tell them what happened. A while later she told a family friend that Augustinho had told her if her father didn't shut up, he'd kill him and the whole family. The fugitive then moved off the settlement and into Trairão. His daughter died sometime later. But not by bullet. The girl caught dengue and the pharmacist gave her a shot of penicillin instead of acetaminophen. She died of anaphylactic shock.

In the following years, tensions continued to rise. And with them, the violence. Discontented settlers began to be executed. In 2011, two killings left the fugitive even more convinced he might be next. João Carlos Baú, known as Cuca, was gunned down while he was dancing at a party in the settlement. The first bullet went straight through his back into his chest. He managed to stumble a few feet before collapsing. When he turned his head to see who had shot him, he took another two bullets to the ear.

After Cuca, it was the turn of Edivaldo da Silva—Divaldinho. The day the settlement was commemorating the arrival of electrical power, there was a knock on his door around three in the morning. Divaldinho answered, wrapped in a towel. Four men stabbed him dozens of times. He lived for many more hours, his guts exposed. First, they couldn't find a car to take him to the hospital in Trairão. Then, when they finally got there, there wasn't any blood for a transfusion. He died at the hospital in Itaituba, after they had sewn up his belly. He had six kids.

The fugitive started compiling police reports and recording denunciations. "The situation is a lot like what you see in Rio's favelas. One crime financing another. Logging financing murder.

There've been fifteen deaths in two years," he said. "When I started reporting this, Augustinho sent me a message that I could start digging a hole because I was going to die."

It is worth taking a closer look at the man considered the most violent grileiro in western Pará in the early 2010s. Carlos Augusto da Silva, Augustinho, came to the region in the 1990s as an employee of Osmar Ferreira, internationally known as the "king of mahogany," and he occupied a vast territory in the area of the Tapajós and Xingu River basins. In 2004, these federal lands became conservation units, which didn't keep Augustinho from continuing to give orders there as if he were the owner. By 2011, he had been accused of instigating murders and had spent years at large. He became the prime suspect behind the ordered killing of João Chupel Primo. I tried hard to contact Augustinho, but he never responded to my interview requests.

Luiz Carlos Tremonte stated that he "greatly admires" Augustinho. "A man who spent twenty years in this forest and put two sons through medical school—I've got to admire him. I think if a fellow had really been accused of so many things, he wouldn't walk around free like he does. Given this whole messy situation that happened now, he's even been saying he's going to leave." In 2018, after spending many years at large, Augustinho was arrested for a triple homicide committed decades earlier. He had beaten the victims to death. It was just one of his crimes.

Luiz Carlos Tremonte, a native of the city of São Paulo, has become a quasi-iconic figure in Pará. In 2010, he actually ran for governor for a few days, and then dropped out of the race. In 2005, when he was in Brasília testifying before the Biopiracy CPI—a congressional committee tasked with investigating the trafficking of wild game and plants and illegal logging—Tremonte made lawmakers' lives hard. It took them a good while to figure out he no longer owned either Amex—which was in his wife's name—or Lamex, although, according to the lawmakers, both were in arrears to IBAMA. After much back-and-forth, the lawmakers managed to extract the information from Tremonte that his current company was Amex. "And is this one in your name?" one congressman asked. "No."

During his testimony before the congressional committee, Tremonte had moments of inspiration. He defended the legality of his operations in the Amazon with these words: "I often say [US missionary] Sister Dorothy [Stang] died, but her ideals didn't." When he was challenged about suspected logging activities inside Amazonia National Park, the first conservation unit established in the forest, in 1974, he said: "Not even familiar with it. Just learned about it yesterday, on the map!" The park lies twenty-five miles from Itaituba, the city where he lived.

When I interviewed him, Luiz Carlos Tremonte kept insisting:

Google me, you'll see my videos on YouTube. You'll discover I'm the biggest defender of the standing forest. People don't understand, but loggers are good for the forest. When we cut down a dense, leafy tree, we're doing a good thing, because it opens up space for a younger one.

He later sent me an article published in the *Economist* in 2006, in which the journalist opens with an apocalyptic phrase by Tremonte: "monstrous misery and hunger"—a reference to how government restrictions had affected loggers. Tremonte would die of COVID-19, in São Paulo, in early 2021.

Another example of an Amazonian man was Sílvio Torquato Junqueira, who claimed he hadn't set foot on his ranch, located inside the Trairão National Forest, since 2006. A soft-spoken fellow from the region of Ribeirão Preto, in São Paulo state, he was a cattle raiser and cat lover. In the 1990s, he had also lived in Brasília, where he was operations director for the Companhia Nacional de Abastecimento (Conab), a state-owned company within the Ministry of Agriculture. All indications are that he didn't much enjoy the attractions in the federal capital on Saturdays and Sundays, since he got in trouble with the Federal Audit Court because most of his business trips coincided with the weekend, when his destination had been his beloved Ribeirão Preto.

At that time, Santa Cecília Ranch did, and did not, belong to Sílvio Torquato Junqueira. This story, so reminiscent of Hamlet, is common in the Amazon. Thousands of hectares were registered in the names of more than twenty of Junqueira's "relatives and friends"—but not one single hectare was in his name. Although Santa Cecília Ranch was located inside a conservation unit, it was still there in 2011, unperturbed by government inspectors.

Junqueira explained the enigma in these terms:

I'm not the owner; I was just looking after lots that belong to people who set themselves up there in 1999, 2000. We went there for the livestock raising; then we discovered timber could be a good thing. We tried to do a management plan, but IBAMA shelved the project. Then they said we needed the deed for the land. I went to INCRA to ask them to give me the title or tenancy certificate, but INCRA said they wouldn't. So I didn't get permission and everything came to a halt. I was in limbo and then, suddenly, in 2006, the president decreed the area the Trairão National Forest. We stopped everything immediately and one person stayed there, Jordão, looking after the lots. We're waiting to see what happens. Since I'd built a house there, lodgings, we receive NGOs, staff from the Chico Mendes Institute. . . . Somebody needs to survey flora and fauna, they stay there. We've given support to the folks from Chico Mendes, right? Everything very easygoing. If they let out a bid in Trairão National Forest to exploit the timber, our idea is to partner with someone to give us some support, because I understand livestock raising, not logging. But today there are some very good international companies in this area. We're there, waiting to see. If the government orders me out, I'll get out.

Sílvio Junqueira's employee was Jordão Ferreira da Silva Sobrinho, better known as Ticão. According to everyone familiar with him, if the world of grilagem had a diplomat, this person would be Ticão. He had excellent relations with Augustinho's gang. And likewise with the beiradeiros from the Riozinho do Anfrísio Extractive Reserve, to whom he offered transportation help when necessary. People described him as extremely well mannered. No one was aware of any reports of violence on Santa Cecília Ranch.

Besides the fact that the land-grabbed ranch lay in a conservation area, timber theft was constant there. The man responsible for the operation would become mayor of Trairão some years later. The road used to transport the logs cut through Santa Cecília Ranch and passed a few yards from the main office. In the report "Via de Direito, Via de Favor" (By law, by favor), the product of a joint ISA-ICMBio investigation, André Villas-Bôas, then executive secretary of the Socioenvironmental Institute, stated:

> Regarding the region of Santa Cecília Ranch, inside the Trairão National Forest, satellite images identified a complex network of roads, some verified in the field, confirming the existence of heavy logging in recent years inside and around the ranch.

Sílvio Junqueira stated he was "completely surprised" by the information that wood was being stolen in the (land-grabbed) area he "manages." He said:

> I'm not aware of this and it must not be true. I've got a gate, I'm in control, Jordão always calls me and says everything is protected. It's not possible, I highly doubt it, there must be some mistake with this image. If anything's going on, I don't have anything to do with it. Nor do my children or any of the people who are there have anything to do with this. If they're doing something wrong there, good God in heaven.

It must be recognized that Santa Cecília Ranch had special status in the realm of the region's grilagem. Given the pedigrees of its front men—known in Brazil as *laranjas*, or oranges—they represented the most refined human citrus crop in the Xingu and Tapajós basins. Most, if not all, were from the state of São Paulo and appeared regularly in the society pages. Marcos de Oliveira Germano, for example, was a champion scratch golfer in the category "pre-senior" (forty to fifty-four years), from Ribeirão Preto's Ipê Golf Club—a somewhat ironic name. "Ever since they killed Dorothy Stang, I haven't had anything else to do with this," he guaranteed. "The idea was to stake a claim. Ever since Pedro Álvares Cabral, people have marked out their land, built a little house, put some crops in, and complied with INCRA regulations to legalize it. But they declared it forest and I haven't gone there since." In 2011, the case in which Germano was claiming land ownership with INCRA was still being processed.

One of Sílvio Junqueira's daughters, present in the orange orchard, worked as an actor and was the organizer of a "hype" party in São Paulo, known as the Gambiarra. "My father set this condominium up some time ago and gave it to us [her and two siblings] as a present," she explained. "He said he'd put it in our name, in case he passed away someday, because it would be ours anyway. But everything is proper, within the law." I've always been fascinated by fathers who pamper their children by giving them a few morsels of thousands of hectares of public forest. "Condominium" was the most extraordinary definition of grilagem I'd ever heard.

The Junqueiras' orange orchard also included people with MBAs from the London Business School; fans of Billie Holiday, Norah Jones, and Melody Gardot; and drum players, windsurfers, and even equestrians. It seems hard to tie the beautiful people of São Paulo's elites to the beautiful people of gunslinging land—people who call grilagem a "condominium" to people who strew corpses in the middle of the street. It's almost impossible to imagine them together, and yet it happened. Only by tying the ends together is it possible to understand the Amazon, and Brazil.

In the Amazon, grilagem expanded under the business-military dictatorship and continued through the subsequent democratic governments. Ten years after João da Gaita's death, as of this writing, it forms a support base for the Bolsonaro government. It finds no resistance, except the bodies of forestpeople leaders and agroecological peasants, something that will be made clear in coming chapters.

I hope João da Gaita got himself right with God—and that the fugitive has located some ground where he could plant his family.

171. the amazon locusts

I am a gaúcha. In the beginning, the gaúcho was a complex, fascinating figure, whose culture was almost completely destroyed along with the pampa, the geography-world they inhabited, the world referred to in lovely terms as the "horizontal vertigo" of the plains. Today, being designated a gaúcho because you were born in Rio Grande do Sul generally has little or nothing to do with these origins. To some extent, what is now considered "tradition" has more to do with advertising and marketing than with any historical realities, much as capitalism often operates. And to another extent, this image serves to foster a vaingloriousness that often flirts with racism.

For many centuries, what we call Rio Grande do Sul was a movable boundary disputed by Portugal and Spain, the two maritime powers reigning from the fifteenth through seventeenth centuries. Sometimes the region belonged to one, sometimes to the other. Even though people in Rio Grande do Sul speak Portuguese, it's not unusual to still find inhabitants of the state who feel culturally closer to the River Plate countries of Argentina, Uruguay, and Paraguay than to North or Northeast Brazil, regions distant both culturally and spatially.

Most gaúchos speak fluent Portunhol, a mixture of Portuguese and Spanish, and those who can, pay frequent visits to Buenos Aires and Montevideo. Unlike in most of Brazil, there are four seasons in the South, and it even snows some places in the winter. The cold doesn't just drape ponchos over bodies, it also sculpts people. Despite these many differences, gaúchos have migrated all over Brazil in search of land, reaching even the Amazon. These wanderings have always been extolled as expressions of bravery, pioneerism, and the spirit of adventure. Brazil shall one day wear *bombachas*—the baggy riding breeches of the pampas.

To understand this gaúcho identity—and its consequences for the forest—we must revisit the past. When the massive wave of European immigration to Brazil began in the nineteenth century, the southern half of Rio Grande (mostly the pampa region but also the borderlands), along with some parts of the north, had been colonized for at least two centuries. Jesuit priests were among the region's earliest colonizers. Clerics from the Society of Jesus subjugated the original peoples, for the most part Guaranis, so they could build what they called "missions," with the rationale that they were "saving" souls.

The political and economic autonomy enjoyed by the Jesuit missions was convenient for the Portuguese and Spanish thrones in the beginning. But by the eighteenth century, it had them gnashing their teeth. After a series of conflicts of interest between the parties, the Jesuits were expelled from the colonial territories, and the Indigenous peoples living inside the missions were massacred. This is a long, complex history, and a few lines of print obviously don't even begin to tell it.

What is left of the missions—notably São Miguel das Missões—is monumental. A thick silence hangs there, perhaps from so much death, audible even to obtuse tourists. I've only ever encountered such dense silence, like a heavy fabric overlaying the world, at the Dachau concentration camp in Germany. The difference is that the missions, as controversial as they are—especially viewed through the lens of our current time—weren't specifically designed for killing. And, to some extent, they averted an earlier massacre of the Indigenous by Portuguese and/or Spanish troops and by *bandeirantes*, the Portuguese descendants who in the sixteenth century began making expeditions into Brazil's various interiors to search for mineral wealth, enslave or kill the Indigenous, and destroy the quilombos of runaway slaves. It makes a difference. While the silence of Dachau desiccates the soul, the silence of São Miguel das Missões stirs melancholy and the urge to cry.

When Brazil began importing European settlers, *latifundiários*—owners of vast ranch lands—were the dominant political and economic force in Rio Grande do Sul. A large slice of the northern half of the state, which has nothing in common with the ecosystem of the pampa, was still what white people usually consider "no-man's-land" or "wilderness." Throughout Brazil's history, whenever these expressions have been used, the lands in question were occupied by the Indigenous or, more precisely, they were lands where the Indigenous had not yet been driven out or fully exterminated. What they call "no man" are the original peoples, people who today are regarded as "almost human" by rulers such as Jair Bolsonaro and by grileiros—the ones in the Amazon and the ones in Congress. During the centuries of the first invasions, the Indigenous people, like Black people, were not considered human, not even "almost." They didn't even have souls, according to the whites who had been endowed with souls but used them to enslave and kill.

In the nineteenth century, Emperor Dom Pedro II lent continuity to the whitening process initiated at least three hundred years earlier by encouraging the immigration of starving people from Europe, who arrived here in search of land. Their settlement experiences differed. In Rio Grande do Sul, they were placed on Indigenous land with the support of the government. They expelled the still remaining original inhabitants from the territories they then began to occupy, and expelled the Black people they found there. The first to arrive were the Germans; then came the Italians. There were immigrants of other nationalities but in the nineteenth century most came from these two countries. Rio Grande do Sul, with its subtropical climate, was considered more suitable than other regions of Brazil for European immigrants.

Slavery was formally abolished in 1888, but without any enactment of inclusive public policies. Apparently, it never occurred to the emperor—who would be ousted by a military coup the following year—nor to the exponents of the incipient republic, that Black people could become settlers of the country that enslaved them. Blacks quit being slaves to become the wretched poor—and part of the racism that structures Brazil today and that reserves the worst life and death statistics for Black people was cemented in this transition. The earliest inclusive public policies, like racial quotas at universities, were implemented more than a century later, starting with Fernando Henrique Cardoso's second term (1998–2002) and then with Lula and Dilma Rousseff, under the PT (2003–2016). They were accompanied by a violent backlash from whites, especially the elites and middle class.

In Rio Grande do Sul's European immigrant colonies, a kind of reverse xenophobia signaled the worldview of the first generations born in the new land and years later would signal the migration of new generations to the Amazon. Those coming from the outside looked down on those from the inside, over whom they felt superior. The more unfortunate they had been and the more they felt driven out of their countries, the stronger their sense of belonging to the land they left behind. I would encounter this same phenomenon in the Amazon when I began living in Altamira.

Around the turn of the millennium, I visited places in Rio Grande do Sul where German and Italian dialects were spoken more than Portuguese. In the 1990s, a particularly annoying bumper sticker was ubiquitous in Porto Alegre, the state capital: *Italiano grazie a dio*—Italian, thank God. When these descendants managed to take a tourist trip to Italy or Germany, they felt more Italian and German than the locals, but they discovered almost nobody understood their dialects, frozen in time, and no one considered them their compatriots. During the 2002 World Cup, foreign journalists were appalled when fans from Rio Grande do Sul who had traveled to Japan to support the Brazilian team declared that Ronaldinho Gaúcho, one of the lead players, wasn't really "gaúcho" because he was Black. At the beginning of World War II, President Getúlio Vargas spent some years flirting with both sides, but in 1942 he aligned with the Allies, and Brazil officially entered the conflict. During the war, speaking German, Italian, and Japanese—the languages of the Axis—was repressed in Brazil. As long as the conflict lasted, the language spoken by grandparents in that era was limited to a restricted space, like whispers at home. It is worth noting that Getúlio Vargas was a gaúcho, a latifundiário from São Borja, and, from 1937 to 1945, during the period known as the Estado Novo, a dictator.

I was born in Ijuí, a town in northwest Rio Grande do Sul that prides itself on being Brazil's "capital of ethnic groups," although dominated politically and economically by the descendants of German and Italian immigrants. My maternal grandfather, a member of our family's first Brazilian-born generation, used to call Indigenous people by the pejorative term *bugres*, while anyone who didn't descend from European ancestors was a "Brazilian." If we asked him what "Brazilian" meant, my grandfather would answer with another expression: *pelo duro*—crossbreed. The gaúchos in the southern half were "crossbreeds." This grandfather of mine always considered himself Italian, although he spent his almost one hundred years of life spreading racism and prejudice without ever having seen even the tip of the boot's heel.

When I lived in Rio Grande do Sul, the usual question was: "What's your origin?" I only found the question odd once I went out into the world. Before that, I too would proudly reply I was "Italian." As for Black people, generally thought of as "even worse than *bugres*," my grandfather saved his best phrase: "I'd rather have a whore for a granddaughter than have her marry a Black." To my good fortune, my father was an entirely different type of human, and he abhorred racism. Yet the fact is that mine was the first generation to "mix." For one hundred years, my family all married within the Italian community.

My father and I had an interesting conversation shortly before he died. As I've already shared in other books, my father was the first person in his family to attend school. All the way back to Italy, you'll find several generations of illiterate Brums. But then a curious pair of outsiders rode a cloud of red dust into Picada Conceição, a village in the rural zone of Ijuí, where my great-grandparents had settled. It was a man and his daughter, both teachers, and they took over the local school to teach the alphabet to the always plentiful offspring of Italian immigrants. Sabino, the father, came from a distinguished family of latifundiários—his ancestors had their names on streets and statues—and Luzia was his daughter with an enslaved woman he'd fallen in love with. Since he had been disinherited—not because he forced a slave to have sex with him, which was considered run of the mill, but because he had acknowledged his love and his daughter—Sabino became a teacher and also made Luzia into one. Luzia's mother died before they reached the community and nobody ever knew her name, which in itself says a lot. It's a rather extraordinary story for the time, and as long as he lived, my father would take flowers to Luzia's tomb, every single year without fail, to thank her for his ABCs and for being a light at decisive moments in his life.

It is revealing that Luzia was never described as Black by my father or any of his contemporaries back in my childhood. When the antiracist struggle received greater attention at the beginning of this century, and the affirmative action policies of Lula's administration were violently criticized by the liberal press and by intellectuals who had previously managed to keep their racism in the closet, I started thinking about the matter of Luzia, and one day I said: "But Dad, Luzia was Black. Why didn't you ever mention it?" My father was surprised. He thought a bit and then said: "We never saw her as Black. She was *morena clara*—light-skinned." I said: "Black, Dad. Black. And that's what matters most."

At that moment, I understood colorism better and why Black

movements say that the darker a Black person's skin color, the greater the racism and its consequences. Luzia, the teacher, taught generations of extremely white and undoubtedly very racist Italian descendants to read and write, but she was tolerated because she was *morena clara*. *Morena* is the word white Brazilians use to refer to a Black person they like. The term indicates a linguistic conversion of Black people, a process typical of a society structured on racism. The goal is to make living together feasible through the symbolic "lightening" of Blacks.

I spent an entire childhood in Ijuí seeing hardly any Black people, who were confined to the city's most wretched periphery by an unwritten law. My maternal grandfather would pick up his shotgun and fire shots whenever a Black person tried to satisfy their hunger by picking fruit from the trees on his farm. These unwanted neighbors were called "the Blacks from Penniless Street." Penniless because they never had any food and hardly any clothing in a region where winter can be as harsh as in Europe, nor did they have homes that afforded protection from the cold and rain. Since they were considered an inferior species, nobody seemed sympathetic to their misfortune. Like the Indigenous, they were considered "intruders."

If Brazil is one of the world's most racist countries, it is also true that there are regional differences in how this racism is expressed. In the Northeast and in states like Rio de Janeiro, where slavery was omnipresent, having slaves and then replacing them with Black housemaids or servants simply represented a change in nomenclature. The same is true for the ranching region of Rio Grande do Sul, where there was an abundance of enslaved labor. In areas colonized by European immigrants, in the north of the state, some of them toward the close of slavery, this coexistence was much less prevalent or even nonexistent. Black people, like the Indigenous, were not supposed to be on land the government had destined for whites. When someone tried to get them to work for food and they refused, they were considered "lazy."

Blacks and *bugres* were no good when it came to work—this was the consensus during my childhood. And if they were no good for work, they weren't good for anything else either.

I suspect, although I have no research to prove it, that in the final decades of the twentieth century, it was worse to be Black in the regions of European colonization in Rio Grande do Sul than anywhere else in Brazil, the reason being that it was extremely hard to find a job. Not even an exploitative job, analogous to enslavement, like the maids who slept in little rooms at the back of the house, with a scheduled time to start work and no scheduled time to stop, receiving disgraceful wages and having few or no labor rights—even these jobs weren't accessible to Black people. Positions considered subaltern were filled by poor white women of European descent. The idea of a Black woman cooking and washing prompted fits of nausea, something I observed countless times in my childhood. It seemed like people thought skin color would soil their white sheets and contaminate their food. Similarly, when an office or factory worker was hired, priority would be given to poor whites—hapless but "equal." The rationale was that "Blacks don't know how to work and aren't trustworthy."

What was left for Black people was the deadliest wretchedness. Black children didn't even dare beg. The children who knocked at our door asking for stale bread were white, always the same ones. In Southern towns like the one where I was born and grew up, a Black man couldn't even knock on a door to ask for food, because the consequences might be worse than hunger. Not only was it risky, the chances of getting even a bit of stale bread were slim.

I found out nonwhite children existed only when a flood left the poor communities on the city's periphery underwater and my father decided the university he had helped found should take in the families. Since he always taught us life lessons by making us live them, he got us out of our pajamas late one night and took us to help lodge those families. I was maybe eight or nine, and I was stupefied to discover this other city existed without my ever having made its acquaintance. I had grown up hearing about the Blacks from Penniless Street, but this was the first time I had seen and talked to them. When the sun came out and the waters receded, these people were submerged again. It's paradoxical but the water had to rise to reveal them; when it subsided, they were hidden once more.

The European immigrants who left their homelands came to Brazil in search of what they didn't have in Europe: land. The idea that a person is nobody if they don't own land was deeply entrenched in their cultural DNA. My paternal great-grandfather, Antonio, left Italy in 1883 because his father, Pietro, didn't want to lose his last son. Pietro had decided to emigrate with part of his family after his other son had been hanged at fifteen because he had let their livestock graze in fields that belonged to the region's big landowner. His punishment for this "invasion" was death. Without a trial, because the lord of the land was the law. The idea that a man can't live or be respected without land was fed from generation to generation like mother's milk. Out of a family of eight children, my father was the only one who relinquished his piece of land to become a teacher. Most of my cousins on my father's side are still farmers who own their own land.

When the Brazilian government began incentivizing the "settlement" of the Amazon, especially under the business-military dictatorship, two types of gaúchos answered the call. Most shared European roots and lived in northern Rio Grande do Sul. They had, however, achieved different rankings within the social hierarchy. One type was the latifundiários, the large landowners who already had plenty of land in their own regions but saw an opportunity to amass more. On various occasions when I was young, I heard certain members of our local society tell stories that evinced absolute disdain for the Indigenous. Roaring with laughter, they would describe how their honchos had swept the *bugres* from their land. Right then, Mato Grosso was the preferred region of the Amazon and these latifundiários didn't travel there much, instead keeping their agents in the field to be responsible for the blood work.

The other type of gaúcho who answered the dictatorship's call included both the mass of small farmers whose growing families meant their children would undergo hardship if they had to further divide land as well as the peasants who owned no land of their own and were exploited as tenants or employees by the same latifundiários. These rural workers embraced the military government's colonization projects and migrated to the Amazon, many to states like Pará and Rondônia in the 1970s. They had no idea what the rainforest was and, like their ancestors a century earlier, they received less government support than promised.

The enormous challenges they faced didn't keep them from cultivating the same reverse xenophobia as their grandparents had when they landed in Brazil. They behaved in the Amazon as if they had more right to be there than the Indigenous people who had lived in and been forest for thousands of years. They also generally felt superior to other migrants, especially those from Northeast states, because they were whiter and "knew how to work." The truth is, if they knew how to work, which is questionable in ecological terms, what they knew was only appropriate for Rio Grande do Sul's climate and geography. In the Amazon, they were completely ignorant, which was bad for them and for the forest.

Besides the matter of social position, there was another difference between the two groups of gaúchos who went to the Amazon. Both groups had learned from their European ancestors that land only becomes property if it is occupied in economic terms. The gaúchos who took up grilagem occupied the land by raising cattle. Chop it all down, sell the hardwood, burn what's left, put in pastureland and cattle to ensure ownership. Land was for exploitation and speculation, not necessarily production. On the other hand, for the rural workers who migrated there to settle on their own land, the goal was to plant, put in fields, make the soil cultivatable and cultivated, eat off the land,

and sell the surplus to improve their own lives and send their children to good schools. They raised livestock, like a milk cow and some chickens and pigs, for subsistence purposes. These migrants also destroyed, but they worked hard. And not to exploit and dominate but to make the Amazon a home for their families. They were wrong, but they weren't criminals. Some would turn into criminals, pressured and seduced by circumstances, but they didn't go to the forest to practice the crime of grilagem like the other group, made up of latifundiários. This difference must be stressed.

On my first trip along the Transamazonian Highway, in 1998, I ran into the second group of gaúchos, the rural workers who migrated to make a life for themselves. They might have been the aunts, uncles, and cousins I'd seen working hard in the fields in my youth. This identification was immediate. On this first foray, I too was gaúcha to the tips of my auburn hair, meaning I was tremendously proud of being both from Rio Grande do Sul and of Italian descent. I took this journey down the legendary road that the military dictatorship had laid over the bodies of Indigenous people, stopping along the way where my intuition told me to. This has always been my favorite way of doing a story. Every time I ran into a gaúcho, we'd both get all excited. Hens were butchered for lunch, I'd listen to their stories with tears in my eyes, and then I'd bid them farewell, my head and backpack stuffed with messages for relatives who had stayed behind in the South.

But I also stopped at other homes and listened to other peoples. I was taken by the language of some of those who opened their doors to a stranger dressed in cowboy boots and then gifted me with the literature that issued from their mouths, a literature that conveyed other experiences of pilgrimage through the land and another kind of living with the rainforest. These words and meanings left marks on my body as strong as the Amazon sun. I generally forgot to apply sunscreen and, after spending a few days the color of a pesticide-covered tomato, I grew tanner than the girl from Ipanema, with millions more freckles and my first wrinkles. I turned white again back in Porto Alegre but never lost the wrinkles.

I aged during the first trip I took through the Amazon, and my vocabulary broadened along with my soul. I was so possessed by new words, by rhythms I had just discovered, and by languages with other textures that I wrote my story practically in a trance, as if my pen were channeling living people. I couldn't put quote marks in this story; I reproduced a polyphonic narrative that was a kind of delirium. Even when reading about it, the Amazon could only be grasped as an experience of the senses. The grammatical constraints of what we call the Portuguese language (which is much less the Portuguese of Portugal now) could only be vanquished if they were persistently breached. I was decolonizing my journalism in my writing as well, not just in how I saw the world. As in much of my life, I was acting from intuition before understanding the whys.

The impact of experiencing other peoples and other, non-gaúcho ways of being in the world stayed with me and started to bother me. I, who thought I would die in Porto Alegre, began to feel cramped in the land I loved, and I was assailed by an insomnia arising from claustrophobia. At the end of the following year, I accepted an invitation to work in São Paulo that would boost my chances of traveling to the many Amazons. Truth be told, I'd said yes before I even received the invitation. I disembarked in São Paulo in January 2000, very much a gaúcha, and immediately began to un-gaúcha myself. I didn't become a *paulistana*—someone from the city of São Paulo—because I never could, nor would I want to. But I lived seventeen years in the capital of the state of São Paulo, and during each one of those years, I devoted myself to journeying all the possible fatherlands and motherlands, brotherlands and sisterlands, that lie inside the city of São Paulo, which I still consider one of the most fascinating places in the world for those who dare step outside their bubble.

Gaúcho journalism had a solid reputation back then and often received awards, but it was journalism done for the state of Rio Grande do Sul, the only planet that mattered. Regional newspapers tend to aim their work inward but a gaúcho paper even more so, to the point that it had become a national joke. People kidded that the world's biggest tragedies would only make the headlines in Rio Grande do Sul if some gaúcho died. It didn't really go that far, but almost. Provincialism was different in São Paulo newsrooms, sold with a cosmopolitan touch. Everything that mattered spoke English, and everything that spoke English was better, even if it wasn't.

I was startled by the number of English words my colleagues used while speaking Portuguese. The talk in our lineup meetings was peppered with corporate jargon in English, which made me feel illiterate until I realized the English language was obviously an instrument of power that indicated one's class. Since being literate in Portuguese was no longer enough to put everyone in their proper place—I myself the granddaughter of illiterates—speaking French, and later English, served to evince the educational superiority of the children of the elites.

That was another difference. In the gaúcho newsroom where I had worked, most of my colleagues belonged to the same social stratus as I did. White middle class, from the interior of the state, tough lives to greater or lesser degrees, public school students, almost all monoglots. During my first years there, I caught four buses to get to the newspaper office at eight in the morning, because I had to hoist my daughter over the school wall, where she stayed by herself until the doorkeeper arrived. Most of my colleagues in São Paulo were wealthier; they owned their own cars, had studied at top private schools, had spent time abroad as high school exchange students or at the London School of Economics, and had traveled much more.

I was a survivor who by that point had already been through a few major battles, which included becoming a mother at fifteen and refusing to get married. I pretended to speak English. And I pretended so much I ended up learning something. After many years, I convinced myself to take English lessons and, three very patient teachers later, I pretended much better. It seems my brain, in addition to being old, was averse to imperialism. I really only learned English when it became a language of love.

While I was at the São Paulo newsroom, I started traveling to the Amazon a lot more. Although Brazil doesn't really have a national press—since nearly 100 percent, or 100 percent, of the newspaper journalists who call themselves "national" are located in São Paulo, Rio de Janeiro, or Brasília—the São Paulo newsroom was much more open to the rest of the country. São Paulo itself is such a vibrant city because it is home to people (sometimes homeless) from all over Brazil and the world.

In all the Amazons I've been to, I've tripped over gaúchos. They're everywhere. The image of the gaúcho pioneer is fed a high-calorie diet inside Rio Grande do Sul and finds some resonance in the rest of Brazil. Just as their ancestors moved from Europe to the "new world" to own land, gaúchos of European descent have scattered across Brazil with the same goal of owning land (in the case of small farmers) and to own more land (in the case of latifundiários).

I'll never forget my interview with Paulo César Quartiero in Boa Vista, capital of Roraima, Brazil's northernmost state, in 2001. I had disembarked in the city to spend a month traveling to all corners of Roraima with the mission of finding stories. I immediately fell in love with one of the most fantastic places I've ever been, where reality itself is madness. Part of this madness were the gaúchos who planted rice on Indigenous land, with funding from Banco do Brasil. Since I was a gaúcha too, these gaúchos felt fully at ease with me, always expecting my news story to show Rio Grande how successful they had become. Quartiero actually said: "We knew it was Indigenous land, but everything was so cheap, it didn't hurt to risk it. The Banco do Brasil would always rather lend money to a gaúcho than to a Northeasterner, you know how it goes. If we lose the land, we've already made money."

Some years later, Paulo César Quartiero became the mayor of Pacaraima, a trading hub for goods and hopes on the edge of Brazil and Venezuela, likewise consciously staked out in Indigenous territory, this one with a hearty trade in contraband Venezuelan gasoline. He soon converted himself into a defender of the Brazilian "fatherland" against some of the Indigenous, whom he now considered invaders, which qualified him to be elected federal congressman as well as lieutenant governor of Roraima. Quartiero and his gang of grileiros accused the Indigenous people of joining ranks with international NGOs to "take Roraima from Brazil." Once again, a curious case of inside-out xenophobia that converts Indigenous people into native foreigners. Quartiero became a cinematic bad guy to some, a hero to others, when he opened war on the ratification of the Raposa Serra do Sol Indigenous Land as part of his offensive against original peoples, particularly the Macuxi.

In 2018, the journalist Naiara Hofmeister interviewed Quartiero on Marajó Island, the new front line of destruction he had opened. Quartiero was inspecting "two uncommonly large columns for a farm entrance gate," which he had ordered to be built. "It's not a portico," he explained to the reporter. "It's a gallows for hanging all the environmentalists who come around busting our balls. Now that Bolsonaro's president, that's how it's going to be." When the flames of the Amazon invaded screens around the world in 2019, Quartiero was exultant: "[The government] started off real bad, but now it's finding its legs." He was at a farm expo in Rio Grande do Sul at the time, and in response to a photographer's request, he put one foot up on a tractor and declared, "I'm going to pose like an Indian killer."

Paulo César Quartiero is a typical gaúcho "pioneer" in the Amazon. I've met a number much like him. These "notables" either continue to live in Rio Grande do Sul and keep their agents in the Amazon, or they alternate between Amazon cities and Brasília, emptying public coffers after taking office as federal congressmen or senators. This isn't to say all gaúchos behave like this when they migrate to the forest or fence off public land in the forest. But most of the gaúchos, even those who work hard—not the case with exemplars of pioneerism the caliber of a Quartiero— share the same way of settling other people's land, or of invading it, leaving deep marks even on the Amazon's urban landscape.

Just as their ancestors replicated their countries of origin and stayed in closed communities when they colonized northern Rio Grande do Sul, those who migrate to the Amazon replicate this form of land occupation when they settle in the forest. All it takes is for half a dozen gaúchos to get together and they organize a Centro de Tradições Gaúchas—Center of Gaúcho Traditions— duplicating a tradition for both internal and external consumption, with traditional dress and dances, a lot of the Brazilian barbecue known as *churrasco*, and, of course, *chimarrão*, the gaúcho version of yerba mate. A gaúcho from a town of Italian or German heritage is as deeply acquainted with pampa culture as he or she is with a funk party in a Rio de Janeiro favela. But just as the descendants of immigrants in Rio Grande do Sul become more Italian or German than Italians and Germans, the gaúchos in the Amazon start believing themselves to be centaurs in bombachas.

This is both an identity statement and a colonial flag. Many towns in the Amazon end up resembling towns in the South, with lots of cement and few trees. The architecture is square and ungainly, turned inward, built from synthetic material with the idea that practicality is what matters. Southern Brazilians don't have a monopoly on this love of cement and reinforced concrete. But gaúchos are great disseminators of the idea that trading tree green for concrete gray is a sign of progress in life.

I was very saddened and somewhat ashamed to realize that gaúchos generally become impermeable to other cultures because they believe they have nothing to learn from people they deem inferior. Their relationship with the forestpeoples is defined by conflict, for countless reasons and also because racism reproduces even more rapidly than rabbits. Incapable of transforming into forest and learning with the forestpeoples, gaúchos try to adapt the forest to the limited world they know, destroying the Amazon and the people that live in it and with it. And sometimes themselves as well.

I am going to dare to lay a group of people down on the psychoanalyst's couch and say that gaúchos will be unable to imagine a future that isn't identical to the past as long as they are stuck in a past that never existed. On the one hand, the past of their great-grandparents and great-great-grandparents, who had issues because they felt they'd been driven from their home countries and then reacted by transforming these places into paradises lost, handing this myth down to subsequent generations. On the other hand, a glorious past that exists only as marketing, since it hides conflicts, slaughters, and terrible injustices that have been committed. Daring a bit more, I would say gaúchos will only be able to imagine a future when they decide to relinquish the gaúcho who never existed, the one who was the "centaur of the pampas." They will then have to come to grips with the various gaúchos who have actually existed and invent a new way of gaúcho-ing. I hope this verb will eventually come to be conjugated in the plural, embracing all beings, human and nonhuman.

The British-born economist Kenneth Boulding (1910–1993), a naturalized US citizen, made a distinction between what he called the "cowboy economy" and the "spaceman economy." Cowboys—and he was clearly alluding to the people who colonized the American West and were mythologized by Hollywood—view the planet as flat earth, as a vast open space with infinite resources, waiting for the strongest to dominate it while they destroy the original peoples, nonbeings, and also nature. It may be no accident that in the time of elected despots like Bolsonaro, the flat-earth theory is in vogue. Spacemen, on the other hand, understand the planet as a spaceship, finite in size and with resources both finite and scarce that must be carefully managed to avoid triggering collapse and the extinction of the species aboard the craft. In Brazil, this concept can be applied to a portion of the environmental movement, with ties to the thesis of "sustainable development."

The challenge to preventing the climate catastrophe will be converting cowboys into astronauts. No easy task in a political-economic system built on the certainty that both the planet as well as other species are objects meant for unbridled exploitation, whose heroes, revered with statues, are precisely the most successful predators. Donald Trump's resonance in the deep United States, with his assaults on climate science and on climate policy, shows how this cowboy economy is alive—and active.

The greater a crisis, the greater the need to bolster a heroic identity, even if false, along with race and gender values that today are combated as never before by those who have always been deemed subaltern, like Black people and women. After all, there's nothing more cowboy than subjugated women and white machos brandishing weapons. In Brazil, the explorers and adventurers known as bandeirantes are now monuments and street names, in São Paulo more than elsewhere. And gaúchos are now cultivating a haughty self-image as "pioneers" more vehemently as Rio Grande do Sul wanes in political and economic importance on the national scene.

How can a people whose pride is grounded in the idea of pioneerism, viewed as synonymous with honor, bravery, and superiority, be made to understand that this form of occupation is a giant mistake that has already brought the planet's climate to collapse and may even cause the extinction of the human species, along with that of (almost) all others?

Boulding's proposition was bold in the 1960s when he conceived it, but it is a typical white US male way of looking at things, contrasting cowboys and astronauts, two characters constructed as heroes by twentieth-century Hollywood. A forest thinker would find them both terribly mistaken because they view the planet as an Other, and a subjugated Other. For forest communities, the planet is neither a ranch nor a spaceship but they themselves and all other human and nonhuman peoples, all of whom are in an organic relationship of intense exchange.

This isn't merely a difference in how one sees and exists, but rather the essence of what can inspire the forging of human communities capable of living with humans and nonhumans on equal terms. While it may be much more advisable to become an astronaut than to continue as a cowboy for the survival of the species, making this switch is not enough. Not to mention, on the few occasions when spacemen have managed to disembark from a spacecraft, they have planted colonial flags on planets and soon begun assessing whether or not there were any resources to be exploited.

I suspect that all spacemen will be cowboys one day, and not the other way around. My proposal and that of others is that we all become Indigenous, in the sense of understanding ourselves as an organic part of a living planet and understanding life as this fascinating relationship of exchange and mutual dependence between different ways of occupying the same body. It seems to me that the only path is to forest ourselves. The future is not in the Old World, Europe, or in the United States, the declining superpower, nor in China, the rising superpower. But in the always-new old world of the original communities, who have resisted all dominators for centuries and who live as an organic part of Earth.

I used to declare myself a gaúcha whenever possible, until I started to understand what a gaúcho is—and especially what a gaúcho is in the Amazon. The more I ventured into the forest, the more I realized that introducing myself as a gaúcha made my interlocutors skittish. And then, in 2004, on the eve of an expedition to Terra do Meio, I was buying supplies in a supermarket in Altamira in the company of a man who worked with peasants who were victims of land conflicts, when we ran into a tall white fellow. My companion stopped to greet the tall man and they exchanged a few barbs. In the course of the conversation, I was introduced, and I said, all excited, "Oh! I'm gaúcha too. Where are you from?" It was a quick chat, and when my shopping mate and I continued down the aisles, he told me, "He's a grileiro." Still naive, I replied, "Gosh, a gaúcho, how disgraceful." Then he explained, "You have to understand that gaúchos are known as the Amazon's locusts."

It took me some years to complete this mental bridge. What was celebrated as heroic pioneerism bursting with bravery in news stories written by gaúchos was interpreted by the forest-peoples as the destruction wrought by locusts, who descend in hordes on something living and only fly off after swallowing up the last leaf. Their legacy is scorched earth, the ruins of what once was forest.

51. altamiracles

I feel physical pain when I open my computer. I know I've reached this chapter, the one where I tell about my arrival in Altamira. Not even I knew until now that this body of mine still ached. Raimunda of the Promised Land always says she changes skin once a year, like a snake. I don't feel that I changed skin when I came to Altamira but that I changed bodies. I know this feeling is real, but I also know this new body has always been mine, it was just another one before. Neither better nor worse, neither more nor less real, neither more nor less authentic, just another me. To become this other, I needed to destroy dams and hurt the people I loved most. This is the pain I still feel, sharp, at this moment when part of my grieving must become word. To stay in Altamira I had to kill myself, cry over myself, grieve my own mourning. I realize now that this grieving isn't over yet, but it is necessary to go on, and to do so in this book as well.

It was August 16, 2017. São Paulo–Belo Horizonte–Belém–Altamira. Four cities, three states, three flights. This is the first onus of living in a city in the interior of the Amazon. Travel will always be much more expensive, take longer, be more precarious and unstable, and just be much worse. If the airline company needs to shuffle its aircraft for some reason, it's certain your city will be left planeless, even if it has only one flight a day. For our move across the country, we had to pay almost as much as the price of an airline ticket for our suitcases, plus photography equipment. I was accompanied by João, who had been my life partner of fifteen years at that point, and the photojournalist Lilo Clareto, my reporting partner.

Lilo and I did our first assignment together in 2001. We were dispatched to Roraima for a month without ever having met, since he had just hired on at the magazine where I worked. After a day in Boa Vista, the state capital, we ventured into Yanomami territory on a cinematic journey into the depths of the Amazon that involved a helicopter, a small aircraft, a voadeira, and a storm. The passage from white people's land to forest inhabited by Yanomamis and so many other beings was my first true experience in passing through a portal. Others were to come. Right then, we were in a helicopter, hanging in the air, waiting for wind conditions to permit a rapid, precise descent. Suspended above the forest, I also suspended my breath. Not out of fear—I'm never afraid of flying—but from the excitement we feel when we're on a trip and know we're going to turn into others of ourselves. And then we plunged downward. To discover that the world was this, that what we had known until then was an un-world.

Our baptism as a reporter-photographer duo happened as soon as we reached the first Yanomami village. No one was there. The Indigenous had temporarily relocated to their camp alongside the fields. It was pitch black by the time we reached them. And pitch black in the forest is something to respect. We were drenched, starving, shivering. The village was nestled in a mountainous region and when the sun vanishes, it is bitter cold, so the Yanomami always keep a number of fires going inside their huge *chabona*, as they call their beautiful collective home.

There was no room for us inside, perhaps because we were still strangers without permission to get so close in the darkness. After a meal of roasted worms, Lilo and I shared a hammock because there wasn't room to hang another one, our feet tucked up against each other's heads, the rain seemingly piercing our skin and striking our bones, with no chance of a fire to warm us. We woke very early the next morning to shouts from members of the accompanying health care team, who were screaming at the Indigenous that they shouldn't spit their phlegm on the ground but instead into little plastic cups. "Not on the ground! No!" and "Spit here!" were the battle cries of the desperate nursing assistants, who were speaking Portuguese to people who only understood Yanomami. They were part of a medical mission to test for tuberculosis, and each bit of sputum was precious. I really wanted to know what the Indigenous were saying to each other amid their chuckles. They must have thought all whites are nuts, and they were right. When we weren't shooting at them, we collected their sputum. That was our good-morning.

Following this debut, Lilo and I had two choices: we'd either love each other or kill each other. We loved each other, and since then formed a reporter-photographer duo madly passionate about journalism and friends forever. It's Lilo who ties my hammock up in the forest, because I'm so bad at it, and when I'm sad, he shows up with flowers he has picked in the woods. He's an intuitive artist whose best photographs are born from the moment, much more than from planning. Lilo sees things nobody else does. And he has the gift of adapting anywhere at all, without ever complaining either about the work hours (always long when I'm the partner on the story) or about food or lodgings. His chief asset is that people usually love him because it's absolutely impossible not to. And so it's obvious I couldn't make such an important move without Lilo by my side. Sixteen years after our grand debut, I called his home in Vila Mariana, in São Paulo, and said: "I'll explain better later. But I need to know now. Are you willing to move to Altamira with me?" Lilo simply replied: "Li-Brum, I'm in. When?"

São Paulo–Belo Horizonte–Belém–Altamira, four cities, three states, three flights. No. Immensely more. A lifetime.

I had a thorn stuck deep inside me. It was the intuition that there was no possible return from that trip. I'm not referring to a return by plane, in physical space, but a return to my body.

We arrived at night. Lilo was to stay at the home of a lovely young activist, Daniela Silva, a Black woman from the periphery of Altamira. The two of them only knew each other from meetings of beiradeiros, where Lilo would shoot pictures as part of our joint work and Daniela was active in the Movimento Xingu Vivo para Sempre—Xingu Alive Forever movement. But they ended up really knowing each other. Pulling a typical Lilo, on the same night that we landed in Altamira, he kissed Dani on the pier along the shoreline and thus set down roots in the forest, the city, and also in the life of the woman he fell for. Today I'm the proud godmother of Maria Clara, the daughter of this union, a little girl with the eyes of someone who has lived a thousand years, raised at events protesting Belo Monte, violence against women, racism toward Black women, and everything that's no good. My partner at this baptism was Erwin Kräutler, bishop emeritus of Xingu, because Lilo and Dani wanted to be certain Maria was born for the struggle.

When we landed in Altamira, Lilo leapt to his destiny while João and I headed to our hotel. We ate a veggie burger at a trailer on the corner and felt Altamira's heavy shadows besetting us on all flanks. We didn't yet know, at least not consciously, that we were beginning to entomb not our love but our marriage. The banzeiro was roaring but I pretended not to hear.

Making a home in a place like Altamira is radically different from spending a few weeks in the trenches and then going back to your couch in São Paulo or some other corner. It was because I knew this that I made the move. But while I had already done so many news reports there, the impact of this move on my regular life only became clear day by day. Not gradually, but always by fits and starts. The first dilemma was the house itself. We wanted a place with a yard because, after all, it would make no sense to leave an apartment in São Paulo to rent another apartment right in the Amazon. The problem is that for many of those in Altamira, trees are trash. The term for weeding is "cleaning up." The only people who haven't paved over their yards (yet) are the ones who can't afford the cement. "Progress" means conquering the forest, even if this means what is left of it in your flower bed. This mentality is cemented in most people's heads, and most people are migrants who come in hopes of getting ahead in life.

Some weeks earlier, a friend had rented a certain house for the sole reason that a lone surviving tree was still left in the yard. When she moved in, her landlord proudly announced, fully expecting gratitude in return: "I've cleaned it up for you." Lilo chose his house because there was a gigantic mango tree in the backyard, absolutely glorious, an abode for lizards and birds of all shapes. Upon returning from a trip to São Paulo, Lilo discovered his landlord had invaded the lot and murdered the mango tree, because the neighbor had complained that its leaves were falling on her roof. The same landlord had "cleaned up" the flowers Lilo had planted in front of the house. That's another characteristic of Altamira: property owners rarely understand renting as a temporary transfer of ownership and continue to think they can invade your home. For people who have traversed Brazil to plant their flag, ownership is fierce.

Whenever I traveled to São Paulo or somewhere else, I would come back to find fewer trees in the city. At each turn, there was always a bit more missing in Altamira. The city moves on by destroying the forest. This is a permanent, steady, and visible war. Every day, Altamira converts more deeply into ruins. The city is the ruins of the forest. As in Hollywood horror films from the 1980s, where some Indian cemetery is always haunting the neighborhood, Altamira is a city built atop several cemeteries. Each brick laid, each additional pound of cement, is an attempt to bury the blood. But sun, storms, and nature counterattack and thwart this erasure, forcing their tormenters to live among the remains of everything that was once living but they killed. More sensitive people, where I include myself, feel this weight. In 2018, one year after my arrival, I released a book entitled *Brasil Construtor de Ruínas*—Brazil, builder of ruins. It was only by living in Altamira that I came to understand that Brazil is a builder of ruins.

We couldn't find a house with a yard. Property owners would explain that they had cemented everything over for the convenience of the people coming for the "project." The project was the Belo Monte hydroelectric power plant. During the years of site preparation and major construction, from 2010 to 2015, rent prices skyrocketed and the former tenants were pushed to the town's periphery. Houses were adapted to receive the new renters from South-Central Brazil, and their wallets readily opened either because public money was involved or because construction companies and subcontractors had been guaranteed hefty profits.

By 2017, this predatory party was over and property owners were smarting from the end of hyperinflated rental prices. Houses were empty, in awful shape, and what had once been alive was now interred beneath cement. When the owners discovered we wanted a yard and liked trees, they were mortified about their missed opportunity and some even offered to rip up the concrete and restore the dirt.

One Sunday we spotted a For Rent sign on a house with a yard. It looked like the place had been abandoned for some time, but we were excited. Renting a house in Altamira, however, doesn't just mean finding an inhabitable place at a good location and affordable price. The hardest part is investigating the property owner. After a few phone calls, I discovered he was a grileiro whom I had denounced years earlier, someone who had committed much violence and destruction but still remained unpunished. One more house lost.

After a series of bitter frustrations, and with our hotel bill accumulating more digits, we decided to adapt to reality. We chose a house some minutes from downtown in a "closed condominium," or gated community. It was furnished, which was convenient for us, and offered the protection of walls and gatekeepers. It was not an easy decision because the concept of a gated community doesn't sit well with me. When my stories are translated to other languages, it's always hard to explain this kind of "condominium," an invention peculiar to Brazil and other countries where inequality is sharp. Much more than an architectural concept, a closed condominium in Brazil is a political-housing project built to leave others out. Not just any others, but the poorest, generally Black people, who only enter in the morning to do the heavier work, for which they are poorly paid; at the end of the day, they leave these walls to return to the city's periphery and to homes lacking basic sanitation. When she was eight, a little girl whom I love asked her mother: "Mom, where do the brown kids live?" She only saw these "brown" people appear in the morning and vanish at night.

Brazil's gated communities are the architectural expression of its racial inequality. They are an extension of the housemaid's bedroom, that little annex at the back with no windows or just a tiny one, where housemaids were, and still are, confined, even in apartments. Brazil likes to portray its architecture through the modernist curves of Oscar Niemeyer. But a more accurate time line of the history of Brazilian architecture runs from the rural aristocracy's manor houses and slave quarters to the tiny maids' rooms of the urban bourgeoisie and, today, to the closed condominium, which emerged as a way of protecting the wealthiest from the increasingly violent response of people violated by some of the world's harshest inequalities.

Choosing to live in a closed condominium in a city in the Amazon was hard for me. At the same time, I was well aware of the murder statistics in Altamira, which in 2015, the year Belo Monte received its operating license, was the most violent city in Brazil—one of the world's most violent countries—with a homicide rate of 124.6 per 100,000 inhabitants. To understand what this means, we can compare this with the rate for the city of Rio de Janeiro, the setting for so many massacres, which tallies 23.4 homicides per 100,000. Altamira's explosion of violence is linked to the building of the dam and hydropower plant. At the height of construction, the city's population almost doubled. By 2017, the figure had dropped a bit, to an estimated 115,000, but still well above the 77,000 inhabitants the city had housed at the beginning of the century. Altamira is the city in the Amazon that kills the most and deforests the most, leaving clear the direct relationship between the Portuguese words *matar*—to kill—and *desmatar*—to deforest. *Desmatar* is one of the most twisted verbs in the Portuguese language. It looks like "unkill" but does the opposite of what it says.

On the morning we were to sign the lease, I took another spin around the living room, trying to find some point of connection with the landlady, who owned a bus company in São Paulo and had done business in Altamira when Belo Monte was under construction. On the shelves, some books by John Grisham, a copy of Lya Luft's collection of essays *Perdas & ganhos*. Not my style, but nothing that offended me either. This wouldn't be the first time I'd lived in a house furnished by someone else. I usually set up house quickly, even in a hotel room.

And then, before we signed, I asked: "Who owns this condominium?" The question occurred to me on the spot; I didn't have time to think before voicing it. I had investigated the landlady but not the condominium's owner. The real estate agent answered without hesitation: "Oh, Regivaldo Galvão." I felt something akin to a shock. Not emotional, but electrical. "Regivaldo Galvão, the man who had Dorothy Stang killed?" And the real estate agent, unruffled and looking at her blood-red nails, replied: "They *say* he had her killed."

End of story. And the house.

This is the first important lesson Altamira taught me. We are part of a long, globalized production chain. We find it hard to recognize (and generally prefer not to) the torturous path traveled by a trendy article of clothing before it reaches some store's well-lit window display, clothing often sewn by a woman or child on the other side of the world working under a system analogous to slavery. We know nonhumans by their cuts of meat—flank steak, rump, tri-tip, etc.—which reach us on foam trays in the supermarket meat case, sparing us all the blood. We also don't concern ourselves, or do so very little, about the path these goods travel once they leave our homes. Best-case scenario, we consider ourselves good citizens because we recycle the synthetic leftovers of our consumption or compost organic waste.

In an Amazonian city like Altamira, such "ignorance" isn't permissible. This chain of relations is short or even nonexistent. Here it's impossible to play innocent, or play innocent so well that we believe it ourselves, as you can do in cities like São Paulo or New York. Our tracks are visible. And other people's tracks too. If there was any risk for someone like me, a journalist who denounces socioenvironmental crimes, it was precisely within the walls of a gated community like that one, and not outside them. I would be living right next to some of those who act against the forest or condone its destruction. In other words, inside enemy territory.

This impossibility of innocence was my first conflict. The only place I could find my vegan milk was at a supermarket owned by an instigator of crime. So I had to quit drinking milk. When I bought a table, I regretted it the next minute because there was no doubt the wood was the product of deforestation. I spent a night researching the type of wood and the risk of extinction for that particular tree species. By the end of my research, I felt like an accomplice in the destruction of the Amazon and it drained all the joy from my first piece of furniture in my new life.

The simplest decision, the most prosaic purchase, each small act, required an investigation. I came to understand that, yes, I would continue doing the best possible but would have to live with the contradictions inherent in existing inside the most predatory capitalism. In Altamira, there was no way I could be free of the blood, as I was in São Paulo. I could never forget this and normalize the unacceptable, while I also had to learn to bear contradictions I couldn't avoid—or life would be impossible.

For me, Altamira's violence materialized in the form of four-wheel-drive pickups with glass tinted so dark you couldn't see who was inside. Drivers speed down the streets, slamming on their brakes and peeling out aggressively and loudly. Only the wealthy can afford this kind of truck, and in Altamira most of these individuals have a past and a present tied up with grilagem, logging, and, not uncommonly, blood. My repetition of the word *blood* in this book doesn't represent exaggeration or a poor writing style or lack of vocabulary. It is life filled with death. Blood asserts itself on the frontiers of the climate war.

I'm a walker, and I never cross the street in front of a pickup. I developed this preventive technique after checking the alarming statistics on vehicle-pedestrian collisions. Even so, these vehicles feel like a threat when I walk down the street. My whole body tenses up. I have a premonition that one day, one of them will run me down. This experience reminds me of *Duel*, a classic 1970s thriller where the driver of a tractor-trailer relentlessly pursues a business commuter down dusty roads. Directed by Steven Spielberg, before he became famous, the movie never shows the driver's face. Just his boots and one arm.

In Altamira, this persecution is subtle but persistent. It's the forest war taken to the streets of the city that builds ruins. Not war—slaughter. The poorest—the deforested forestpeoples—walk, bike, or ride small-displacement motorcycles, the consumer's dream come true for most. Scenes of entire families piled on the backs of little bikes—father, mother, and as many as three kids—are commonplace. I've seen women with nursing babies strapped to their chests zipping along on two wheels between pickups. A lot of blood is spilled even on urban streets.

I gradually realized Altamira is a land of amputees. People go about losing territory, identity, and pieces of their bodies in the streets. They often lose their very lives, run down during a clash between unequal forces, steel against flesh. There have been many days when this loss has been unbearable for me. When this happens, I retreat to my house for a day or two, to remake the skin on my body so I can once again expose myself to the sun and, especially, to the pickup trucks.

Before living in Altamira, I would just pass through the city, getting off a plane to catch a boat into the deep forest, and then a second time, boarding a plane to return to São Paulo. In my move to the center of the world, what I hadn't expected was this relationship with the city. I had been captured by the deforested peoples, overcome by immense tenderness for the human and nonhuman ruins, and invaded by the understanding that a modern city is, by definition, ruins of nature. Up until then, I had thought I could understand the forest without understanding the ruins of the forest, that I could tell about forestpeoples without telling about deforested peoples. Living in this Amazonian city, I could almost feel these connections being completed within my body, the bridge between a forest in the process of conversion into ruins and a forest already buried by the ruins called city. All of this is the Amazon.

It isn't just the chain of events—between the wood of your table and the tree toppled by an enslaved worker, or between the meat on your plate and the cattle enslaved to deforestation—that grows shorter and painfully visible. The decisions made in Brasília crash down on people's lives like the acts of some Old Testament god. When Michel Temer's administration and the Congress of the corrupt pushed through a "labor reform," it was literally the next day that many of the workers formally employed by companies in Altamira became freelancers without any rights, earning day wages. Not only are laws imposed by the strongest; it is also the strongest who choose the laws or parts of them that serve them best, disregarding all the others. Ignoring this reality when lawmaking is to ignore the majority of the Brazils. How can you protest if protesting means you'll never get a job in the city again? How can you protest if protesting means you'll be forced to migrate yet again? I've witnessed workers simply lower their heads and prepare for hunger.

When I lived in São Paulo, I chose, given my profession and my convictions, to travel to the territories of tragedy and then return to my middle-class apartment. Not in Altamira. I was in the banzeiro, and choosing not to live in it would put me alongside the killers. One day, reality literally came through my door, aboard the body of a friend, both rapper and woodworker, who arrived to deliver a bookcase. He sat down to have a glass of cacao juice and told me the police had raided his house. They grabbed his friend, who was spending a few days with him, and stuck his friend's head underwater, over and over again. And hit him. And beat him. All my visitor could do was watch the torture and pray not to be tortured himself. He was tired because he couldn't sleep at night. Police gunfire, yet again. And he had to throw himself on the floor, and sleep there. He couldn't always do it. Then he added: "Once I dated a white woman. And I almost felt white too, because I could walk around the city at night." I could no longer pretend I was capable of doing anything for him or for anyone else. He continued to make small pieces of furniture for me. Our friendship was an illusion, like friendship between whites and Black people in a country where the first group is always the first group. An illusion, like Saturday.

In Altamira, it's mandatory to try to identify and classify everyone quickly, as if we ourselves were airport X-rays. Who is she? What does he want? Why is she here? Those were the questions I started asking. One night, when I was still coming and going between south and north, a friend and I were with some people at a corner bar. Suddenly, a man at a nearby table got up and pointed at my friend's T-shirt. Defying my recommendation that he never wear any clothing with symbols or words on it, my friend was wearing a T-shirt from Urihi, an NGO that does Indigenous health care work and that for many years provided excellent services in Roraima, working with the Yanomami, until the NGO was criminalized so the usual suspects could resume their lucrative misappropriation of public money. But the problem at that moment was something else. His shirt was stamped with Indigenous symbols, so the man identified us as "Indian defenders," and he became increasingly aggressive. I had to use all the diplomacy I'd learned in my years of wanderings to get us out of the bar as fast as possible.

Living in Altamira, I tried to disappear, which means I tried to make myself hard to identify. The wealthiest women, the daughters of grileiros and large landowners, as well as liberal professionals and all the women who are trying to climb the ladder, wear skin-tight jeans and high heels. Long hair, usually with highlights, long perfectly manicured nails, lots of makeup, gold jewelry, and glitz. There's another layer of women, female professionals who come from outside, generally with ties to socioenvironmental organizations or public institutions. You can recognize them by their Indigenous-crafted bracelets and necklaces, colorful light-weight dresses or skirts, and flip-flops or flats.

And their Kayapó shifts. This story is both terrible and raving mad, like all good stories about Altamira. Women of Mebêngôkre ethnicity, which includes the Kayapó and Xikrin, all wear the same style of dress, lightweight and well-behaved. The only thing that changes is the print. The explanation is that in the mid-twentieth century, Evangelical missionaries enforced the wearing of shifts so the shameless nudity of Indigenous women's bodies would have a little shame. And the shift became an institution. There's a seamstress on the Altamira market today who makes practically nothing but these dresses to supply Xikrin and Kayapó clientele. Lightweight and colorful, they've also been adopted by anthropologists and the like on the streets of Altamira. The little post-missionary-post-Kayapó shift is ever more the rage in the world of Amazon and climate activism, my favorite gift for friends in São Paulo.

When I disembarked in the city, I made it a point not to wear jeans tighter than Scrooge or ultrahigh heels, which was impos-sible anyway, given my noted lack of motor coordination, and also not embrace the use of Kayapó dresses, which actually made me look like a sack of potatoes. I knew I couldn't go unnoticed, but at least I could try to be beige. I was immediately picked out by a man on a passing bike, who stopped so suddenly at my side that it startled me. He approached me, all excited: "Where's your church? I want to attend!"

We finally found a house. Not the one we wanted, the one that was possible. It was one of five two-story homes built by a family of fazendeiros and merchants so they could all live together in a well-to-do area on the edge of the river. Since the family ended up occupying only two of the five homes, they rented out the other three. We began living in this extremely private place, a kind of small gated community, among people from Altamira society. There was a large lot on the other side of the very high walls, occupied by many trees, dirt, and the homes of families with children of various ages. Opposites, shoulder to shoulder.

The people on the other side of the wall were often my refuge, although they didn't know it. I would open my bedroom window and accompany their lives of work and joy, their pickup soccer games, the tire swing the father hung in the tree one day for the kids, heartbreak songs on the radio. At night, the lot became the realm of frogs of varying sizes and songs that filled me with life so I could get through the night in a city of so many deaths. All that noise was my lullaby and one of the things I missed most when I had to leave Altamira. One day I returned from a trip and there was nothing there anymore. The families had been expelled, the trees ripped out, the frogs murdered. The lot had been "cleaned up" to receive tons of concrete. I felt brutalized and also guilty for not even having known about that unequal fight. The violence had unfolded right beside me and I had preferred not to see it.

We stayed in the house for over a year, and during this time the owners' two chow chows treated us like intruders. They were the furry version of four-wheel-drive pickups. Those enormous dogs with their bearlike faces and thick fur coats, imported into the Amazon heat, came at us whenever they saw us, blocking our way across the lot. We had wrangled a yard out of concrete by planting vases in every corner and even adding a suspended garden, and the dogs always shat there. It seemed like they were shitting just to be mean and show who was boss.

On the first day I woke up in the house, I understood where I was and how I would have to live there. I opened the living room window and my view was the neighbor's enormous pickup truck, a little more than three feet away. Plastered across the door was an XXL poster with the face of Jair Bolsonaro. Other posters would appear, because my fazendeiro neighbor was one of the most active propagandists for Bolsonaro's 2018 presidential campaign in Altamira. From then on, Bolsonaro's psychopathic features would be my first sight upon waking. Day after day. It was hard, but I remembered where I was and stayed alert.

On the hardest days, when the city flays my skin and soul, I cling to a memory of the exact moment when I fell in love with Altamira, even before I moved there. It was early 2017, and I had just left a colorful, noisy multilingual meeting of Indigenous peoples early one evening. I walked several dozen feet and stumbled upon a kind of rave at a gym. Several dozen more feet, and my ears were surprised by the sound of off-key but poignant hymns coming from an Evangelical church. One city block, three worlds. And I could walk by them all and still eat a bowl of açaí at the end.

4.0. the children of altamira

The young woman had black hair and looked to be of Indigenous and African ancestries. At that moment, she didn't know whether her twenty-year-old brother's limbs were all in place. She didn't know whether the head of the person she loved was on the same body as its arms. Nor did she know whether the arms were near the legs. Or if that wasn't the case at all. Whether he'd been burned to death, whether the body of the brother she'd grown up with was a carbonized mass amid bodies of other brothers, fathers, children. Human people.

She screamed. Her mother was there with her. The mother of the twenty-year-old young man. She had conceived him and carried him in her womb for nine months. And right then was searching for his head, trying to guess which was the flesh of her flesh within that mass of incinerated bodies. She was a mother, and she didn't know whether her son's final breath had been drawn during the excruciating pain of having his head severed or the excruciating pain of suffocating as his body burned. She didn't want to, but she couldn't keep from wondering if it took him long to die, and she prayed it had been quick. These were the mother's questions. Not only hers but the same questions asked by all the mothers, first in front of the prison gates in Altamira and then in front of the gates of the Medical Legal Institute, the morgue.

It wasn't just because her son was dead—an inversion in the order of life, a pain (almost) anyone can imagine even if they can't quite comprehend it. It was even worse than this pain. It was the pain of a tortured death, of the certainty her son had died in terror. The mother screamed and screamed. Because there were no words to name what she was living through. The sister screamed and screamed. Another woman, her face also furrowed by suffering, embraced the body of the dead man's sister, as if wanting to contain the scream that was lacerating the world. A man embraced the mother's body, but he seemed to feel too weak to contain the scream issuing from her like a tsunami swallowing up one person alone and everything she knew and was known of her.

There are images documenting this moment. But the photos cannot be published. There's that too. The images can't have a face, they can't have a name, they can't have a voice. Nor can the story's details be told, the details of the young man killed in the custody of the state at the penitentiary called the Regional Recovery Center of Altamira. If the two women are identified by criminal factions, their heads might also roll—literally—down the streets of the city's marginalized peripheries. They are ghosts. Living ghosts.

I'll never get this image out of my head. The massacre of Altamira, which took place on the morning of July 29, 2019, was the second largest in the history of Brazil's prison system: fifty-eight men in the custody of the state were killed, sixteen of them decapitated and the rest turned to flames. Yes, before the forest had gone up in flames on the world's screens that same year, bodies of deforested people had done the same.

Yet that wasn't all. Shortly after the massacre, four survivors were strangled during their transfer to another prison. They had been handcuffed. This was the final tally: sixty-two people under the responsibility of the state were killed, first on the premises of a state building and then inside a jail truck belonging to the state. Nearly half were still awaiting trial. Most were Black and under the age of thirty-five; few had finished school.

The massacre has been attributed to a war between the organized crime factions Red Command and Class A Command. The

National Justice Council classified the prison's conditions as "terrible." Though it was designed to hold 163 inmates, more than 300 were packed into the space. The number of prison guards was well below what was needed, and there were always weapons around.

When he was questioned about the massacre, President Jair Bolsonaro had this to say: "Ask the victims of those who died there what they think about it. After they answer, I'll answer you." Bishop Erwin Kräutler reacted with these words: "I've read in the paper that our president is saying we should ask the victims of those who died. That is not the kind of answer, for the love of God, that a president [should give] these families here. Every inmate has a mother, a father. Their mothers are there crying." When four inmates were strangled during the transfer, Bolsonaro said: "Problems come up."

These were the words family members heard from Brazil's antipresident. And these were also the words the mother heard. And the sister. And there's still the little girl. She's five years old and has the name of a street in São Paulo. The dead man the two women are screaming for is her uncle. She wants to know what happened. How do we explain it?

I could tell you the story of Brazil starting when the original peoples first caught sight of stinking white men disembarking on the coast, before the peoples knew the men carried the apocalypse on their crosses and would exterminate 90 percent of their population. I could tell you the story of the Amazon starting from when the ancestors of today's Indigenous helped plant the forest, later to be destroyed along with them. I could tell you the story of Belo Monte starting from when the Kayapó Tuíra held a machete to the face of a representative of President José Sarney, the big boss of Brazil's oligarchies, back when the power plant was still on the drawing board and was called Kararaô. I could tell you that this symbolic gesture of resistance would delay dam construction for decades, but twenty years later, Belo Monte would be forcibly built by a political party with popular roots. And, despite all this, I would not know how to explain what happened to the girl who has the name of a street in São Paulo.

Violent death is no stranger to the girl. Less than two years earlier, the police had executed her father in one of the Collective Urban Resettlements built by Norte Energia. The father of the girl who has the name of a street was a brickmaker. Like her grandfather too. When the dam arrived, the government expropriated the area where the brickyards stood, which means people were expelled from their way of life. Until then, the family had lived in poverty but not gone hungry. The small family brickyard produced enough so the adults and children could enjoy at least minimum dignity. When they lost what allowed them to survive, their poverty turned to penury.

The girl's father looked for a job, but he hadn't gone to school. Before he died, he was arrested for holding up a gas station. When he was killed, according to a police officer, "he was the wrong person in the wrong place." The fellow who should have died, according to the same officer, was the friend who was with the father. The police had executed the wrong man. And the man's mother and sister were told this, as if the state were legally allowed to carry out an execution. But the family is afraid to confront the state. And they should be. If they protest, others might be killed. So this is how things went: "Excuse us, ma'am, we killed your son by mistake."

Today, the girl without a father lives with her paternal grandmother in a housing project that is part of the Minha Casa Minha Vida program—My Home My Life. There, public transportation is in short supply, the only leisure area has been abandoned, and the neighborhood is ruins generating ruins. Eight children and four adults live in the small house. Most of the children have lost their parents to violence, and that is why they're being raised by their grandmother, who works as a street cleaner. Last year a drunk merchant ran over the grandmother on the sidewalk and she lost part of her foot.

The children are sometimes left alone at home. Their grandmother needs to work to get food. She turns herself outside in, now with only a foot and a half. Shortly before the prison massacre, she made a trip to take one of her grandsons to his mother, who had been shot by an organized crime faction and had to flee the city to keep from dying. The mother's partner, who was along during the attack, was shot in the head and fell into a coma. She herself was shot in the hand. She only survived because she set her four-year-old child down on the ground and fought. This four-year-old boy, cousin of the little girl who has the name of a street in São Paulo, witnessed all of this violence. When you're poor and have to flee, without being able to count on anyone other than other poor people—this falls into the category of terrifying. Another daughter of this grandmother with a foot and a half is also in hiding, in another city, because an ex threatened to kill her.

Domestic violence is a normalized part of life for many women on the peripheries of Altamira, almost as certain as the daily birth of the sun. In their stifling houses, children watch as their mothers, aunts, and sisters are beaten. One teenage girl explained it to me this way: "It's part of men's nature not to control themselves. That's why I don't know if I want to get married." Her leg was also bashed up when she was hit by a vehicle, at a time when the city was transforming and filling up with cars. Expelled from the riverbank by the company that built the plant, she didn't have time to learn to walk down those streets before the wheels found her. She limps along with a disfigurement that hampers her growth and makes her a target of mockery at school. The Trans-Amazon Regional Public Hospital, the biggest in the area, hasn't yet been able to do an operation that would allow her to recover much use of her leg. She reached adolescence while still waiting in line. And she might yet become an adult while still in line.

At her father's funeral, the girl who has the name of a street explained to everyone who arrived for the visitation: "The police killed my daddy. The police killed my daddy." The father's blood-ied, gunshot body suddenly appeared on an aunt's cell phone screen. Next came a video where his body was being dragged by the police. Bodies are often photographed and filmed by "jour-nalists" who are accompanying the police or even by officers themselves, and the images are distributed on WhatsApp groups. Bodies become things when people dehumanize themselves by dehumanizing others. For the girl who has the name of a street, that blood-covered "thing" was her father. And she explained to everyone who arrived: "The police killed my daddy."

The girl's brother rejected the word of death. He's nine years old. He seems to have developed a way of dealing with a reality that is almost nothing but violence. He keeps repeating: "I'm going to stay here [next to the coffin] until my dad wakes up." He has the same name as a soccer player and is still waiting for his dad to wake up. He doesn't have a cognitive problem; he knows his father will never wake up, but that's what he says. He's telling himself a different story. And perhaps this is the best choice for someone who has no choice and wants desperately to live. It's either this story, or: the dam robbed my family of its sustenance, my father was killed by those who should protect him, my grandmother was run over by a wealthy drunk man and lost half her foot, my aunt is in hiding so she won't be executed by a criminal faction, my other aunt had to run off so she wouldn't be killed by her ex-husband, my half sister's uncle turned into cinders in prison.

I look at him and know he knows all this. But he saves a small part of himself when he looks off into nowhere, which he often does. The boy has nightmares. Lots of them. Nightmares he doesn't want to share. Secrets, he says. Then a sadness unfurls into the distance.

I need to say something about this boy. In my lifetime as a reporter, I've seen many children with elderly eyes. I've written about them. They are children who live with death every day, children who are afraid they'll die and run the real risk of dying at any moment. Children for whom death is more certain than life.

When we meet children with elderly eyes, we know a crime has been committed, because children just shouldn't have elderly eyes. But whenever I talk about them, I always mention their eyes. That look of someone who has already lived several lives in just a handful of years, the look of someone who has seen too many deaths before they can even process what death is, the look of someone who lives with the fear of dying before getting to live. What I saw in the boy who has the name of a soccer player is different. The boy has wrinkles under his eyes. I had never seen a child with wrinkles.

He is the girl's half brother by way of their father. Their father, who was executed before he turned thirty. A brother-in-law murdered the boy's mother when the boy was less than a year old. The family was gathered in the front yard when the brother-in-law showed up. He was drunk. And fuming. Military police officers had doused his face with pepper spray. The boy's mother was laughing about something else, but when he heard her laughter, he thought it was at him, at his humiliation. His humiliation turned to anger, and he wanted someone to pay. She was the weakest. He pulled out his gun and shot her. The woman was breastfeeding the boy. The bullet struck her chest, and almost the baby. She didn't let go of her baby. She protected her son and died four days later at the hospital.

The boy is an orphan, no father, no mother. When I met him, a month before the massacre that would kill his sister's uncle, he was happy. And the pupils above his wrinkles had suddenly lit up. There was a procession on the river and for the first time he was sailing down the Xingu. I couldn't believe it. The boy had been born in a city on the banks of the Xingu and he had never been on the river. He had been born on the river but amputated from it.

Since then, I've included this question in my interviews. And I've discovered that many children on the periphery of Altamira haven't been to the river, which lies barely a hundred feet from downtown. Many of them don't leave the periphery because public transport is difficult, because no adult can take them to the riverbank, because it's all so wretched. Unless public transportation functions, and fares are accessible, what is close becomes distant, what is close becomes never. The only world these children know are homes that lack everything and potholed streets that lack everything. And this is another form of unnameable violence. This is a prison, although these children haven't committed any crime. And because they are have-nots, many of them move from this prison to the official one. And die before the age of twenty.

I remember the demonstrations in 2013, among the biggest in Brazilian history. They were sparked by a twenty-centavo hike in public transportation fares—less than a dime. Many people made fun of these twenty centavos, the many who don't know they are in fact the few couldn't imagine someone rebelling over twenty centavos, coins they wouldn't bother to bend over to pick up. In the Brazil of the boy who has the name of a soccer player and the girl who has the name of a street in São Paulo, however, twenty centavos could make all the difference. And these Brazils are vast, although television anchors don't live in any of them.

The boy is in the fourth grade. Ask the boy: What is the Amazon? He doesn't know. At the age of nine, he is told he lives in a city in the Amazon rainforest. He's never been to the forest, just as he had never been on the river. Ask the boy: "What is your country?" He answers with the name of the neighborhood where he lives.

This answer isn't wrong. It's the most precise answer the boy can give. His neighborhood is his country. And his country pens him in—and determines him. Then you show him a map. And the boy gets all excited, almost like when he was sailing down the river. He sees Brazil and he sees the Amazon and, suddenly, there's a planet that isn't flat.

I've lost track of the adults and children for whom I was the first to show them a map of Brazil and the world. And explain where we were in relation to the world. The children of Altamira's peripheries remind me of the teens I interviewed in a favela in Rio de Janeiro, a favela without any view or any glamour. They told me they had never been to the sea or had gone only when they were very little—teens from Rio de Janeiro who had never seen or no longer remembered the sea. If they left their territory, the rival gang would kill them. None of them had turned twenty. And they knew their future would be a prison or a cemetery. In Altamira, the children were wrenched from the river and the forest. The Xingu, the river to which the boy should belong, is one of the most incredible, and the Amazon is the planet's most biodiverse forest. But the boy was born already deforested.

Only a minority of children in Altamira live in homes that offer both comfort and basic services, children whose parents are grileiros or ranchers or merchants or state or federal workers or liberal professionals. These homes usually have a lot of tempered glass, the mark of Belo Monte imprinted on the city's architecture. Tempered glass has become a status symbol, making the city even more raving mad. Children from the wealthiest families attend private school. They live where they have a view of the river or at least spend leisure time along the waterfront. Some go to Disney World with their parents for vacation, with a layover in Miami. A good share of the girls take ballet. These are the children of the few.

The children of the many are exposed to extreme violence. If Brazil suffers from a chronic lack of public policies concerned with the peripheries of the largest cities in the South and Southeast, it's easy to imagine just how paltry public services are in a city in the interior of the Amazon. Children in their final years of elementary school often can't write much more than their own names. In the case of the descendants of forested communities, broken ties to the river and the forest lie at the root of their relationship to the city. In the case of migrants, most of whom are from the Northeast, the broken ties are to the land left behind.

These children's parents (or grandparents) came from somewhere else in Brazil, in search of a better life through a job on one of the region's pharaonic public works projects, or else their parents (or grandparents) were expelled from the river and forest by one of these pharaonic public works projects. Very often, someone who came to work on a pharaonic project will be converted into someone expelled by a pharaonic project years or decades later. This is the fate of someone enslaved, to build their own slave quarters even though they think they're opening a road to freedom. Between the Transamazonian Highway, begun in the 1970s, and Belo Monte, a project from the 2010s, thousands of lives were destroyed. And children were condemned to be born without roots. And humans need roots as much as trees do. Without them, they die early. Even when their death is by natural causes, the truth is that their death is unnatural.

From the time they start walking, the forestchildren, whether Indigenous, beiradeiros, or quilombolas, begin their educational process through knowledge passed down by their parents and grandparents. Still young, they already know how to fish, hunt, and navigate, they know which plants they can eat, they're able to extract water from specific plants, they learn to do what they need to do with their hands, they are peopled with stories that say who they are and where they came from. Like the offspring of other species, these humans soon learn what is most important for living. Like trees, they are planted, and their roots, firmly formed by the oral transmission of knowledge, dig deep into the ground.

Children whose parents and grandparents were expelled from the forest and therefore from themselves, and thus converted into urban poor, are born uprooted from everything. When a boy doesn't know what the Amazon is and believes his country is his neighborhood, it evinces the violence of his deterritorialization. He is lost in the deepest way someone can be lost, because he has been deterritorialized not only from the ground but also from his own body. He has no north star, nor any south, east, or west. These are children without a past or future, whose present is violence. Violence from the outside, generally in the form of a bullet, but also violence from the inside. Violence is the very condition for a body that is born violated and violenced because it un-belongs. This is why the children of Altamira are born old and, like the city, already in ruins.

The Brazilian press labeled what happened at the Altamira prison a revolt. The problem of the precision of words. What happened wasn't a revolt but a massacre. It would have been a revolt if the prisoners had joined forces to demand that the state enforce the Constitution, but what happened at the so-called Regional Recovery Center of Altamira was that inmates killed other inmates because the state allowed it, by commission or omission. And then, by commission or omission, it allowed four more to be executed while they were handcuffed and on their way to another prison. Barbarism has already been proclaimed when more than three hundred people are incarcerated in a space that is meant to hold only half that. Barbarism is there. There were dozens of inmates in containers. It's easy to imagine what it means to be imprisoned in a container, with others who are imprisoned, in a city that seems to boil. If that's not torture, we need to rediscuss what is.

When the grandmother of the girl who has the name of a street discovered her son was not among the decapitated but among the incinerated, she took the news like a new death. There is no way to recognize a body deformed by fire. She needed to wait for the DNA testing to find out if his genes were jumbled in with the carbonized mass. Family members waited days to receive a body to cry over, while the city forgot about them once again. Or hadn't even remembered, because it doesn't recognize them as inhabitants of the same world.

There's no way you can live in a country with a level of violence like Brazil's, in all areas taken to extremes following Bolsonaro's ascent to power, without also being infected and transformed. If sixty-two middle-class white people had been decapitated or carbonized or strangled, the reaction would have been infinitely greater. The pressure for change, and the eloquence of the reaction too. If sixty-two Indigenous people had been decapitated or carbonized or strangled, the reaction would have been much smaller. But, given the international impact, there would still be significant visibility and pressure. But when sixty-two people belonging to a category that reduces them to one noun—*inmate*—are decapitated or carbonized or strangled, the reaction, pressure, and ensuing measures are much less and the outcry dies away much faster.

The incarcerated are seen as leftovers, even by many human rights defenders. Not in formal discourse or even rational thought, but in the way indignation rarely leads to action. Brazil doesn't stop for such deaths. Nor did Altamira.

On the weekend after the massacre, a letter from one of the gangs circulated on WhatsApp groups, threatening retaliation if any parties were held in the city following the massacre. There's no way to know if the letter was authentic or not, but it exposed a moral abyss. When criminals need to threaten society into respecting the dead and the pain of those grieving the dead, something fundamental has been lost. It would have been appropriate to close all the doors, lower the blinds and shades, hang a black banner in mourning, and join with the inmates' relatives to demand dignity and justice, similar to what has happened following other Brazilian tragedies. This didn't happen in Altamira. Even those who decry dehumanization dehumanize themselves over time. And I say this looking at myself too.

After the massacre, I wrote an article about the children of Altamira. The girl who has the name of a street and the boy who has the name of a soccer player wore their best clothes to have their picture taken, even though only their backs would show because they couldn't risk being identified. It was a report about severed heads, and the children were wearing their Sunday best. For them, it was a rare moment of happiness. After the photograph, they dove into their city's river for the first time. For the first time in their entire short, barbarized lives. They played a lot, as children do. "The Xingu is my favorite river," the girl said over and over. And over. This is the Xingu. This is the Amazon. The boy's eyes were shining above his wrinkles.

Then the boy and the girl went back to the Brazil that is builder of ruins. He, an orphan without a mother or father, she, an orphan without a father but still with a mother. A year and a half later, in December 2020, just before Christmas, the girl's mother was murdered by an ex-boyfriend, and then this child also found herself completely orphaned. The girl's mother, the young woman who was screaming at the opening of this chapter, not knowing whether her brother had been incinerated or decapitated, no longer exists. Her screams were never heard. She has been crossed out of the photograph. The two children have been left. And a grandmother with a foot and a half.

2018. the first generation without hope

You cannot understand the Altamira of this century without understanding Belo Monte's impact. It is as if a huge alien spacecraft had landed in the forest and its ruins, the city, and then built new ruins of a proportion and at a velocity much greater than at any other time. At the moment I write, in the early 2020s, it has been ten years of accumulated impact. Even before this, when the project was still in the planning stages, the hydropower plant was encouraging Brazilians to scale their country's map in a march of the desperate, of the self-employed, and of prostitutes, all drawn to public works projects for another chance to make a life. This march of bodies disquieted by hunger, or the memory of hunger, are the open veins of Brazil, overflowing with human blood that breaches borders because it never reaches home.

The girl who has the name of a street in São Paulo and the boy who has the name of a soccer player embody the first generation of urban children split off from river and forest, a product of Belo Monte. When the construction process began, their parents were adolescents, who reached adulthood only to be shot to death between the ages of twenty and thirty as violence exploded, driven in large part by the breakdown of community ties and the destruction of ways of life. The impact of Belo Monte has deleted a generation of young adults and led to a phenomenon where children are raised by grandparents who have suffered various forms of amputation (some literal) but are still alive. This reality holds true in other urban peripheries in Brazil. But, once again, Altamira exposes the extreme face of this reality, which is, bottom line, a country's suicide.

Altamira is the city that has taken the experience of a forest in ruins to a radical extreme, making it a kind of harbinger of the climate collapse. Altamira portends what will happen to the world if adults continue to allow this planet-house to burn, as we have been warned by Greta Thunberg, the Swedish teen who inspired the largest climate movement in history. To understand the Greta Generation—mostly comprising white teenagers, children of humanity's dominant minority, the same humanity that has superheated Earth by eating the planet—we must understand Altamira.

"Our house is on fire." When Greta Thunberg began hurling phrases like this in the faces of adults, she was giving voice to the greatest historical inflection ever produced by one generation. For the first time in the human story, offspring are caring for the world that adults of the species have destroyed—and continue to destroy. This is an inversion not only in how our species works but also in how any species works. And this shift corresponds to something equally monumental: the climate emergency is the greatest threat ever experienced by humans. The cry we hear from Greta and the millions of youth inspired by her, a cry that reverberates across languages and geographies—this is the order of magnitude of what we are witnessing.

In the course of three short months, Greta became one of the most influential people on the planet. She was fifteen years old when she stopped going to class and sat down in front of the Swedish parliament, in August 2018: "You grown-ups don't give a shit about my future." What good does it do to attend school if there won't be a tomorrow? While this question may have sounded insolent to many, it was a fair one. More than fair, it evinced a clarity society doesn't expect from children and adolescents. Soon, Greta wasn't alone. The Fridays for Future movement began carrying thousands of students into the streets every week in school climate strikes. In March 2019, the first global strike saw 1.5 million adolescents take to the world's streets, and other strikes followed. At the turn of the decade there were millions of Gretas, from the Amazon to Australia, from Siberia to New York.

European children and adolescents suddenly realized their world was ruled by adults like Donald Trump (and Recep Erdoğan, Viktor Orbán, Rodrigo Duterte, and others). In 2019, to make things worse in the global scenario, Brazil—the country that holds 60 percent of the Amazon, the rainforest strategic to regulating the climate—came to be ruled by Jair Bolsonaro, a man who calls global heating a "communist plot."

If these are the adults in the control room of the world where you live, and are going to live, you only need average intelligence to enter panic mode. Then you look inside your house, the one made of walls, and realize your parents are preoccupied with more mundane urgencies, like paying the monthly bills or trying to decide whether the most cutting-edge cell phone is a Huawei, Apple, or Samsung.

Children and adolescents from the Greta Generation have realized the obvious. Their house is on fire, and their parents and rulers are going about their lives as if nothing were happening. One year after Greta Thunberg's first protest, the burning Amazon, with the region of Altamira as its epicenter, made this image all too literal. When this teenager began her solitary protest because adults had denied her a future, these adults had already proved themselves stupid enough to elect liars who deny global heating in the name of the interests of large corporations in the areas of fossil fuels, mining, and the most predatory agribusiness. When the planet most needed climate policies and global alliances, Trump was in charge of the world's biggest power while Bolsonaro was the front-runner in Brazil's presidential race and was announcing, among other horrors, his project to transform what remained of the Amazon into a commodity.

When adolescents like Greta realized adults had abdicated their role as adults, they took up the task of caring for the world. "Since our leaders are behaving like children, we will have to take the responsibility they should have taken long ago," the girl declared at the UN Climate Change Conference in Poland in December 2018. At the same time, these young climate leaders are smart enough to know volunteerism won't suffice; political spaces must be occupied and debates waged with the adults who hold public policymaking power. This too is something new about members of the climate generation: they are children and adolescents, but they are not naive.

Whenever Greta Thunberg has spoken out publicly, she has demonstrated a clarity absent in adults, owing more to the latter's opportunism than to incompetence. As she stated to the select audience of billionaires in attendance at the World Economic Forum in Davos in January 2019:

> Some people—some companies and some decision-makers in particular—have known exactly what priceless values they have been sacrificing to continue making unimaginable amounts of money. And I think many of you here today belong to that group of people.

We don't know the subjective effects of this radical inversion in what it means to be an adult and what it means to be a child. This hasn't been a slow, evolutionary inversion, unfolding over centuries or millennia, but a brutal break. It is the generation prior to Greta's that has arguably been the most consumerist, spoiled generation in wealthy nations and the wealthy slices of poor countries. People who are now in their thirties and forties were molded to see consumption and instant gratification as imperatives. Many specimens of this generation have probably refused to become adults because this would mean accepting limits. Shaped by the capitalist rationale that freedom means doing whatever you want, that you have a basic right to indulge yourself in every possible pleasure, many of them believe the planet fits inside their navel.

And so adolescents with braids in their hair wag their fingers in the faces of these adults and say: "Grow up!" These babyfaced teens, some still with pimples, not yet knowing how to walk on legs that have suddenly grown too long, condemn the twentieth century's great object of consumption, the car, along with the plane. Instead, they pedal about and take public transit. They condemn the fossil fuel and plastics industries, while corporations set their lobbyists to spreading lies about them. They condemn the consumption of meat, and it is not just the meat industry that feels threatened but a constellation of starred chefs as well. They say it's better not to buy clothing and other goods but rather to exchange and recycle them, and so call the fashion industry into question. And they do this quickly, because velocity has shifted as well.

What is at stake today is whether Earth will very soon be just a bad planet or an openly hostile one for the human species—and for many others. The young climate activists know there's a tremendous difference between bad and hostile. But how can adults and decision makers be convinced of this if they are living as if there were no tomorrow and, because they do so, there might really not be one? How can those who exhaust resources in the name of immediate satisfaction be convinced that tomorrow is at hand and will be bad for everyone, although much worse for those who have contributed least to exhausting the planet?

The Greta Generation has proposed a radical shift in our experience of time and space in response to the climate emergency. "Stay on the ground," they tell adults, declaring that planes should only be used when urgently necessary, since aviation is a major emitter of carbon dioxide and other pollutants. To set an example, Greta traveled by sailboat from Europe to the United States to take part in the UN's Climate Action Summit in 2019.

It is a strong image. Through their actions, instead of colonizing America with this contemporary version of caravels, these adolescents are advocating the decolonization of Europe (and the United States) and of minds that are also intent on eating up time. One country should no longer be just a hop away from another. The journey must be experienced and distances understood with our bodies. We must produce locally and consume locally. Without poison or genetically modified organisms. The superfluous is now just that, contrary to what advertising has pumped into our minds in recent decades. This isn't a choice, these adolescents point out. The time for choosing between good and better is past. This is the only option we have, or the catastrophe will be greater still.

Greta and her generation tore a huge narcissistic wound in the bodies of their parents and older siblings. On the far right and far left alike, the truculent reactions to these adolescent activists have been proportionate both to the powerful interests at which they take aim and also to the immense changes in habits they demand. Even people who have always believed themselves to be in step with the environmental agenda, thinking it's enough to recycle their garbage to be a "good person," now feel threatened.

Adults often tell the climate kids: "You give me hope." And Greta and other leaders reply: "I don't want your hope. I don't want you to be hopeful. I want you to panic. I want you to feel the fear I feel every day."

This is not rhetoric. These well-informed youth know the clock is running out. The planet may heat up much more than what has been discussed at climate summits, climbing three, four, or even five degrees Celsius. Unless global populations stage an uprising to stop it. What we are witnessing with the youth-led movement is the most vital human adaptation to the climate emergency: a generation that dispenses with hope precisely so they can put an end to paralysis and fight. More than adaptation, this is transmutation. To relinquish hope but not the joy of fighting together— that's the power of the Greta Generation.

This very new generation of climate activists reflects our historical moment and anticipates the future. Some are boys, of course. But just a glance at the movements tells us the main leaders are women. Even though Greta's doll-like face may be the face of this generation, each country has leaders of inspirational discourse and strong action. It's not just that females are taking the lead; each one of these women brings important characteristics to the fight. Greta is vocal about having Asperger's—not as an illness, disability, or burden, but as a difference, sometimes even a "superpower." According to her, it endows her with an ability to focus and concentrate that, "given the right circumstances," has been determinant in the climate struggle. Anuna de Wever, of Belgium, identifies as gender fluid. And she argues that this condition allows her to see other possible worlds, without holding her captive to an imposed "normal."

What these leaders bring to the fight for life on the planet is the potential to see differences as a strength, as a positive asset in the face of the challenges presented by the climate emergency. In this world of walls, barbed wire, and armed borders, what is most insubordinate about this generation's message is their entreaty for us to create a global community and fight for our shared house. In this fight, the Amazon is one of the centers of the world.

68. hope is overrated

Hope has been an issue for me ever since I started following the Belo Monte event. Watching Belo Monte crush rivers, forest, and beings, and in the name of the state as well, has forced me to confront certain questions profoundly. This includes forgoing hope—an unpopular stance that is often poorly understood and invariably causes me trouble. No, I don't have any hope. And no, I'm not unhappy or happy. Nor am I pessimistic or optimistic. These polarizations don't matter to me. My inner world does not move between these dichotomies, nor does the outer world.

In May 2019, I gave a talk at Harvard University about the Amazon and the creation of futures, and in it I stated that hope, like despair, is a luxury we can't afford. With our planet over-heating, there's no time for melancholy or lamentations. We need to move, even without hope. As soon as I had finished my talk, a well-known Brazilian businessman made an impassioned defense of hope and received an enthusiastic round of applause from some in the audience. Hope, and not the accelerated destruction of the Amazon or the global climate emergency, was the topic of the ensuing debate. Some thought I was a kind of enemy of hope and therefore an enemy of the future (theirs). I'm concerned that the same thing might happen in this book.

At some point in my first (and so far only) novel, one of the characters kills a cat. I would never have imagined it, but the cat's death proved a problem for many people. It was also the way some readers found to avoid the question really bothering them: the taboos that had been broken in a mother-daughter relationship— a relationship deemed holy by the sensibilities of multiple eras, including ours. I'm concerned that hope might turn into this book's cat and an excuse to avoid facing either the destruction of the Amazon, now headed to the point of no return, or the climate collapse currently underway. But I need to, I must, run the risk.

Hope has a long history—and I'd like someone to write it someday—from religion to philosophy, from political marketing to the world of capitalist goods. On a planet where the ground is ever more like quicksand, in which nation-states are collapsing, hope has increasingly replaced happiness as a commodity. Do you remember how, until just a short while ago, everyone was obliged to be happy? And whoever said they weren't either had a deformed soul or was chronically depressed?

The notion of happiness as a commodity has been dissected by various fields of knowledge and also through our own daily experience. Converted into a product by capitalism, where it is a consumer good whose supply is supposedly guaranteed through more consumption, happiness no longer has the same market value, though books on the topic may still occasionally crowd the shelves of self-help sections. Likewise converted into a commodity, hope has been supplanting it, at a time when a future on a worse planet looms darkly.

My personal investigation of hope began in 2015. I'll get back to it in a few paragraphs. In the last part of my talk at Harvard, I spoke about what I believe to be one of the most fascinating events of the late 2010s: the emergence of history's first generation without hope. A fascinating generation because it has ripped the ground out from under those who are dogmatic about hope by also becoming the first generation to shake off the paralysis of its era. And in shaking off this paralysis, the new generation has suffered the vexation of hearing their parents tell them their movement gave them hope. The impasse over hope sheds light on the impasse between the generation that took consumption of the planet to dizzying new heights—their parents' generation— and the generation that will live on this depleted planet.

After their initial fright over Greta Thunberg's words—"I don't want your hope. . . . I want you to panic"—adults usually "give her a break" because of her age. "She'll grow up," I often hear. (And maybe set her butt down next to theirs, resting on fluffy pillows of hope while the house burns?) Even climate scientists and activists, who know the reality of the climate emergency and check the catastrophe's numbers at breakfast just as obsessively as investors check the stock market, have trouble with the topic. They're afraid if there is no hope, people will become paralyzed and fail to react or to pressure those in power to implement public policies to combat global heating. They're also afraid that, without hope, people won't make the effort to transform and transmute in the face of the changes (for the worse) already impinging on our daily lives.

In his latest book, *The New Climate War: The Fight to Take Back Our Planet*, the US scientist Michael Mann wrote about the new strategy employed by the fossil fuel industry and other climate villains. Given that denialism became unsustainable after a virus brought the human population to its knees, corporations have started focusing their discourse on blaming the individual. The climate catastrophe and pandemics, which will now be increasingly frequent, are portrayed as a consequence of the sum of individual habits, which is very far from the truth. If habits need to change, it is also a proven fact that these corporations are the main culprits behind our planet's corrosion.

Mann mentions yet another strategy employed by the marketers of evil, which is to use bots to spread "doomerism" on social media. Doomerism is a kind of climatic nihilism that sees everything as a lost cause, leaving the human species with no chance of salvation and the planet on an irreversible path to destruction. This behavioral phenomenon—which, according to Mann, is being fostered by corporations that want to continue racking up profits—leads to inaction at a moment when the need for action is urgent.

I dare to disagree. I believe hope also presents a risk. Life will not get easier in the coming years and decades. We need strong generations. We need to become better than we are and do things we don't yet know how to do, because what we know now is no longer sufficient. In this context, if hope is a prerequisite to action, at some point it may no longer be available, even for the followers of religions grounded in it. And then what would be left, collective suicide? In all these years listening to very diverse peoples and observing different worlds, I've learned it never works to skirt around contradictions. We must confront and move ahead with them. And so I dare to question the dogma of hope, or, in the language of capitalism, to question hope as a political asset.

In trying to decipher the very extreme moment we are living through, I've noticed a profound shift in mindset, in step with changes to the planet's climate and morphology. It is my hypothesis that were it not for this shift in the way of thinking, teenagers from Greta's generation wouldn't be able to do what they're doing. I don't think they have issues with hope, nor is hope on the immediate horizon of their concerns. It simply isn't as important in their lives as in their parents'. Hope turns up in their talk because adults spur the topic.

When these young people say they don't have hope and don't want to give hope to anyone, much less to those largely responsible for bequeathing them an exhausted planet, they are displaying keen intuition. They are rejecting the hegemonic discourse and even the idea of a hegemonic discourse. Europe, which is where Greta and most of the student climate leaders come from, is the place that developed a discourse not only about what Europe itself is but also about what other places are, a discourse about humanity and also about civilization and barbarism. Hope is part and parcel of this "Western tradition." In rejecting the facile idea of hope, these teens intuit—or conclude—that if they want to face life on the coming planet, they will have to reject this way of thinking—or they won't have a chance.

They also refuse to be consumed by frightened adults, who

are always eager for young bodies as they begin to fear death, like every aging generation. One feature of the current generation of grown-ups is that they have been heavily influenced by the United States and its hope-for-export, packaged first by Hollywood and then by Silicon Valley. If climate students let themselves be transformed into wellsprings of hope, they'll immediately become cute little tokens in times of darkness, collectibles purchased to place alongside others in a curio cabinet. Greta would then be reduced to a sweet face—and not recognized for wielding the power she effectively does.

Refusing to be an object of hope means refusing to be consumed by the cogwheels that swallowed much older, more experienced rebels and chomped up insurrections to then spit them out. Somehow, the climate youth also seem to intuit that they must make these adults relinquish the crutch of hope, because it allows the adults to stay put on their metaphorical couches in a state of stupor while our planet-house burns.

I can imagine how scary it must be to have my generation as parents, or even the one immediately after mine, which to me seems even more numbed, since it has been more spoiled by its supposed "right" to consume. These children and teens watch their house blazing away and they burn from the heat of the fire. And their parents go about tending to other matters. Then these youth realize if they don't do something, they're screwed, because they're the ones who'll have to live on a much worse planet. At the same time, these adults are the ones in power and (not) making the needed decisions. When confronted, these "grown-ups" either respond with repression, since they sense their age-granted authority attacked, or demand hope. Exasperating, to say the least.

The adult demand for hope is belied by reality. The general discourse is that without hope, people won't fight global heating. Yet reality shows that the people who are changing the paradigm of the climate struggle—and the most veteran climate scientists and activists recognize this change—say they have no hope, or at least that having hope is not the most important thing. The ones who have shaken off our species' stupor are teenagers who want adults to panic.

Instead of rejecting what these young people have to say, adults should be listening hard. We are witnessing a new form of thought, a transmutation to the planet's new reality, one that is also changing language. In May 2019, the *Guardian* announced it would change its style guide to lend greater precision to the language used in its coverage. Instead of "climate change," it now favors the terms "climate emergency, crisis or breakdown"; instead of "global warming," "global heating." The pressure to make changes to language was produced in part by the Greta Thunberg generation. I have also adopted these words in this book and in all my articles because I consider them more precise.

Movement and hope, as the (extremely) young climate activists prove day after day, are not linked. It is possible to act without hope, but rather—as Anuna de Wever told me—with the joy of being together, doing together, fighting together. Her words allude to something else urgent: the need to weave the commons, to make community. Not family, clan, or nation. Community. Community is also what the new generation of climate activists is creating in the world, with each student climate strike or, during the COVID-19 pandemic, with each action on the internet. They are obliterating borders and tearing down walls in the name of the commons: the fight for climate justice, the battle against the masters of the world who are stripping the planet, and the confrontation with the capitalist logic of the commodity people who swallow up worlds.

Though many don't realize the full dimension of what they see, we are watching our species reinvent itself to live in a hostile environment. The present fight can be summed up as one between those weaving the commons and those shredding the possibility of the commons, like the new old fascists.

It is no accident that far-right populists deny global heating.

They know it may be through the climate struggle that people will be able to unite to weave the commons. Today, they tremble in fear before children who point fingers at them, and then they try to transform these children into objects of consumption. When they fail, they invent conspiracy theories to discredit them. Or they wave the lovely demand for hope in an effort to attract the herd.

I was grappling with this topic when I read a text about the commons by the philosopher Peter Pál Pelbart:

> Perhaps the challenge is to abandon the dialectics of Same and Other, of Identity and Alterity, and recover the logic of Multiplicity. It is no longer merely a matter of my right to be different from the Other or the Other's right to be different from me, in both cases preserving an opposition between us; nor is it a matter of a relationship of peaceful coexistence between us, where each is tethered to his identity like a dog to a post, and thus entrenched in it. It is a matter of something more radical in these encounters, of also embarking on and assuming some of the Other, and thus at times even differing from yourself, detaching from yourself, coming unstuck from your own identity and constructing unprecedented shiftings.

This passage evokes my quest to unwhiten myself, a movement only possible by assuming the Other's traits and thus differing from myself, adhering by choice to the endless path of dis-identity and dis-identification. Always adrift. It also evokes this new generation of climate activists, who aren't "new" simply because they were born in this century, but because they call for what is new. And because, more than calling for what is new, they *are* what is new.

It also points to how necessary it is to stop being a dog tied to a post, the one Pelbart writes about, and run the risk of other possible identities in a world where the impossible is breathing down our necks. How necessary it is to displace yourself from yourself to try out a new experience in being—and in being together. This begins with understanding that my framework of experiences does not encompass the world. That is also why I need the Other, so they can teach me to see, and by seeing through another experience in being, I take on some of their traits, without fearing I'll lose my own. And I transform into a translingual being.

In this same text, Pelbart refers to "Counterpoint," a tribute to Edward Said written by Palestinian poet Mahmoud Darwish:

> The best answer still lies in Darwish's poem, which puts [the answer] in Edward Said's mouth: "If I die before you, I entrust you with the impossible." And Darwish asks, "Is the impossible far off?" And Said's voice answers, "A generation away." It's almost Kafka: "Oh, plenty of hope, an infinite amount of hope—but not for us."

I believe the impossible is the condition facing this generation right now, no longer far off. I believe that as we face the impossible, we need to create a new experience in being a person, do something we've never done, risk being what we don't know.

As I've said, the question of hope surfaced for me while I was following the construction of Belo Monte and the destruction of the Xingu River. One thing, construction, resulting in the other, destruction. It was only when they witnessed Belo Monte damming up the river, with its steel and concrete claws, that people who had fought against death in the past and seen their friends slain by gunshots in struggles over the forest felt as if they'd reached the end of history. Belo Monte was erected by violating all of Brazil's laws and likewise violating the bodies of the weakest, under an administration led by the party these people had helped found. Their homes were destroyed and set aflame, the forest burned, and convulsing creatures drowned. The Amazon world was transforming.

What we witnessed and lived in those years was excess clarity—submersion, almost a drowning, in the deepest darkness of power arrangements and structures of submission, of politics and policies to control bodies, all bodies, the bodies of the river, of the trees, of nonhumans and humans.

But history doesn't end as long as we have memory. And so I, like others, have devoted myself to memory. There I realized I had become another me, together with others who also became me and others. I discovered myself to be a self without hope. And discovered I wasn't sad, or even in despair. These contrasts no longer found resonance in me. Hope was no longer an issue because I didn't feel it, and I didn't miss the feeling. Hope unmattered to me.

What fascinated me right then, and still fascinates me today, was the joy of being together, even during catastrophe. This was a "phenomenon" I first witnessed, and later experienced, alongside the beiradeiros expelled by Belo Monte, refugees inside their own country. Joy as an act of insurrection, like a finger plunged into the eye of the hurricane, into the oppressor's eye. Let me say, before I am misunderstood again, I haven't replaced hope with joy. Mine became another being-and-becoming in the world, a being that laughs if only out of insolence and is capable of fighting even knowing she'll lose. I've been overtaken by fierce life. I've transformed and transmuted.

In 2015, I wrote a column about hope for *El País*. Today, that moment seems like a distant past, and what was bad is now much worse, as already foretold. In the Brazil of 2015, people were afraid the year would never end, and I thought I could help by telling what I had realized and learned. I wrote this:

> Perhaps the time has come to overcome hope. . . . I would like
> to state here that in order to take on the challenge of building
> a political project for Brazil, hope isn't all that important. In
> fact, I think it's overrated. Given the current state of affairs,

perhaps the time has come to understand we must do something much harder: create and fight even without hope. It isn't hope that will mend Brazil's gashes, but rather our ability to take on conflict even when we know we're going to lose. Or fight even when the cause is lost. Act without believing. Act as an ethical imperative.

As the following years have shown, most Brazilians—on the right but also on the left—have preferred not to address conflicts and contradictions but instead spout hatred and falsification. The result was the election of Jair Messias Bolsonaro. Let me repeat the memorable words of Eduardo Viveiros de Castro: "The Indigenous are experts in the end of the world, because their world ended in 1500." And point out that his provocative statement referred to the fact that perhaps, if they are willing, Indigenous peoples might teach us to live after the end of the world represented by the climate emergency.

Other ways of life are also other ways of thinking. It was by plunging into this river of divergent logics that I was able to understand that the catastrophe isn't the end but the middle, and the means. I understood this with my body—which makes all the difference—by living alongside people who had lived through various catastrophes, people for whom the world had transformed itself various times and for whom life was rewoven through resistance. But resistance of a dimension unlike what we know through white Western experience. Resistance not entailing a heavy burden or the cross, that of martyred resignation, nor resistance through vengeance or the sword. Insolent laughter has been part of this resistance, which Viveiros de Castro calls *rexistência*—resistance for existence: "Indigenous peoples cannot *not* resist at the risk of not existing as such. Their existing is eminently a resisting, which I condense into the neologism *rexistir*"—resist to exist to resist . . .

On the Xingu, where the Brazilian state and Norte Energia

have built ruins of incredible proportions, I witnessed and lived alongside people who existed because they resisted—and who resisted to exist. What amazed me when I listened to the girls and boys of the student climate strike was that these young Europeans, mostly white and middle class, had come so close to the worldview of the forestpeoples without ever having met them, joining in a struggle much older than themselves and echoing a tradition they had previously never been part of. Along what invisible pathways did their thoughts meet, how did they engage in this dialogue that took place without ever taking place?

Maybe, but just maybe—because I'm still investigating—it is the catastrophe in the middle of lives, the catastrophe not experienced as the end of history. The history of the forestpeoples, who have already lived through catastrophe and face the threat of having to do so again, the history of the teenagers who know they'll have to live on a postcatastrophe planet, or on a midcatastrophe one. This perception of the world, that of a midcatastrophe life, alters the whole body, as well as how this body is placed in the world. This is a body in a state of transmutation.

As I said early on in these pages, Donald Trump and then Jair Bolsonaro have embodied the dispute over histories past. In the 2010s, from Brexit to Trumpism and from Trumpism to Bolsonarism, our present debate has abandoned the horizon of the future to dedicate itself to pasts that never were. Caricatures like Trump and Bolsonaro have garnered so much support (not only) because it has never been harder to imagine a future where we can live. For the first time, tomorrow is an impending catastrophe. Not a potential catastrophe, as during the Cold War, with the atom bomb always threatening destruction. But a catastrophe unlikely to be averted.

The subjective product of this feeling that there is "no future" is the invention of pasts to which we could return. The British voters who approved Brexit believed they could return to a golden era, to a powerful Anglo-Saxon Britain. Middle America's poor whites swore Trump could give them back a country where Black and brown people, immigrants, Jewish people, women, and the LGBTQIA+ community were subaltern. A country where, like these subalterns, every single "thing" was in its place, and where everyone could live with the certainty of knowing where everything belonged. Bolsonaro's voters denied, or justified, all the torture and murders committed by agents of the Brazilian state under the dictatorship, because they'd rather have the illusion of living in a country where there was "order" and "safety," where a man was a man and a woman was a woman, where men had sex with women and women with men.

Everyone wanted desperately to go back to living in a country that never was. Portrayed with the paintbrush of willful belief, these pasts immune from immense conflict and tremendous violence never existed, but who is to say what once existed? Neofascist populism disputes the past as a strategy for holding power while systematically working to destroy memory, often destroying the bodies that produce and shelter it.

The neofascists who reached power in the 2010s received the support of followers who behave in politics like religious believers, even when they're atheists. This phenomenon is because, for the first time in human history, the future is in large part a given. We know we'll live on a much worse planet. What is up for dispute, repeating once again, is whether living conditions on Earth will be bad or hostile. What is also up for dispute is how we'll deal with it. Those who deny reality, however, are falsifying a past so they can use it to replace the future they can't face. Denial is generally desperate. And despair is a great impetus of hate.

But what is the future, after all? The future also needs to uninvent itself as a concept and go back to being imagined. Or the future needs to detach itself from hegemonic interpretations and open up to other potential ways of being conceived. Maybe it won't even be called "future" but something else. Maybe it isn't even something that belongs to tomorrow, at least not in linear terms, on a continuous time line. I propose we stop clinging to European ways of thinking and logic structures devised by the inventors of the civilization that brought us to this point of extremity. This future uninvented from the future is being woven by the experiences of peoples coming from other cosmopolitical territories. Amid so much bad news, here is some great: the new generation of Swedish girls is crossing paths with the Indigenous.

1937. self-extermination as a gesture

But what about the generation of deforested adolescents who have
been flung into the past before they become future, what happens
when they are converted into the remains of a systematic process of destruction? In Altamira, the poor peripheries are filled
with people expelled from the forest. Expelled by Belo Monte,
expelled by other public works projects. There are organizations
fighting for the forestpeoples to remain forest, because this is the
Amazon's best chance to remain standing. But few are fighting
for those already converted into the urban poor—people who are
treated like the ruins of war, considered lost, beyond any salvation. They too become ruins.

The Brazilian elites have grown accustomed to the logic that
for them to keep their privileges, others will have to lose their
bodies. This logic has infected the entire society, including its
victims. In countries like Brazil, the idea of progress is bound up
with access to privileges. And it is a matter of individual progress,
since the very notion of community has come to ruin. Even the
subjugated aspire to be "above" others socially and racially, an aspiration that increasingly outweighs the desire for emancipation.
The poor enjoy hegemony over the wretched, the middle class over
the lower, and lighter-skinned Black people over darker.

When capitalism met up with slavery, it deformed thought. It is
no accident that it was a Black intellectual from the United States
who best defined this mechanism. In 1935, the thinker W. E. B.
Du Bois, one of the twentieth century's most brilliant minds, introduced the concept of "psychological wage" to explain one of
racism's prime purposes: to give whites who have been screwed

over a feeling of superiority because some people—specifically, Black people—are worse off than they are.

Nearly one century later, this same concept—expanded to include women and LGBTQIA+ people—can be used to explain the phenomenon of elected despots. For the psychological wage to work, the subjugation of an Other must continue, especially at a moment when the usual subjugated people have begun protesting more vehemently.

Bolsonaro has governed by sustaining his racist, homophobic, and misogynistic attacks and by contriving fake news to shore up the value of this psychological wage. This is the best explanation for why even some impoverished people continued to support Bolsonaro during the pandemic in 2020 and 2021, even as they were watching relatives die of COVID-19 while waiting for a bed at a collapsing hospital. So dependent were they on the psychological wage that they embraced what was destroying them. Subjectivities are not side effects. To the contrary: they move the world.

Living among ruins and finding myself in ruins too, I understood that nothing changes, nor will the forest have a chance to continue existing if people—all peoples and not just human peoples—are treated like remains. This is why it's so important to treat those who have been pushed to the peripheries of Amazon's cities as "deforested" rather than apply the generic term "poor" to them. This isn't a mere rhetorical flourish, but a radical shift in viewpoint and concept, altering how one understands the world and decides to address the climate collapse.

The generic term "poor" erases a person's origins, along with the process that led them to this condition. Someone who is deforested came from a place, from a forest, and suffered a process of being wrenched from their ground, the ground of land and water, the ground of culture, the ground of bonds and affections. We cannot reduce reforestation to trees but must expand it to include humans, because the forest is an integral whole of organic exchanges and varied relations between different species of beings, human and nonhuman alike. The children of all the Altamiras must be given back their roots. They must be forested, these children who were born unforested.

Since Altamira is a harbinger, and a vanguard, it shows us what happens when a generation is suddenly uprooted. Belo Monte's impact on the region of the Middle Xingu has been like an episode of acute climate collapse that has altered an entire ecosystem in just a few years. In January 2020, almost a decade after construction began, it became apparent that something remarkable and terrible was happening to adolescents who had only been children when the city initiated its process of transformation. Altamira was hit by an epidemic of suicides. Sometimes, a number of attempts were made in the same week or even the same day. A portion of these adolescents had begun a process of self-annihilation.

By late April 2020, in four short months, fifteen people had died by suicide. Nine of them were children and adolescents from the ages of eleven to nineteen. This meant the number of suicides in Altamira in the first four months of 2020 was equal to the city's total for all of 2019. In a city whose population was then estimated at 115,000, fifteen suicides in four months put the number of self-inflicted deaths in Altamira at nearly three times the annual average for Brazil. While a city cannot be accurately compared to a country, this information nonetheless hints at the dimension of what was happening in Altamira. The community asked itself: Why? Why here? And why now?

Worldwide, suicide is now the second leading cause of death among youth, outranked only by traffic accidents. In Brazil, suicide rates among youth ages fifteen to twenty-nine rose 8.3 percent from 2011 to 2018. While the trend was global, with Brazil offering one of the sharper examples, evidence indicated that Altamira had once again outperformed the statistics.

In the past, the press didn't publish anything about cases of suicide, in order not to influence other people to commit the same extreme act. But widespread access to the internet has made this kind of preventive caution obsolete. People post farewell letters on social media, while suicide handbooks circulate on the deep web, along with photographs and videos of children and adolescents self-mutilating or dying by suicide. There are even transnational groups that help adolescents kill themselves.

I did my first story on suicide in 2007. It was about a teen from Rio Grande do Sul who had killed himself with the help of cybernauts from other countries on a website. He used the method known by the macabre name "barbecue": charcoal is burned in a confined space, like you're grilling out; the smoke soon thickens, consuming oxygen and asphyxiating you. The Brazilian boy ended up setting himself on fire in the bathroom of his family's apartment, where his body was found burned. The whole episode was followed, and abetted, in real time by people around the world, people who still haven't been held accountable. The Brazilian Federal Police were notified by an officer in Canada, who had in turn been notified by a young Canadian woman who watched these scenes of horror unfold on the internet. It was a transnational crime, incitement to suicide. This was the only reason I allowed myself, and was allowed, to report on the topic.

Writing this story was a very painful personal process, and I still bear its marks. When adolescent suicides began surging in Altamira in 2020, it took me months to persuade myself to do a story about it, and I only did so then because I felt ethically obliged. I had committed myself to seeing the world from Altamira and I was witnessing something very serious taking place. I had a duty to tell the story.

The Altamira report was published in a whole new context. By 2020, suicide was no longer a stifled, taboo topic. Three years earlier, in 2017, the "Blue Whale Challenge" had been blamed for a rise in teen suicides around the world. Streaming television series like Netflix's *13 Reasons Why* also helped break the silence. Talking about suicide became a public health measure.

In Altamira, some of the adolescents who died by suicide left farewell notes on Facebook or sent WhatsApp messages to family and friends. These messages were blamed for sparking an outbreak among youth whose main means of communication were WhatsApp and other social media. Most of the teens hanged themselves, but at least three jumped from towers in Altamira, taking their act outside the secrecy of their homes and turning it into a public spectacle. Their funerals became occasions where other families asked for help, breaking through the barriers that so often surround this type of death.

Every suicide is an individual act and should be analyzed in terms of its singularity. At the same time, a string of suicides can only be understood within a socioenvironmental context. The main hypothesis raised by health care workers and representatives of the groups who mobilized to address the tragedy in Altamira was that the suicides were the result of the social disruption caused by Belo Monte. The youth who took their own lives had gone from childhood to adolescence during the violent process of dam construction, when the city was transformed along with the lives of its families. Within a few years, Altamira went from being a city of countryside habits, like sleeping with your windows open or strolling the streets worry free at night, to being one of the most violent cities in Brazil. It also came to have one of the highest rates of vulnerability to violence among youth ages fifteen to twenty-nine.

Four of the teens who died by suicide lived in neighborhoods built by Norte Energia to house people expelled from areas the company flooded: Jatobá, São Joaquim, Água Azul, and Casa Nova. Another four lived in neighborhoods where Belo Monte had wrought profound changes: Paixão de Cristo and Jardim Independente 1. One family residing in one of the Collective Urban Resettlements lost two children in early 2020. Both hanged themselves. The youngest one first, just before he turned sixteen, and then his twenty-six-year-old sister. She was found hanging near her baby.

While adolescents on the other side of the planet were leading global climate strikes to denounce the extermination of their future, inspired by Greta Thunberg, Altamira's adolescents were witnessing their friends' self-extermination. So they created a movement to confront both self-extermination as well as the extermination engendered by police forces and clashes within organized crime. The hostile future decried by European youth was already a daily reality for youth in the Amazon. For the deforested, the destruction of bodies was neither a metaphor nor an image nor a scientific prophecy. They were already experiencing the post–end of the world. Belo Monte had anticipated their climate apocalypse.

On March 31, 2020, when two young people died by suicide and a third was murdered the same day, organized youth in Altamira published an open letter to the authorities: "They say we are the country's future, but how will we be the future if we don't have a present?"

1987. belo monte refugees

Érika Pellegrino moved to Altamira from São Paulo in September 2017. Petite, with long black hair cascading down a very pallid back, Érika reminds me of a manga character. The banzeiro pulled her in too. She had first set foot in Altamira eight months earlier, as part of a team of sixteen volunteer mental health care providers working with the Belo Monte Refugees movement. In January 2017, the team had lent form to the name and concept of Care Clinic by listening to the beiradeiros expelled by the hydropower plant and also to families displaced from the central area of Altamira to its peripheries. Lilo and I had documented the experience so that the Care Clinic might inspire similar interven tions in the case of other catastrophes in Brazil.

Érika was the only psychiatrist among psychoanalysts and psychologists. And she was also a very unique individual. The daughter of a firefighter and a bank worker, she was from a working-class background but had studied medicine at one of Brazil's top universities, Unicamp, a school attended by members of the elites. After graduation, she took a year off to travel the world, spending more time in Asia than in other geographies. Her various interests include Japanese culture and tarot, of which she is a serious student. For ethical reasons, she embraces polyamory in terms of her sexuality and emotional bonds.

After listening to the Belo Monte refugees for two weeks, Érika decided to close up her office and apartment in São Paulo and give up her job at a public mental health clinic in Cracolândia, or Crackland—an area of downtown São Paulo christened with this explicitly biased name because it is a gathering place for a large number of crack users. Érika wanted to work as a psychiatrist in Altamira so she could continue caring for local populations who were experiencing intense psychic suffering. She was joined by her life partner Thiago Leal, another distinctive figure. A graduate of the very traditional University of São Paulo Law School, Thiago doesn't get along well with the field of law and neither often with lawyers. Altamira is like a street corner where disconformed people hang out.

Érika's arrival in Altamira was the result of an intervention that began with the act of listening. This was my second effort in doing what I didn't know how to do, in response to the urgency of this historical time. The Belo Monte Refugees movement was fully crowdfunded over the internet. It stands as proof of the power of listening, and the power of being with others.

It's interesting to try to figure out where a story begins, but always rather arbitrary. I'm going to choose a beginning for this next story that for me is a middle and, for the protagonist, an end. For me, the beginning was the voice stuck in João da Silva's throat—João, whose legs had suddenly become paralyzed at the Norte Energia office; João, Raimunda's husband, the man whose brain had given way to a stroke when he realized they had torn everything from him.

Note that the banzeiro has brought João to us a second time, so his return can be understood at another moment along the river that takes us, drowns us, and spits us out farther on.

João had once been a man-boy traveling the various Brazils alone, earning a living by the strength of his arms. He had fallen in love with Raimunda at a dance party, sanctified this love at a collective wedding, and gone on to have seven daughters, their names all beginning with the letter L, for liberty. He had helped build the Tucuruí dam on the Tocantins River and then been expelled from there in consequence of the barrier he had helped build. He had traversed the world, traveling to Iraq to build a road for tanks, taken there by large Brazilian construction companies, the same ones that built Belo Monte and would later be accused of corruption under the extensive investigation known as Operation Carwash. He had fainted from hunger after going days without food during hard times. And, finally, he had found a place on an island on the Xingu.

Finding a place was a huge thing, because the island didn't just guarantee him ground and plenty, which is already a lot. The island on the Xingu also guaranteed him recognition, the eye of others who saw him as part of it. Soon after his arrival, João understood that there, between forest and river, he was the one possessed. João had arrived because arriving is belonging. And he believed he had arrived at a forever.

But then the corporation and the state materialized on the Xingu in the form of Belo Monte, and João, along with Raimunda, was expelled from the island to which they belonged. On March 23, 2015, there he was, expecting to receive a sum of money that would allow him at least to rebuild his life, because at the age of sixty-plus, João was afraid he wouldn't have the strength to begin another saga. But the sum the authorities stipulated (because there can be no negotiation between such unequal parties) condemned him to no longer belong, or be beiradeiro, but to return to the generic mass called "poor."

At that point, João decided to kill the representative of Norte Energia, the company that was bloodlessly murdering him. Not murder for revenge, this must be made clear. But as a sacrifice. In João's words: "If I was to do damage to some big guy, some big guy inside there, maybe it'd make things better for others. I'd be sacrificing my own life, but other people's lives would get better."

But João isn't a murderer. Instead, he dammed himself up and had to be carried from the Norte Energia office. In his paralysis, he gave his silence a body, because with Belo Monte, even when he had a voice, he didn't. And João's silence castigated the ears of whoever was listening more than any scream could. João's silence pained the body of whoever dared listen. João's silence, when it was heard, produced movement. Indignation, disgust, discomfort, anger, unease, pain . . . the names were many. João was the immolated and self-immolated man of Belo Monte. He was the first to choose self-extermination.

When I first listened to João, I was accompanied by Maíra, my only child, who is a psychoanalyst. It was a big moment in my life with Maíra, because it was her first time in the Amazon, a mythical place to which her mother had been vanishing from time to time ever since she was a teen. A place that for me has always been female.

We were sitting in the living room of the house they had built on the margins of the city after they had been expelled, Raimunda, Maíra, and I. Lilo was in a corner taking pictures. Suddenly a man burst in. Shirtless, eyes overcome by blue—and by wrath. It was João. And he wanted to talk. João was no longer a thundering silence. João was voice and João was word. And João didn't have a little to say. He had a lot. First standing, pointing nowhere. Then seated, his eyes stabbing us.

João said, and said loudly, and said without leaving any room to dam him up: "I lost the end of the thread. I'm inside this house today, but truth is, I'm outside, I don't have a house. I don't have a house. Understand? I'm outside. I get lost. I don't know where I am. I've lost my way from everything."

And João went on: "When I lost the island, I lost my life. I lost the thread. It stopped there, understand? From here on, I only see darkness in my sight. I don't see a clear world anymore. I see nothing but darkness. I stay here staring at the world, looking for myself. Who can answer this search for me? Nobody.

"The hole in my life, the hole in my life . . ."

It was the week of Brazilian Independence Day, September 7, 2015. Days before this meeting, João had wanted to go to the island to kill himself, as a martyr. He wanted to incinerate himself on the scorched island, along with his family. Raimunda stopped him. "I want the world to know Belo Monte killed me," he said.

Perhaps this is the beginning of the Care Clinic's story. Or at least one of the beginnings. By the time I heard João, I had already listened to a number of people hit by Belo Monte. And, in different ways, these people compelled me to continue this story. But the power of João's words struck unknown layers within me. I too left the house (which wasn't a house to him) de-territorialized. And, blending what I heard with what Maíra heard, I realized that for many reasons it would be important to tell João and Raimunda's story, as I have done in three different languages, but that this wouldn't be enough for João to traverse the darkness. I also knew João wasn't the only one who lived in the dark after being expelled by Belo Monte, expatriated from his own country inside his own country, inside and out at the same time.

De-territorialized, the word I use to define the feeling that cut through me right then, pushed me toward another word, one that would allow me to move. The word I'm looking for might be *trans-territorialize*—to traverse territories, breaking down dams and blurring boundaries. This is clear to me today, but it wasn't then.

Shortly after meeting João, I had an interview in Altamira with Thais Santi, an attorney with the Federal Public Prosecutor's Office. Before we began, I felt the need to break interview protocol and tell her about what I had been listening to and feeling. I talked about the physical pain caused by João's words. And I told her: "I feel like what I know how to do isn't enough. People like João have been traumatized. They've been dammed up too, like the Xingu River. And they need a kind of help they can't find here. The horror of it is so great that we have to invent another way of doing what we know how to do. We have to create things that don't exist."

It was then that the webwork of listening began: João spoke, Maíra and I listened. And now the voice continued to be his, but it traveled through our bodies to echo farther than the room in the house no longer a house. The force of this voice pushed me to breach the boundaries of journalism's circumscribed territory and start inventing something that didn't exist and that could never be invented with only one voice. It had to be a net, woven voice by voice.

With João's words speaking inside me over and over, I went back to São Paulo and began knocking on the doors of psychoanalysts and people who work with what is known as testimony therapy. I wrote emails to various people I admire. Some I knew personally, others I'd only met through their books. A number of them heard me. I told them what I had seen and heard and then said: "There are all kinds of people in Altamira today, because of the resistance to Belo Monte. Many fewer than there should be, but they're there. Lawyers, documentary filmmakers, journalists like me . . . but there aren't any psychologists or psychoanalysts, people who work with mental health. So here's my question for you: Why aren't you there?"

This provocation was meant to break through a barrier, an invisible one—to incite psychoanalysts and psychologists from South-Central Brazil to journey to the Amazon, to displace themselves in various ways and also to blur the concepts of center and periphery.

This took place in September and October 2015. Some of the people listened. And some came up with their own answers, following other paths, because there are many possible routes. Among those who listened was the psychoanalyst Ilana Katz. One beiradeira looked at Ilana and, startled by her petite size, defined her in these words: "Gosh, she's just a little bit!"

Well, Ilana is a lot. Or a little bit that produces a lot of movement. Ilana listened. And the voice traveled through her too. So she told another psychoanalyst, Christian Dunker. And Christian listened. Ilana told the psychologists Cássia Pereira and André Nader, and they listened. And this listening, the movement of listening, produced engagement.

There were two trips to Altamira in 2016 so the group could

introduce themselves to people, grasp reality with their bodies actually incarnated into the landscape, and create what did not exist. On this first trip, I made myself into a bridge, introducing the group both to the territory itself and to the leaders of social organizations and movements in the Middle Xingu. As a bridge, I shared with the group the confidence that had come to be placed in me over all my years of reporting in that geography. I would impart what is to me my most valuable asset, the trust and credibility won through the craft of listening to and telling of lives.

On this first expedition, our pact was to: (1) listen and learn; (2) understand how people named their suffering in words, because words are not all the same and words also name what isn't the same; (3) discover if our presence made sense for those who were there and, if it did, by what paths mental health intervention could produce care; (4) make no promises we couldn't keep. There was another imperative as well: each of us was forbidden to be yet another colonizer, and we were very aware of this because we know the worst colonizer is the one who doesn't know they are one. And only by listening, the listening that engages our whole bodies, could we protect ourselves from the temptation to believe we knew what we didn't know.

On the second trip, I accompanied Ilana, Cássia, and André, who tested what they called a "device." Working in pairs, they listened to the people who had been referred by the social movements. They also met with public health agents from Altamira, because it was clear to everyone that mental health is a right—and rights translate into public policy. This intervention, which then received the name Care Clinic, would be a one-time event. Public policy, however, is what endures. So dialogue with those working in the territory as public health agents could never be auxiliary but was instead vital.

Ilana, Cássia, and André met every Thursday for most of the year to design the clinic's care model. With the support of Christian, who opened the University of São Paulo's doors to the movement, the three of them devoted that which is most precious and delicate in our human lives: time.

The next step was to share on the internet what we were hearing. João's voice, after traveling through our bodies, reached 1,305 people, who listened and also made donations that allowed the project to unfold as a gesture. We became a poem, like Carlos Drummond de Andrade's "Square Dance": "João loved Tereza who loved Raimundo who loved Maria . . ." We just switched the verb *love* for the verb *listen*, never forgetting that listening is also a form of love.

It would take me more than forty minutes to recite this living poem if I were to name all of the listeners who became givers. From September to November 2016, Ilana and Christian coordinated an open course entitled "Psychoanalysis in a Situation of Social Vulnerability: The Belo Monte Case," which was offered in person and online through the University of São Paulo Institute of Psychology and attended by around one hundred people. Anyone interested in volunteering at the Care Clinic in Altamira in January 2017 was required to take the course, in person or virtually; those who could only attend virtually had to write a text about each class.

Applicants' résumés were analyzed to assess the candidates' experience and motivation for participating in the movement. Those selected in the first phase were then interviewed. Lastly, the team took part in a second course to prepare for the actual intervention in January. In short, it wasn't easy getting chosen to work in Altamira for two weeks without earning a centavo. Ilana later articulated an idea I think is quite important: There is no such thing as volunteer work. Something is always earned. Not necessarily money or material goods. Value is different from price. Price is something monetary, while value isn't always monetizable. The team who went to Altamira earned a lot. A real lot.

And so our living poem went on. Our poem of listeners. Now with eleven more names: Ana Carolina Perrella, Anna Mariutti,

Flavia Gleich, Flavia Ribeiro, Layla Gomes, Luciana Guarreschi, Noemi Bandeira, Pedro Obliziner, Rodrigo Souza, Vivian Karina da Silva, and Érika Costa Pellegrino. On January 15, 2017, the listeners disembarked in Altamira. When they returned to their places of residence in South-Central Brazil, on January 29, the Care Clinic had received sixty-two cases and held 171 appointments (each case entailed more than one visit). Sometimes more than one family member was seen, so the sixty-two cases represented eighty-two people. Additionally, twelve meetings and four actions took place. In order to reach people where they were, the teams drove more than sixteen hundred miles and made five expeditions on the Xingu.

Every day, André and Cássia worked out the logistics for this operation in care. Early on, André articulated something fundamental: logistics, or how to reach the people who needed to be heard, and how the listeners would get to the people they needed to hear, was itself a form of care—caring for the people who were seen, caring for the team. The team needed to feel supported on their forays into the field, and those who would be seen needed to feel safe so they could receive the strangers who would listen to what was rumbling deep inside each one of them. André and Cássia spent most of their time at the hotel, working all day and into the night so the listeners could be in town and on the river, where people were listened to—in the tract housing units known as RUCs, built by Norte Energia, and also on islands and riverbanks. The teams went by taxi, transported by Celso Rodrigues and Erasmo Araújo de Melo Filho, the drivers who became part of the team. And by boat, in the voadeiras of Leodegário Oliveira da Silva, nickname Bago, an irreplaceable team member; João Barbosa do Nascimento, nickname Joãozinho; Leonardo Baptista; Aranor; and Socorro Arara. The name of Bago's small voadeira, written on the hull, was inspirational: "Everything Changes."

Christian and Ilana provided supervision more than ten times a day, when the listeners arrived from town or the river. And they also saw people. Lilo and I documented this web being woven by the Care Clinic team. And every night, starting at eight, there was a meeting to discuss the day and to share concerns. And there were also meetings with health services, the university, and social movements.

I think the team cared for others and was also cared for. Everybody cared for everybody, each through their act of listening. Every day was exhausting, and one day's exhaustion piled on to the next day's exhaustion and even so we were thoroughly vitalized by the experience. Our hearts are always beating and our lungs expanding, but even if our vital signs are steady and stable, some days we're more alive. We were very alive in Altamira, listening to the life that escaped through the cracks in the dam to stand as resistance.

The word we generally use in Portuguese for this type of experience is *construção*—construction. The experience with the Care Clinic made me think that *construct*—a word that evokes verticality and also hardness, the hardness of concrete, of iron and steel—might be replaced by the verb *weave*, a horizontal web, delicate, open to many pathways, its threads never spinning to an end.

The word *construct* has always bothered me during my experience in the Amazon and, even more so, in my experience with Belo Monte, because the word itself contains the very violence of dam construction, of tons of concrete damming up the Xingu. I think *weaving* is a more emancipatory word. Not the hardness of concrete, but the delicacy of thread. Not the verticality of a pyramid, but the horizontality of a web. The five men who were part of the mostly female Care Clinic also wove. This verb shift was fundamental to achieving what Christian defined beautifully: "We did the improbable while respecting the impossible." Because caring also means respecting limits—others' limits and also our own.

The opportunity for an experience in psychoanalytical listening in a territory where most people had never had this experience, and offering it to people no one has ever listened to this way, proved tremendously powerful. The first week, we visited Maria Francineide Ferreira dos Santos, an Evangelical beiradeira who became a leader when Belo Monte was expelling people, and we asked her to suggest other people who might need to be seen. I was present at these meetings, but obviously not during the sessions themselves. When the team saw people, they became patients.

I sat on the ground in a corner of Francineide's yard, generally my place as a "listeneer" reporter, while Ilana and Rodrigo talked with her. Ilana began by explaining what a psychologist does. Then this beiradeira, who is one of the smartest women I know, interrupted Ilana to explain what she, Maria Francineide, understood:

> This is how I understand it, in my way of speaking. You know that I've started going to school now, right, so I'm starting everything in my life after the age of forty-eight. The way I think of it, you're people who will help us find a door when many can't find a way out anymore. There are cases of people who come from this dam here, who isolate themselves to the point where nothing else matters. Not their children, not food, not work. You die, you know? People don't understand. There's a sadness born inside you that, no matter how much you want to get rid of it, sometimes you can't. That happened to me. Then the pain is awful. You always want to be alone, you don't want to talk to anyone. So it kills you. So you're the people who help us find this door. I went through the door they put there. They made a little box, put me inside, and left a real tiny little crack. But they put some dark paper across the crack. As hard as I looked, I couldn't find the crack. And we go into certain places where you have to dislocate your arm, neck, leg, hips, to be able to get out the other side with the rest, and then there's still the work to put

it back together, because many times your bones don't stay in place. So the way I see it, you're people who help us find the crack, the door, when it's not there.

Silence.

Near the end of my trip with the Care Clinic, there on the big banks of the Xingu, a beiradeira pulled me under the shade of a tree. She wanted to tell me her story. I was quite worried that people might confuse our roles, mine as a reporter, the others as psychologists or psychoanalysts. But they understood, perhaps even better than we did. I'm the writer who for years has listened to their lives in order to help open doors to the world outside. And the psychologists, as Francineide said, were listening to their lives to help open doors to the world inside.

Once in a while, beiradeiros in the Amazon will pull me off to a corner, at a party or a public meeting, and say they need to "talk to the writer." This time, the woman who pulled me over to a tree wanted to tell me what had happened the day before, when she was seen by a pair of psychologists:

I thought I'd never tell anyone this secret. I'd never spoken to anybody about my past. And yesterday I told the psychologist. It was like ripping a rusty nail from my guts. I woke up this morning at four, like always, but I was free. I don't have anything to eat, and I carry a very heavy burden on account of what happened to us because of this Belo Monte. But today I woke up weighing just a gram.

5. the resistance equation: me + 1 +

The Care Clinic experience invoked the power of listening as a political act of resistance. Not just psychoanalytic listening, not just journalistic listening, but a listening that crosses fields of knowledge and bodies as well. The voice passes from one body to another. And because it leaves marks during this passage, it earns the name "transmission." What begins with the words of João da Silva ends in a symphony of voices.

When he breached the dam that had silenced him, when he spoke, João transgressed. He didn't commit murder, he didn't die. When he spoke and was heard, João began weaving a movement of life. Unlike a letter lost along the way, João's words reached their destination.

I learned from this process that we don't need to make sacrifices; we need to listen. While I can find points of connection with Judeo-Christian religions even though I'm not religious, I am wholly averse to the idea of sacrifice. I don't believe in it. I believe in choosing to lose in order to be with others. But never through sacrifice—a factory of saints that chews up flesh to spit out statutes on the other end.

I believe in poets, not martyrs. Resistance to Belo Monte has created at least one poet of the Xingu. The village of Santo Antônio, Élio Alves da Silva's community, was swept away. It became a ghost and produced living dead. Élio ached. He became a fisher without a river. He found he was a poet when he was lost in brutal loneliness after the diaspora. He found he was a poet when he felt the urgent need to go to the Xingu he had lost and hear the call of the limpkin, the crying bird. Élio needed this other sadness to be sad along with him. And then, suddenly, as he says, "the story needed to come out." And he made his first poem. He wrote it with his voice, in his memory, because he is schooled in the river, not the alphabet.

Poetry is what voices the ineffable. For Élio, the violence produced by Belo Monte had been ineffable until that moment. To speak, he became a poet. We were on the edge of the river, the macabre landscape drawn by Belo Monte lying before us. In this scene, drowned trees were dying slowly, their naked, scrawny limbs pointing fingers of blame. Even when the Amazon sun is there, omnipresent, we still see the gray behind the blue. Against this landscape, Élio explained to me that, alone, he only counts as one. And anyone who only counts as one doesn't count, in more than one sense. To count, again in more than one sense, you have to be with the Other: "Me, alone, I can't do anything. But if I go over there and call one more, it'll be me plus one. Then that one calls one more. And then it's me plus one plus one . . . plus . . ."

In the years that followed, I felt the political-poetic formulation "me + 1 +" become a resistance equation that seeped into movements in Brazil and beyond.

100. about ties

When adolescents began hanging themselves and throwing themselves off towers in Altamira, it was the psychiatrist Érika Pellegrino who understood this best. As I wrote in my article about this series of suicides, Érika developed the hypothesis that we were witnessing the result of a decade of unprocessed collective trauma. The eruption of violence triggered by the Belo Monte event has corroded both the mental health of this community where bonds have been broken as well as the mental health of every family that was affected. If nobody ever, or only rarely, listened to these adults, certainly nobody ever asked the children anything, children who had been left homeless in so many ways, watching their parents in a state of perdition day after day. Not just those who were hit directly, but also those who suffered the consequences of life in a city they no longer recognized. The most fragile felt it first and more deeply.

Érika had this to say in her first days grappling with this series of suicides:

The main [suicide] risk factors among children and adolescents are mental disorder and family disintegration. While various cities in Brazil face social problems and challenges in accessing a public mental health network, the dimensions of what has happened in Altamira because of Belo Monte has altered the municipality's epidemiological profile in mental health. We don't have any quantitative data on this yet, but it is something everyone brings up. The Belo Monte event was very sudden and very big. [This is true] both for the families who suffered its impact directly—the case of those removed by force—and for the families who suffered indirectly—the case of those subjected to the eruption of violence. It makes sense to believe that this sudden, radical increase in sickness and the disintegration of bonds will have a bigger effect on the most vulnerable, like children and adolescents. This doesn't happen overnight. It's a process. One that is still unfolding and accumulating, which also helps us think about why this is happening now, in 2020.

Dorismeire Almeida de Vasconcelos, the aunt of one of the teens who threw themselves from a tower, followed this same thread:

> To understand these suicides in Altamira, you have to understand that we're fighting to survive here every day. Here, we experience the whole weight of the capitalist system that governs the economy and doesn't allow for the humanization of society. We're failing to care for our youth properly. We're always firefighters in Altamira, always putting out fires [very often literally, as when the forest burned in 2019—and continued to burn in the following years]. In Altamira, we wake up every day wondering how we'll manage to survive to the next day. . . . What we're reaping in 2020 is the result of everything that happened to us in the past and everything we didn't do in the past. Suicide is the result of what we're doing to our future generations.

Given this literal death of the future, what was left of the community in Altamira united and took action. The teenage friends of the teens who had killed themselves, mothers grieving other deaths, and social movement activists soon devised a system for detecting farewell messages on social media. Volunteers would then show up at the poster's house to keep them from going through with it. They interrupted dozens of suicides. Consciously or unconsciously, these people understood they would only have a shared future by stitching the community back up. Or that it would only be possible to guarantee a future for the community by creating the commons. At that moment, the commons quite literally meant removing the cord from around the neck of those who would rather not become adults in a world undergoing transformation. As one of the teens said in a farewell letter posted to his Facebook page: "I'll be dead by then. But first, I want to ask you, adults: What will you do so other adolescents like me don't die by suicide?"

I've always listened to a greater number of adults expelled by Belo Monte than to adolescents. These suicides showed just how invisible, even to me, was the pain of those who watched in terror as their elders transformed. And how much they rejected an adult life they could no longer want. After all, why would they? Yet at the same time, they couldn't find any other possible future. During the years when Belo Monte was under construction, ties with life began fraying, until they eventually broke in those early days of 2020.

In 1993, I was in Dourados, Mato Grosso do Sul, to do a story about adolescents of the Guarani-Kaiowá people. These youth, mostly male, were dying by hanging themselves from the branches of the few remaining trees on the Indigenous "reserve," a space incompatible with their lifeway because it was too small and too degraded and too penned in by the whites, who were still killing them. They were living the postapocalypse in a concentration camp. And they continued to hang themselves into the following decades.

These Guarani-Kaiowá teens were the first in Brazil to die of suicide in series owing to the corrosion of nature and thus of themselves. They put the cord around their necks, but they were murder victims. Their suicide was the result of a process of genocide executed by the Brazilian state and white society. Decades later, in 2020, non-Indigenous adolescents in the Amazonian city of Altamira began tying cords around their necks. We call this phenomenon "suicide," but perhaps we must find another name for an event that may now begin multiplying across a planet in climate anguish.

It is inevitable that we ponder the aesthetics of death, how the ties broken by the Belo Monte ecocide were refashioned as cords round the necks of those who hanged themselves. The ties that no longer existed—ties with others, with the community, with river and forest, with culture, with life—gained literal form, as deadly nooses. The cords took these teens to the limit of existence while also sustaining their bodies—bodies left to swing in the air, also literalizing their uprootedness from the forest, and thus from life.

9. pigeon claws on the roof

When I moved to Altamira, I expected to run into various challenges and was concerned about the more obvious risks. But I didn't take into account how living on a front line of the climate war would affect me. Trees were ripped out and the landscape transformed so fast that you couldn't even rely on the view from your window not to change from day to day. The soundscape was also being destroyed, because when a piece of land is cemented over, everything alive goes dead, like what happened to my frog neighbors one day. Our senses were under constant attack. Even restaurants, bars, and shops were ephemeral. You couldn't count on anything in Altamira—what was there one day might not be there the next, including people, since so many of them migrated from one place to another in search of ground that is always slipping out from under them. Coming from a place far away, I was always lost because it was hard to establish references. Making a home somewhere means you create a map of emotional bonds. In Altamira, the ongoing, accelerated building of ruins thwarted the geography of emotional bonds.

I discovered that living in Altamira meant inhabiting a landscape at war. And in this landscape of continual disintegration, people die. There is a lot of dying in Altamira, much of it due to unnatural causes. And death is never far away. It's close. And gets closer every day.

Grappling with an undeclared and therefore unrecognized war is especially hard because what is in fact an attack is treated as something normal, what is in fact devastation is treated as normal, what is in fact extermination is treated as normal. I suspect it's much like living in a favela in Rio de Janeiro, for example. But it's also different because Altamira's war extends well beyond human peoples; it is simultaneously the war of the beginning and of the end of the world, the war of the planet against the dominant minority of humans.

Before changing my address to Altamira, and the other changes that followed, I had witnessed conflicts as a journalist. I'd spent the previous thirty years covering a number of undeclared wars in the various Brazils. But when I Altamirized, things altered so much that the war began entwining with my daily life as well, invading my dreams, defining my schedule, contaminating my habits, shifting my perception of reality. The experience of living in the company of deadliness seeped down into me.

In June 2019, before the outbreak of teen suicides, I moved house. I'd left my marriage behind, and that meant I was left without a home as well. João had been my home during the previous fifteen years but could no longer be, because I was no longer who I had been. So two friends and I rented a house together, and since both of them had commitments in São Paulo, I finished setting it up myself. I was finalizing my book *Brasil Construtor de Ruínas*, which analyzes nearly two decades of Brazil, from Lula to Bolsonaro. I've never had trouble moving or being alone; I've always made sure to be good company for myself. But who was I, in that new now?

The first sign was the pigeons. They were sickly birds, visibly affected by environmental corrosion, their feathers jagged and dirty. And they were all over. When I woke in the middle of the night, the pigeons were there, making that sound they make, which to me became the sound of the apocalypse. Dozens of them scratching at the roof above me, their sharp claws and beaks scraping my head as if it were ground. Screaking. Cooing their incessant muffled messages. They too were an army of the desperate, well organized, perhaps the best survivors I knew. I felt like a character out of a Hitchcock film. The pigeons lurked there day and night; wherever I looked, there another one would be. I felt spied on. And those claws and beaks grating away on the roof . . . grating away and away. They were aliens in the Amazon, a planet to which they didn't belong. Small invaders who hadn't asked to be there—but, since they were, they took up the fierce life.

Loneliness dug its chipped and infected nails into me, pecking at my guts with its beak. Being alone is entirely different from being lonely. Loneliness is a cloak that envelopes you, isolating you from everyone. Nothing and nobody reach you. You become a kind of single-specimen species. The name of the pigeon was depression. I was headed there, but it took me a while to realize it. It wasn't Prometheus's eagle nibbling at my liver day after day, but a fat gray flea-infested pigeon with only one eye. The yellow eye of those who kill to live.

This wasn't my first depressive episode. Maybe it was my fifth. It's hard to pinpoint exactly when I had my first encounter with this darkness that emanates from within. I suspect it began during my childhood, this phase of which we are all survivors. My grandmother used to spend her days sitting alone in the same chair in the kitchen, her sadness seeming to encompass the whole house, until it slowly, eventually paralyzed her legs. For years she underwent painful treatment to restore movement. Those were times when no one spoke of depression, much less of antidepressants. What my sharp ears of a child heard was that so-and-so "has bad nerves." I didn't understand what that meant, or where those nerves were located, but I knew it was serious and had no cure.

Only more recently was I actually diagnosed with depression. What had triggered my episodes were journalistic ventures where writing proved tragically insufficient. My depression has always been linked to impotence. In the short book where I narrate the history of my relationship with words, I explain that ever since I was a child, I've written so I won't die, and won't kill. This is a profound personal truth. Writing is what mediates my relation to the world. It's also the weapon that replaced the burning match-stick of my childhood, from when I attempted to set my home-town's city hall afire. Once I could arm myself with a pen, I was able to take on the world outside. But at times, writing fails. Then the monster opens its eyes inside me.

My crisis in Altamira was different from my earlier ones, and it didn't have to do with the insufficiency of writing. To the con-trary, I was writing nonstop, my head clear. I had flirted with death before, but only as an idea. I'd never felt the summons of suicide in my adult life. Almost imperceptibly, the desire to die intruded upon my mind. Or perhaps just woke from its restless sleep. I didn't sense this desire as despair, but as what was right for me. It seemed to be a sensible, rational, even obvious decision. I no longer wanted to live. I was tired. Period.

My first plan was a symbolic death. I wanted to be nameless, identity-less, history-less. To be *not*. I planned to catch a bus at the Altamira station, headed anywhere, and let myself go with-out a destination. I would catch first one bus and then another, and then another. I would simply vanish into the world, and to the world, like so many other disappeared who never return but remain alive in other lives. I was fed up with being Eliane Brum and I was fed up with being all the other mes. I wanted to be none of me.

When I realized there was no way for me to be not, I began researching the best way to die by suicide. I didn't want a pain-ful death. Nor did I want to cause trouble, much less guilt. I truly didn't. I planned to leave all my bills paid, I planned love letters to all those dear to me, leaving it clear I was making a coherent life choice, although it was death. I was outraged at how hard it is to die with dignity, because suicide is taboo. I researched and researched.

At some point, I began suspecting that my desire was mis-placed. I continued to research but asked for help. I notified my psychoanalyst, Miriam Chnaiderman, as well as a soul sister,

Viviane Zandonadi. I told some people who were physically closer to me, but they were incapable of listening. This happens to people like me, who are seen as caregivers. When you ask for help, nobody believes you really need it. And since you play an important role, that of caring for others, no one wants to remove you from that position because it would mess up the tidy order of everyone's world.

These two women from São Paulo cared for me, materializing into my daily life even though they were thousands of kilometers away. I went back on a low dose of antidepressants. And plunged into reading the best books on depression I could find, bringing the power of words back into my life. I accepted the fact that depression walks beside me. And today I'm able to identify its proximity. The monster sniffs at me, and I feel the air it displaces inside me. So I get ahead of it, create mechanisms for coping with it, let those around me know I'll be "strange" for a while.

I came very close to dying this time. And that woke me up. When I realized how close I had come, I decided to look the monster in its yellow eyes and demonsterfy it. Some days later, a close friend of mine arranged his own method of death. He was careful to leave the groceries in the car so his significant other would find them. It was his first attempt too. We weren't the only ones to flirt with self-extermination in those days. I think we were—and are—experiencing war trauma, but the fact that it was an undeclared, unrecognized war left us fewer tools for coping with the deadliness of our days.

I'm sharing this personal experience because I don't believe it was by chance, detached from the ruins surrounding me. When adolescents started hanging themselves and jumping off towers, I remembered how I, a grown woman over the age of fifty, with myriad psychological resources and decades of psychoanalysis, had tried to engineer my own death in Altamira, as if it were the most tranquil conclusion, almost cold and even obvious. And around me, other adults who had confronted bigger crises than the ones experienced at that moment also pondered the act of dying for the first time.

Little is said about suicide during times of war, because bodies are already too shattered by bombs, grenades, and machine guns. And also because while suicide may still be a taboo in times of "peace," it turns into a betrayal of the species at a moment when so many are fighting to stay alive. But suicides happen. And they aren't rare. I think my own experience, along with the experiences of other people I'm not authorized to share, and especially the string of suicides by adolescents in Altamira, signal how self-extermination may eventually have a much greater impact than we suppose, especially as the effects of the climate crisis become more visible, present, and routine. Altamira transformed by Belo Monte can be seen as an experiment in what happens to a community when its ecosystem is destroyed and violence replaces law.

My hatred of the pigeons subsided. I still don't like them. But I've realized that what I hated about the pigeons were the things about them that reminded me of humans. What terrified me was their humanization. Their incredible resistance and capacity for survival turn them into pests that can multiply in new, degraded environments, occupying all the cracks and crannies and feeding on almost anything. Pigeons, cockroaches, and rats are the nonhumans we resemble most. They are humanities too. In that house, my hallucination was that one day it would be just me and the one-eyed pigeon. One staring down the other, one the mirror of the other, amid the planet's ruins. One and the other, the same. This is my climate apocalypse, and I anticipated it during those days of 2019.

2018. alice

If the pigeons were a disturbing mirror in Altamira—such a troublesome Other that refused to allow humanity to drive it to extinction and went about humanizing itself—vultures were a revelation. Only a deformed mind could have produced our image of them, associated with death and plunder, darkness and filth, an image that inhabits our common thought and our literature too. Under the impact of the climate crisis, our contemporary eye sees vultures as beings who have adapted to destruction without becoming destroyers.

A frequent, plentiful presence on the streets of Altamira, vultures eat death's leftovers. They don't kill, they just clean the city of its remains, whose rotting could produce more death. Spurned by humans, they still render a service. But this is simply how vultures adapt to the city. When they aren't in the ruins of the forest but in the forest itself, vultures are majestic. They soar to the very heights and glide through the sky for long distances, their huge, unfolded black wings appearing to stop time. During the season when giant South American river turtles—yet another endangered wonder—lay their eggs on the beach, vultures wait. And then land on the eggs the turtles have failed to bury fast enough. And feed themselves. Here, they are no longer subservient, as in the city, but move in synchronized flocks, opening their wings from on high.

From our hiding spot in the vegetation, we watch this struggle of life and death without interfering. At times we can't see the huge turtles, shrouded by the waves of sand they kick up while interring their eggs for the purpose of life. And then the vultures' flight obscures the sun and brings on night. Vultures don't threaten giant river turtles as a species. Humans do that—poachers arrive at the beach when we're no longer there and kill huge numbers of these mothers. If anyone ever asks me what bird I'd like to be, I'll answer without blinking an eye: a vulture.

In 2017, I saw these turtles reach the Tabuleiro do Embaubal Wildlife Refuge to lay their eggs after an epic journey. And because I wanted to tell their story in a news report, I ended up spending that New Year's Eve gathering up little baby turtles, as hundreds emerged from the sand after birth like mythological creatures. We were interfering so they could be taken to a safe place, where they would have better chances of reaching adulthood and saving their species from extinction. It was the best New Year's Eve of my life, the only one when I felt something new birthed inside me as well.

My most intense experience on this "job," however, had come ten days earlier, on December 20, when I saw Alice give birth to herself on the sand. This is how I tell the story:

A little head peeps out. Sprouting from the sand. *Ploft.*

Her head isn't much bigger than a fingernail. But a fingernail could crush her. I'm the first living being she sees, my stare her first contact with the outside world, the planet beyond the sand. Life with life.

The ecstasy is all mine; she might just be frightened. Or curious. The rest of her tiny body is still inside the sand. Open your thumb and index finger, but not much, and you'll have an idea of her size. I'm calling her Alice, like my granddaughter, born less than two months earlier, because we humans like to give names and I already love her a lot. But she must know herself by paths unknown to us.

Alice is a giant South American river turtle, also known as an Arrau turtle, one of the world's largest freshwater chelonians, and year after year her species reedits an amazing saga. Her little green head represents a monumental effort by an increasingly endangered species to survive. To lay the egg from which Alice hatched, her mother had to confront dangers as great as Ulysses did on his mythic odyssey. And Alice, this tiny collection of frailties that hasn't yet stretched her snout toward the sun, will face a journey rife with true traps. Alice is tiny but valiant. Very. Not valiant as a moral quality but as a force of life. Were she not, her little head wouldn't be there, pondering the world beyond the world.

I'm going to tell you about Gumercinda, who could be her mother. We don't know who Alice's mother is, but we know that Gumercinda was there, on Tabuleiro do Embaubal, or Embaubal Nesting Beach, in the Xingu River basin in Pará. This is the breeding ground for Gumercinda and another twenty thousand turtles, as well as for other types of chelonians, like *tracajás* and *pitiús* (six-tubercled Amazon river turtles). Embaubal Nesting Beach is a space that at first glance makes the world seem good—at first glance, it's nothing but beautiful. And inhabited by species who converse without disturbing the silence.

Gumercinda is one of eight turtles monitored by the biologists Cristiane Costa Carneiro, nicknamed Turtle Cris, and Juarez Pezzuti, or Juca, professor with the Center for Advanced Amazon Studies at the Federal University of Pará. In 2013, they attached a radio and an antenna to each of these eight turtles to monitor them by satellite. The beiradeiros call this antenna a *chifre*, like a creature's horn. Four years later, Gumercinda's was the only horn still working. The batteries on the others might have died, or the horn gotten lost, or something more brutal. Not Gumercinda's. She's still under surveillance, as if she were on a reality show where she's the only one who doesn't know she is the star. Or do you suppose she does?

Turtle Cris and Juca both have academic careers, but much of what they've learned has been with the beiradeiros in the Tabuleiro region—their mentors, as Cris explains. Antonio Davi Gil, or Tuíca, is one of them. Nearly blind, he sniffs out the turtles;

as he explains, they know a lot about human people and also about the forest, more than any human, more than any PhD, even more than he, who was practically born in the river. "Turtles are big, and they know a lot about water. They know more than I do." Tuíca is building a very large canoe, big enough to hold his eight children, because ever since they dammed up the Xingu, he can't find any fish for food. He says he's going to load the whole family in it and head off to some place in the forest where the men of progress can't reach them. Tuíca is more like Gumercinda, whom he knows well, than like me, though we formally belong to the same species. He and Gumercinda are forest; I'm not there yet.

Gumercinda is the only one of the eight turtles who wasn't named in honor of a woman from Juca's or Cris's families. Angelina is Juca's grandmother. Carmela is Juca's other grandmother, on his father's side. Maria is Juca's mother. Dany is Juca's wife. Tereza is Juca's daughter. Lúcia is Cris's mother. Then there's Cris, christened after the biologist herself. But what about Gumercinda?

The name honors Uncle Murilo's dog. Juca's uncle Murilo has a beagle named Gumercindo who, according to his nephew, is nothing special. If Gumercinda the turtle knew this, she might have shoved the antenna up some caiman's butt and eaten the radio herself. But she doesn't know it. While Gumercinda is named after Uncle Murilo's dog, Carmela and Maria bear almost legendary names drawn from the history of the battle against Brazil's business-military dictatorship. In 1971, Carmela Pezzuti, Juca's grandma, who passed away in 2009, was imprisoned, tortured, and deported to Chile, along with seventy guerrillas who had been exchanged for the Swiss ambassador after his kidnapping by the Popular Revolutionary Vanguard (VPR).

Maria do Carmo Britto, Juca's mother, has "little cotton curls" now, according to her son. But she was a militant with the National Liberation Command, or Colina, and with other clandestine organizations that fought the dictatorship. Under the code name Lia, she planned and helped carry out the notorious theft of former São Paulo governor Ademar de Barros's safe, hidden at the home of Ademar's lover. As commander of VPR, she may have been the first female to head a guerrilla organization. Maria was imprisoned, tortured, deported as part of the group of forty who were freed in exchange for the German ambassador in 1970, and exiled to Algeria. "When I gave them those names, I did it to pay silent tribute," Juca says.

Gumercinda, who pays homage only to Uncle Murilo's wily dog, weighed 77 pounds the last time someone checked, but her species can reach 130 pounds. She lives in the Marajó Archipelago at the mouth of the Amazon River. More specifically, on Ilha de Salvador in the municipality of Afuá. That's where she spends most of the year, eating and trying hard to stay alive. Gumercinda has proven faithful to what scientists call "feeding grounds" and "nesting grounds." The turtles only abandon the former when food grows scarce, and the latter when the place gets too risky for their offspring. It's possible to know where Gumercinda is, but what do you suppose she feels? What does it feel like to swim, or lie in the sun? How does she experience her instincts?

What we do know is that on August 6, 2017, something stirred inside Gumercinda, something that compelled her to leave home and set off. In prior years, she had begun her journey a few weeks later. But this time, Gumercinda and the others sensed the big rains would arrive early. Gumercinda then began a 530-mile sojourn—equal to driving from Detroit to Washington, DC—with many chances of dying along the way. And she did this swimming. Some of her horned colleagues often conquer even greater distances, at times more than six hundred miles. Neither Gumercinda nor the others do it alone. The mothers travel in groups, or bales, numbering more than fifty strong, urged into movement by an imperative instinct.

Gumercinda is traveling with more weight, at least six and a half pounds more, comprising some one hundred eggs. This figure is just an average; the number might reach a few dozen more.

And she travels slowly, perhaps out of caution for her precious cargo. In their bale, the turtles are like a group of mothers, traveling first up the Amazon, then the Xingu. Swimming the big rivers against the current, but not joyfully. Alert, cautious, listening and sniffing. There are risks in the Amazon River, but they are smaller. The occasional caiman. Beiradeiros looking for a turtle to feed the day's hunger. Some commercial hunting. Heading into Pará, in the region of the municipality of Gurupá, the number of turtle poachers grows. But it is in the region of Porto de Moz, on the Xingu River, that Gumercinda's and her companions' lives become lives of danger.

Turtle Cris grows tense when Gumercinda approaches the region of Porto de Moz. Her eyes are glued to the computer screen as she watches satellite signals. In this territory, the predator is human. And only that which is human knows how to destroy en masse. The poachers there use an *espinhel*, a type of weir with up to a thousand hooks attached. They bait each hook with *mucajá*, a fruit that tastes like candy to the turtles. Hundreds die each day on these spiked weirs. Each one of the turtles murdered on their motherhood voyage carries within it one hundred more possibilities of life. Each carries one hundred Alices who won't be born.

It is criminal. The hunting of giant South American river turtles—*Podocnemis expansa*—has been banned. Only the beiradeiros are legally allowed to capture turtles to feed their family, if they don't have any other available source of protein. And only under those circumstances. But what's the law anyway? If humans are killed with impunity in the forest and across Brazil, what are the chances for this freshwater turtle? These mothers are sold to restaurants and turned into prizes at competitions. In 2017, a turtle fetched up to sixty dollars on the black market in full daylight. And this is their life, interrupted.

Abrupt, excruciating pain. Blood.

The turtles are no longer creatures capable of an extraordinary

feat, reduced instead to a commodity. Humans are the only predators who rob the living of their dignity when they kill. A turtle killed
by a caiman, being against being, is still a turtle. A turtle killed by
a beiradeiro who needs to satisfy their hunger, being against being,
is still a turtle. A turtle killed by poachers to sell on the market is
turtle meat. Drained of substance, it only has a price.

At this point on the journey, we look at Cris and notice she
doesn't seem to be breathing. Gumercinda has swum through
Porto de Moz, an accomplishment she repeats year after year.
The biologist breathes a sigh of relief. She suspects Gumercinda
has learned she shouldn't eat the candy in the region of Porto de
Moz. That she passes under the weir and swims on. Alert and
cautious, listening and sniffing out her most ferocious predator.

It is only on September 8, thirty-two days after her departure,
that Gumercinda reaches her destination, Embaubal Nesting
Beach. She is exhausted but not yet safe. Since 2016, the nesting
beach has been part of what is legally designated a wildlife refuge,
which is a conservation unit created to protect the chelonians
who turn the sands into a gigantic nursery at this time of year.
But even there, the poachers don't give them a break. This year,
in 2017, the inspectors arrived late because their voadeiras broke
down. Gumercinda and the other turtles divined the threat. They
witnessed other mothers being hunted. They escaped the weirs in
Porto de Moz, but were captured in the area protected under law,
where law is a mirage.

Gumercinda sniffs out the beast that is human. And fears it.
Gumercinda listens. She's skittish, frightened. She can lay her
eggs on Piteruçu, a beach that has seen no human-made changes,
or on Juncal, an island that was artificially raised to provide more
sand for the nests. Gumercinda seems to prefer the softer, cooler
sand on Piteruçu, where her eggs have greater chances of hatching. But, since the poachers have attacked there, Gumercinda ob-
serves. And hesitates.

Now she has to make the toughest choice: laying her eggs on

Piteruçu and thus running a greater risk of losing her life and one hundred eggs but giving her offspring better chances of being born, or run a less deadly risk by digging her chamber on Juncal, where her nestlings will have lower chances both of leaving their eggs and of surviving, because the sand is coarser and hotter.

It takes Gumercinda more than twenty days to make the choice. She comes and goes with the others, venturing a little farther on the beach each day, sniffing the ground, assessing and experimenting. Deciding. Then she lies on the sand alongside the rest of her bale, and they bask in the sun to stimulate both their metabolism and ovulation. Eventually, one or two of the more courageous ones start digging a chamber, and the others follow.

Gumercinda the turtle ends up choosing Juncal Island, like most of her bale. She takes a final swim in the river before scaling the sandy beach. Slowly. Sniffing and listening. If she senses any danger, she will retreat. Gumercinda chooses the spot. There aren't many available. Hundreds of turtles are digging nests. *Whoosh whoosh whoosh.* The sound they make doesn't fit into words. Each one of the hundreds of turtles raises a cloud of sand nearly six feet high. They dig and dig and dig.

Nonstop.

It is three in the morning when our boat pulls up to Juncal Island. This is when I have my most profound experience of being a foreigner. (Two years later, I would take part in an expedition to the Antarctic, where this feeling expanded.) I feel like not just a foreigner but an astronaut. The landscape is illuminated only by the moon. And seagulls are sentries to our footsteps. They immediately denounce us with their squawking, a warning that beings who shouldn't be there are stepping on the ground of more-than-humans.

We advance in silence.

The turtles are more frightened than usual because of the violence they have experienced recently. Weeks earlier, three inspection agents went to the beach drunk and walked through the laying grounds, messing with the turtles. The stress felt by the mothers limits our efforts to document them. We crawl to the edges of the nesting grounds. And don't move beyond this boundary. We stay there nearly three hours, belly down on the sand. We can see nothing but stars, so many stars, above our heads. What is happening close at hand, we can only hear. *Whoosh whoosh whoosh.* And darkness.

We're there so the turtles can get used to our scent and our presence. So they believe we won't hurt them. Or else they will return to the water.

Day breaks on Embaubal Nesting Beach. And what we see lies beyond the scope of adjectives. I realize our limits are not just about proximity but also about words. And it is honest for me to recognize this up front. Lilo Clareto and I know that images and words will convey only a part of the enormity that is life narrating itself. Beautiviolence as a single noun, melded into one sole body of letters.

Our wonder is interrupted by a squadron of vultures. *Awk aawwk.*

Hundreds of them. And they are imposing. In an instant they drop from the sky onto the beach. They are a threat not to the turtles, protected by thick shells as much as thirty inches long, but to their eggs, whenever one accidentally gets pushed out. In the mothers' eager digging, they sometimes end up kicking another one's eggs out of the nest. That's when the vultures move in. And the turtles accept them as a part of it all.

Gumercinda chooses a spot. She'll keep digging nonstop for an hour. Until the hole is at least twenty inches deep, sometimes even more than two feet. This will be her offsprings' nest, and she makes sure it's nice and deep, so the beaks and claws of predators cannot reach it. Gumercinda goes motionless. She'll spend about thirty minutes laying her clutch of one hundred or more eggs. All around, *whoosh whoosh whoosh.* Sand flies all over. The vultures are meddlesome, but Gumercinda doesn't seem to care. What is she feeling right now? I can't understand Gumercinda's language, nor she mine.

Half an hour later, Gumercinda gets up and starts covering the hole. There is an atavistic technology to this act, as to all of them. She uses her hind feet to kick sand into the nest and then compacts it by pounding against it with the bottom of her shell, called a "plastron" by biologists. Cris can't contain her excitement with the nest. "It's perfect, it's perfect," she whispers.

It takes another hour before the sand shields the eggs. Each of these turtles is an artist, sculpting out reproduction. The laying period will end with a treasure trove of two million buried eggs. That's an estimate. It might be half that, or more than that. It depends on increasingly intense climate variations and on the competence of the human inspection system, generally quite questionable and sometimes intentionally incompetent. In 2009, the year there was no protection, some two thousand turtles were captured on Embaubal Nesting Beach and became commodities.

I remember my first appearance in the rainforest, in 1998, when I traveled the Transamazonian. The first ground I stepped on with my gaúcho boots was Itaituba, on the banks of the Tapajós River. I was received by a high-ranking military officer—if I remember right, an army colonel—who was keen to know exactly what I was doing and to "help" me however I needed. The night I arrived, there was to be a big party for the soldiers stationed in Itaituba. As I've mentioned before, it seems that soldiers serving in the Amazon have never been informed that the dictatorship ended, so they march about city and forest clad in military boots and arrogance, certain of their supremacy over civilians. Later, in 2019, when Jair Bolsonaro reached the presidency of Brazil, I had a clearer understanding that, to some extent, the dictatorship never did end and a spangled portion of those in uniform still want more power. This is a legacy of many distortions, including a republic that began with a military coup.

On that particular party night, a truly giant South American river turtle was the main dish. Placed in the middle of the table, the turtle was the banquet. I took a bite but couldn't keep eating. At one point, the colonel came over to "ask" me not to mention that the soldiers were eating a forest creature whose hunting and sale were prohibited. I replied neither yes nor no, something I excel at when necessary. But I felt sick to my stomach all night. When I wrote the article, I ended up not mentioning" the fact because the colonel was a colleague's source. But I've never shed my sense of shame. I recall this low moment as I observe Gumercinda digging to survive.

Gumercinda finishes, seemingly satisfied with her work. She looks up to the sky. At no point does she stop sniffing, listening, observing. And then she makes her way back to the water. She's exhausted. Since the sand on Juncal is coarse, she's injured, her feet now raw, bleeding flesh.

The turtle-person dives into the Xingu. On October 5, the twenty-seventh day of her stay on Embaubal Nesting Beach, she sets off on her long journey back. She's thinner now, because there's not much fruit in the nesting region and competition is stiff. She no longer carries her precious cargo. This time she swims with the current. But the beast who is human is there. With its weirs and nets. Gumercinda doesn't let exhaustion dull her senses or hunger trick her. She swims fast, veering away from dangers. She's a great survivor. Gumercinda and the others are magnificent.

Cris follows her by computer. The biologist shares the base at Embaubal Nesting Beach with twelve inspection agents, another biologist, and military police officers with the environmental patrol. She is tense again. Her "office" is located under her house next to the hammock where she sleeps. The headquarters is a stuffy structure infested with cockroaches. Below, between the pillars, a breeze wafts by as this turtle doula follows Gumercinda's path on the screen.

And then, relief. On October 17, Gumercinda has returned to

Marajó Archipelago. It took her only thirteen days to conquer over five hundred miles along these great rivers. She swam an average of forty miles a day. Gumercinda now eats and builds up her strength. In a year, if she isn't killed by some predator, she'll initiate her saga yet again. What I call a saga is simply life to Gumercinda.

From September through January, Juncal Island is a gigantic nest, populated only by birds and manifold insects. The green pellicle that once coated part of Gumercinda's skin like a very fine silk thickens at the end of every year. The Amazonian winter has arrived, and waters descend from the sky. Some days there is one river above and another below. Everything grows ferociously. It's time for the first eggs to start hatching, about forty-five days after their mothers nestled them in a bosom of sand. Embaubal Nesting Beach turns into a nursery of babies so fragile and so valiant.

Like Alice.

Once again we are astronauts landing on an earthly moon in the middle of the night. This time, we arrive earlier, around midnight. And once again the birds divine and denounce us. It is now that tiny turtles begin sprouting from the sand. Juncal Island has been surrounded by a screen fence as part of a management program. Tiny turtles are gathered up and thrown into boxes. They'll be counted and released in selected spots, where they are supposed to have greater chances of surviving.

Some of the more daring hatchlings manage to leap the fence and head toward the water, where, with luck, they'll find adult turtles who have chosen to live year round in the region of Embaubal Nesting Beach. They gather in close to these females, whose robust presence protects them from some of their predators. They build up their strength, eating leaves, slime, and small algae. Growing. Maybe next year they'll migrate with their mothers when they return to lay their eggs, but there is no proof this happens. As many as twenty thousand babies are born in the middle of some nights. Twenty thousand—the population of some towns in the interior of Brazil.

Now we can walk across the nesting beach. But carefully. Foot after foot, very slowly, because infant turtles are hatching all over. Just fledglings, they stare at the weird giants that walk on two legs, that are us.

We want to watch a birth. That sounds easy, but it isn't. You have to guess where there's a nest out of which a baby will be born in the next few hours. You have to see whether a small swirl of sand begins expanding on the surface. We position our video camera in front of one of these and film virtually imperceptible movements. We celebrate each change in hushed voices. And then, two hours later, bodies and camera in the same position, we witness the "birth" of . . . a mole cricket, an insect that hides in the sand. The hatchlings scurrying around us must think they were born on a planet of tall creatures with dim wits.

With the help of Cris, who can't quit howling over our misadventure, we shift our camera to another swirl in the sand, a few inches away. Alice is there, but we don't know it.

We wait.

There is no question she'll be female. Since the beach on Juncal Island was artificially built up, the sand there is coarse. When the temperature of the sand is above ninety degrees Fahrenheit, the female reproductive system develops. If it is lower than this, the male reproductive system develops. Since the coarse sand on Juncal is above ninety, 100 percent of the hatchlings are female. And so, year after year, males grow scarcer. Decades ago, the beiradeiros say, you'd always see various males surrounding one female. Today, that's an unlikely scene.

We, who don't know how to see, see nothing but a stunning landscape. But a constant explosion of simultaneous events is taking place. Sex, birth, death.

We've been here an hour without anything apparently happening. And then . . . *Ploft*. A tiny head pokes out of the sand. It's

3:12 a.m. on December 20, 2017. And Alice makes her first contact with the world outside.

She is minuscule. And grandiose. She seems out of the blue. But isn't. This little one spent at least ten days in an underground world of sand, in total darkness, after cracking out of her shell. While she was in the egg, she fed on the vitellus, or yolk, through a kind of umbilical cord. Yes, Alice has a belly button. When the yolk is finished and her navel healed over, she leaves the egg. But she carries a bit of this food inside her, a reserve to sustain her on her long journey toward the surface. She spends days and days digging with feet she has only just recently tested out. Upward, ever upward, through sand coarser than ideal, compacted by the first rains and the rising tide.

For a baby turtle, birth is an epic. Even more so for a trailblazer, like Alice, the first to leave her nest. Her sisters will follow the tunnel she has opened. Alice hasn't even seen the world yet and she's already exhausted. Her eyes are still closed and she breathes through her mouth, gasping. In this gesture alone she is already a survivor. Of some two million eggs, Alice is one of the four hundred thousand tiny turtles who managed to sprout. This is yet another estimate—some years it has been half that, others much more.

The average birth rate is only 20 percent, according to Cris. The rest of the eggs won't even hatch, due to flooding or high temperatures. Millions of the eggs laid by Alice's ancestors were once used for oil to light cities. Today it is human poaching and the climate crisis that threaten her species' survival.

But Alice doesn't yet know her life is destined to be a drama, or perhaps a tragedy. There she is. Trying. She only opens her eyes—green—for the first time when an insect alights on her. Next, it's a beetle who uses her head as a landing strip, in a dreadful display of bad manners. Then it's time for a grasshopper to find her fascinating. The light from our camera disturbs her birth; sometimes she seems to close her eyes in hopes that when she opens them, we will have disappeared. In vain.

Alice wriggles, trying to shake off pesky bugs, drawn first by the camera's light, then by Alice herself. Once rid of them, she goes back to sleep. Sometimes she tries to ignore them, because she is very, very tired. But all sorts of insects are disturbing her. She's forced to open her eyes again. She takes a swipe with her tiny foot. And goes about extracting her little body from the sand. This movement alone wears her out, and she breathes through her mouth a number of times. Then she sticks her snout up high and looks around. She looks hard. She seems to be seeing the stars for the first time. This is the world, after all.

Through her powerful instinct, which will sustain her as long as she lives, Alice knows she needs to emerge during the night, before vultures and other birds descend on the beach to hunt her. Alice appears to be late. And we start getting worried. But then the sun peeks over the horizon, a mere promise of light. Alice opens her eyes. This time, she doesn't close them anymore. She cleans the sand from her right eye with one foot, from the left eye with the other, and starts hurrying toward the water. She is more than three hundred feet from the river, and the journey is perilous.

Alice hastens up and over the dunes, which must seem like mountains, given her tiny size. She stops only once, when she hears the shriek of a seagull. And then resumes running. When she gets closer to the river, she must cross not just sand but also ground plants, which must look like a forest to her. Alice doesn't hesitate but moves right along. Running, running toward life. She finally dives into the Xingu. For the first time. And swims without being taught. She vanishes into the water.

Minuscule.

From a distance, the little turtles all look alike. But when we get up close, they become unique, with their own singular traits as well as personalities. Alice had an especially large snout and was almost clumsy. There were cuter hatchlings, bigger hatchlings, smarter hatchlings. None of them was Alice, whom we saw come to life and fight to become a being of this world.

Alice has her chance. She has managed to escape vultures on land. But her journey by water has barely begun. If she escapes peacock bass, piranha, and other fish waiting for her just up ahead—as if lined up at a company cafeteria—if she escapes caimans and long-beaked birds, if she finds a bale of adult females to serve as a shield, one day Alice will return to Embaubal Nesting Beach to lay her eggs. And, like her mother, she will also be persistently preyed upon by the beast that is human.

Alice vanishes into the water to live. Her existence might last a second—or a century.

69. translingual

I have chosen to journey, to traverse worlds, as a way of life. Not as a way of moving from one place to another but as a choice to never cease journeying. And journeying always onward means accepting that there is no conclusion to be reached or any definitive understanding to come to. There is no where. And, harder still, no shelter to be found in a language, as a tongue, or in language, as worldview. I believe this is the condition common to us all, though many don't realize it. You can only be, by being translingual—and translanguage. Languages, and language itself, are bodies, if not our very bodies. Just as our cells are constantly renewing and our neural connections adapting, what we call "I" is movement, mutation, transmutation. We are all in transition.

Being translingual and translanguage means you're at a permanent loss and because you realize this loss, you are more filled with your senses. To take the glass-half-empty, glass-half-full cliché, it's as if you realize—and above all accept—the fact that your glass is quite empty, and this makes it fuller. I've always known how impossible it is to convert life's complexity into words, just as it's impossible to convert a body into words. Life and body evade words, or words fail to encompass life and body. This is a permanent condition for anyone who tells stories, whether through writing or the spoken word.

When I intuit the banzeiro and embrace it—because I'm tired of pretending I don't hear it, and because I've chosen to travel to its eye to find out what it wants of me—impossibility and loss grow. And keep on growing. The experience of living with other worlds and other peoples evinces how the tongue and the language I inhabit—and the body I am—are radically lacking. My challenge in these pages and in everything I write is how to express this loss, not covering it up but marking it with words. As I've said before, and say once again because it's important, if I've learned anything, it is to never, in any situation, run from contradictions. I carry mine in my body, laid bare for anyone who wants to see.

And now, instead of saying "humans and nonhumans," as I generally have—using "nonhumans" to refer to those who are others—I am going to use only "humans and more-than-humans." This choice is meant to express both loss and contradiction. It has been a tremendous challenge deciding how I should refer to all others who don't belong to the human species. I haven't arrived at a good term, nor, in my opinion, have the other people also pursuing this challenge. It's obvious I would never opt for "animals," a concept tainted by centuries of ignorance, even though we are "human animals." I too was taught at school that "humans are rational animals," whereas all other animals are "irrational," a statement that hasn't held up to science for a long time.

It is highly limiting to view life's multiplicity of forms through the concept "species"—another perspective that accedes to the hegemony of biology, as if this view were a consensus across all universes. Yet I don't know how to undermine this hegemony at this point on the journey. I use "humans and nonhumans" in my talks and news stories because, if I used other terms, it would take me as much time to explain them as I need for the actual subject. And also because, as a first reaction, people find it disturbing enough to see "nonhumans" cast on the same level as "humans." Not to mention the gender-neutral language I've tried to use in these pages (a challenge much greater in the original Portuguese than in English), groping my way, searching, but accepting the challenge of groping and searching, jettisoning the binarism contained in terms like *mankind*, translating ourselves to the translingual translanguage of livingkind.

But right now, on the journey across the pages of this book, I must move beyond the term "nonhumans," which I use elsewhere. Reducing all livingkind to a negative of the human, referencing them to something they are not, is extremely feeble. Not to mention, we know that a nonbeing—a being who is not part of a positive referential—is considered "less." Even if a body can only express itself from its "place of speech" (in my case, as human, female, white, middle class, etc.), we must make an honest effort to try harder.

In opting to use the tentative term "more-than-human," I believe some suggestions from the field of politics are of value: the idea that there is more, much more, than humans at the centers of the world, or as worlds themselves, and the message that the whole of those who are Others, even if viewed through the limited concept "species," is necessarily more important than one single species alone. "More-than-human" is a less feeble designation than "nonhuman" and, at the same time, an instigation. I feel that turning loss and difficulty into instigation is the best way to bring readers face-to-face with their own contradictions.

The region of the Middle Xingu alone, where I came to reside and belong, is home to nine original peoples, each with their own language, and then there are all the variations of Portuguese spoken by beiradeiros and even by Altamirans, who are from all over. My lifetime wouldn't be enough for me to learn all these tongues; even if it were possible to speak all of them reasonably well, I would never encompass all of their forms of language. Good anthropologists live with an Indigenous people for years, or decades, not so they can understand the people, but so that, in the little they do understand, they betray them less. The same holds true for journalists like me. All we can manage to do is narrate another experience, after it has journeyed our body—always after journeying our body.

At first, I refused to write about the original peoples at all, because I felt my ignorance barred me from it. I only allowed myself to tell about the beiradeiros, with whom I share a common linguistic base and with whom I've shared experiences for nearly twenty years. I don't regret that I did write about the Indigenous in the past, but I'm ashamed of what I wrote. Only in recent years did I come to understand that I do indeed need to write about them, but while emphasizing my ignorance. I realized it would be omissive not to write about the violence they suffer. And also some Indigenous groups asked me to write. However, it still leaves me quite uncomfortable. I try to rely on knowledge gleaned by anthropologists, yet there is very little available.

In recent years, the Indigenous have become journalists to better tell those who oppress them about their bodies, their distinct tongues, and their language. I think this journey is both necessary and invaluable, but I hope the Indigenous know that journalism, as it still stands today, is a white invention. I also hope that, in addition to counterinvading the territory that constantly assaults them, the Indigenous penetrate journalism with their own way of narrating. In fact, I hope they *devour* journalism, which would be the best possible news.

Thais Mantovanelli is an anthropologist who works mainly with the Mebêngôkre Xikrin and Juruna Yudjá of the Middle Xingu. When she is not in the villages, she lives in Altamira. Thais says that in the Mebêngôkre language—spoken by the peoples who call themselves by this name but are known in the white world as Kayapó and Xikrin—it is common for speakers to use the expression "Gamá?" when talking over the radio. This translates something like: "Was your ear able to hear to understand?" The interlocutor then replies: "Arup ba kumá." Which means: "Yes, I was able to understand what I heard in my ear."

As an *escutadeira*, a listeneer, I try to understand what I hear with my ear. And with all my other senses, intuition included.

I suspect this is what "ear" means in the Mebêngôkre tongue—it is a more-than-body-part. When I listen to the Indigenous, "hear in my ear" is about hearing what I understand them to say, when they say it in my own tongue. But what tells me more is what I can grasp from their words when they are spoken in a tongue I don't understand.

When speaking in their native language, the Indigenous sometimes have to use words in Portuguese that don't exist in their mother tongues—because they don't exist in their linguistic worldview. These words mark their speech with the invasion suffered by their bodies. This is what happens with words like *development, progress, corporation*, and *businessman*. When they speak these words, they're assaulted yet again, because the words are invading their tongue—the intangible one—and also their tongues, the ones that enable sound.

My foundational experience with listening, the one that changed my way of coping with my ignorance about the bodies of Indigenous peoples, occurred at one of countless hearings that the Federal Public Prosecutor's Office held in Altamira to listen to those hit by the impact of Belo Monte. When I write "Indigenous peoples" here, now, I feel coarse, because I'm grouping into one adjective-noun pair all these bodies that have nothing or little in common with each other, other than having been assaulted by the dominant human minority. I think the Indigenous should perhaps be called "extra-human" or "beyond-human." Jair Bolsonaro, it's worth remembering, considers them "almost-human-like-us." Here again it is explicit how language is a field where truly important battles are waged, thwarted, or silenced all the time.

At this "hearing" (another of those untranslatable words for the Indigenous), I was captured by a scene where I couldn't do anything other than hear in my ear what I couldn't understand. What I *dis*-understood would later become a lament for strings composed by the maestro Alexandre Guerra and performed by orchestras from Manaus to Budapest. In the impasse between languages, the maestro used his own language to create chords that grieve without aggrieving.

He was an elder. His people, Araweté. His body was red from annatto, his hair in a bowl cut. And he sat up straight, hands embracing the bow and arrows in front of him. He sat like that for nearly twelve hours. Without eating. Without bending. I looked at him, but he never made eye contact with me.

In front of him, taking turns at the microphone, were Indigenous leaders from several of the peoples hit by Belo Monte, demanding that Norte Energia make good on its agreements. Like others, he didn't understand the Portuguese language. Forty years earlier, neither he nor his people even knew something called Brazil existed, and it is possible this still didn't make any sense. But the Araweté elder was there, under the lights, sitting in a red plastic chair, waiting for his fate to be decided, in Portuguese, in a place they called Brazil. What did he see?

I don't know what he saw. I know what I saw. And what I saw allowed me to grasp a dimension not of him but of myself. Or of ourselves, "whites." The language of justice, like the language of bureaucracy, with all its acronyms, was designed to make illiterates even out of those who hold doctorates in literature. But what is left for the Indigenous, who try to express themselves in the language of those who are destroying them—and who try to do so even while being destroyed by that language? What was left for the Araweté elder, sitting there for nearly twelve hours? He had no choice, since it was through those words that his existence was annihilated.

The leaders of various original peoples hit by Belo Monte, the ones who can speak Portuguese, had decried the impossibility of life after the hydropower plant was inflicted on the Xingu. They reported hunger, they reported disease. The dam had altered the river, endangering Indigenous survival further still. In Volta Grande do Xingu, the river is drying up and the fish are dying.

Norte Energia controls the river water. How can you explain this to the Araweté elder in any language?

Pressure is on to build another mammoth project in the same region, a project that the Canadian mining company Belo Sun has touted as the biggest open-pit gold mine in Brazil. How can the Araweté elder understand this, he who doesn't even understand a language in which the word *beautiful* can name something that destroys and kills?

Painted with annatto, clutching his bow and arrows, sitting in a red plastic chair, not understanding the language in which his fate is decided and his hunger decreed, there is the Araweté elder. How did he get to the convention center? What paths took him to this moment, to this chair, this setting so exposed by lights and at the same time so obscured by negotiations, subterfuges, and erasures?

The Araweté have known about us whites for a long time. Whites are present in their mythology. But "official" contact occurred only in the twentieth century, in the 1970s, when the Transamazonian Highway was forced on the region. It was then that the business-military dictatorship began what they portrayed as the "attraction and pacification" of Indigenous peoples. (But in the understanding of the Araweté, let me stress, what happened was the opposite: they were the ones who tamed the whites.)

In 1976, Brazil's federal agency of Indigenous affairs, FUNAI, found the Araweté camped alongside peasant fields. They were starving and sick from this first contact. In July of that same year, agency staff decided to take the Araweté on a sixty-two-mile, seventeen-day walk to a FUNAI post. Adults and children died along the way. Even worse, with their eyes glued shut by infectious conjunctivitis, the Araweté couldn't even see their way. They got lost in the woods and starved to death. Small children, suddenly orphaned, were sacrificed by desperate adults: many grew too weak to walk and asked to be left to die in peace. By journey's end, 73 people had ceased to exist, killed by the contact and the march. FUNAI's first census of them registered 120 survivors. At that point, these 120 people were the sum total of Arawetés on the planet.

The elder sitting in the red plastic chair, clutching his bow and arrows, is one of the survivors of this "official" contact with whites forty years earlier. He is one of the children who was found, to be lost forever. And there he is. What does he see? What are those whites who are negotiating his life on the stage at the convention center? What are we?

Leaping forward. It is no longer the Transamazonian slashing through the homes and lives of the original peoples of the Xingu. It is Belo Monte. In 2013, the anthropologist Guilherme Heurich, with Brazil's Museu Nacional, submitted a trenchant text to the Federal Attorney General's office in Brasília:

> What Norte Energia did, during the Emergency Plan [which would supposedly protect the Indigenous from the impact of dam construction], was provide a constant influx of goods to the villages. Norte Energia posed as the big donor of non-Indigenous products, universal and infinite, with the only intermediaries between them and the Indigenous people being the lists [of products offered as part of so-called impact mitigation measures].

Once again, government administrations abstained from fulfilling their constitutional obligation to protect the original peoples, leaving them at the mercy of negotiations with the Company (yes, with a capital *C*, as if it were God) and of its unlimited power, since part of the state was actively omissive.

FUNAI at first rejected requests for things like luxury mattresses. Then *caciques*, or Indigenous leaders, began negotiating the product lists directly. It was like a sales counter where the classic allegory of the 1500s, when European invaders traded the lives of the original peoples for little mirrors, was being replayed. Five hundred years later, the mirrors became motor canoes, fuel, television sets, junk food, soda. Indigenous people who didn't eat sugar began consuming it daily.

During a conversation with an Araweté, Heurich discovered how these people interpreted the influx of commodities into their village. The commodities were *pepikã*, reparation for everyone's future death. Like compensation paid out in life for a decreed death, a shabby last supper for the condemned, consisting of ultraprocessed food that would also poison them, hastening their end.

"And what will kill you?" the anthropologist asked them. "The water." "The water?" "Yes, the water from the dam." The Araweté analysis of this influx of commodities into the village, as Heurich points out, couldn't be clearer or more precise: "Everything the Emergency Plan has unloaded is an advanced payment for the death that will occur when the village is flooded by the waters of Belo Monte." Declining this future, another Araweté created a different one: "We're going to build a really big canoe . . . so everyone can live in the middle of the river."

The Araweté elder, who is here at the Altamira convention center now, clutching his bow and arrows, had experienced, together with his people, the certainty that the end of the world had arrived. How can you gauge and respond to an impact of this magnitude, the impact of living with the certainty that the world will end the next day? And now here he is. Sitting in a red plastic chair. Motionless. Almost twelve hours without eating, without bending.

The Xingu and its peoples are no longer the same. On the banks of the Ipixuna, the Araweté feel the rivers and their branches sicken day after day. First, the water was transformed into a commodity, now it is the gold. Other peoples take the microphone to tell how Belo Monte has crushed Volta Grande do Xingu, drying up its present and sending its future up in smoke. If the Belo

Sun Mining project is approved, they warn, today's world will end. The Yudjá are one of these peoples. Called Juruna by whites, they are now relearning their own tongue from their relatives in the Upper Xingu and recouping their right to name themselves: Yudjá. "What does our name mean? Our name, Yudjá, we have it because we are of this river." Of this river that now kills. The cacique who is speaking at the microphone has just lost his brother, who drowned in the river where he was born but could no longer recognize.

These violations are denounced, but nothing happens. The violence is announced but not impeded. The law, like the river, has been dammed up on the Xingu. How can the Araweté elder comprehend a law that exists to not exist?

And nevertheless, there he is, sitting tall, almost twelve hours without eating, without bending. In a red plastic chair. The meeting is necessary, but it is also an assault. The language is different, the ritual different, the social and political organization also different. The Araweté elder is there, sitting among the representatives of other Indigenous peoples who have been his enemies as far back as his ancestors could think, hearing words his ear cannot understand. How is so much impossible, possible?

We call them the Araweté, but this name doesn't make sense in their tongue, which is part of the Tupi-Guarani trunk. The name was given by someone from FUNAI, but there is no such reference in the language of the Araweté, who don't know why they're called that. They call themselves *bïde*, which means "us," "us folks," "human beings." Whites are *kamará*. And also *awi*— "enemies," "foreigners." And there is the elder, sitting with his bow and arrows, and not even the word used to summon his people to the microphone makes any sense to him. Called by a name that isn't theirs, they have to respond in a tongue they don't speak about a violence they don't understand.

Tension advances, and time feels like a fabric about to tear. The microphone is dominated by leaders from other peoples,

who are good at speaking the whites' tongue. Little is left for the
Araweté, their ancestral knowledge reduced to half a dozen fal-
tering words in the murderer's language. The Indigenous raise
their clubs, their words harsh because life is turning toward
death. "What you all do is create conflict, you put nation against
nation to fight. This is a crime," says one leader. "There are miners and loggers looting our lands and you do nothing," another
shouts. "You have to respect us, respect our elders, respect our
tongue. The river is dry, the river is dirty. We're suffering. You
have to hear!"

They don't. The president of FUNAI asks for a "vote of confidence," pointing out that he has just taken office (he won't last
long at his post, but he doesn't know that yet). He promises everything will be different. When an Indigenous man interrupts him,
he says: "I heard you out, now I ask you to please let me speak.
That's democracy." Democracy. If the Araweté elder understood
Portuguese, what would he think about "democracy"? What does
"democracy" do for the Araweté elder?

Expressions like "income generation," "productive activities,"
and "mobilization logistics" come up often over the hours. How
can we understand this raping of the ears? Sitting there, what
does the Araweté elder see?

A disembodied tongue is much worse than a ghost because it
can't even haunt. If a word disincarnates, if the one who speaks
and the one who listens can't see the blood in the word *genocide*,
in sounds or in writing, they can only write lost letters. And what
about the Araweté elder who dies slowly at the meeting, without
even knowing the word that names his extinction?

It is already the middle of the night when the meeting ends
and the leaders gather to sign yet another document in which
Norte Energia and FUNAI pledge to keep promises they've failed
to keep so many times. The Araweté elder finally moves. He moves
like a cat, threading his way across the room as if in foreign territory, which in fact he is. Very slowly, he goes over to a computer

keyboard and cautiously stretches out an annatto-covered finger. He touches a key, then quickly withdraws his hand.

He waits. Nothing happens.

Then he says a few words in his language, says them to no one. He presses his body against the white wall, protecting his back in a hostile environment, while he ponders the scene. Then he returns to hazarding his catlike steps. He approaches the table where the authorities sat, now empty. He picks up the microphone and taps it a few times, cautiously. Nothing. It is off now. Not a word comes out of it. The president of FUNAI signs off with a routine goodbye: "God bless."

god.

What does the Araweté elder see? Ignorant, I know only what I see.

I wish we, whites, had never touched him. I wish none of the original peoples had ever known of us. In Cao Hamburger's 2021 film *Xingu*, where the anthropologist Cláudio Villas-Bôas is trying to "save" the Indigenous, his character has this to say: "There's something in them that dies forever as soon as we touch them." I remember another phrase as well, the title of an invaluable book by the anthropologist Jorge Pozzobon: *Vocês, brancos, não têm alma*—You, whites, have no soul.

We touched them. And whenever we touch them, we bring on extermination. Like fiction's worst aliens, we landed and killed them in so many ways. And we learned nothing, because we just keep on exterminating them.

We are still, in large part, the same people who prompted the first genocide, in 1500. The Brazilian Constitution of 1988, which guarantees the protection of original peoples, has been suffering attacks on all flanks. And it suffers the worst of assaults every day: the assault of not being enforced. Whites do not keep their word. They have words to write the law but do not keep them.

I don't know what the Araweté elder sees. I know what I see. Before me is someone who is a world unto himself. Someone who should not need to be here. And all we have to offer are red plastic chairs and disincarnate words.

He takes out a kind of long cigar. Lights it. The Araweté elder descends the convention center stairs with difficulty. And vanishes into the city that smells like sewage.

I leave there a monster.

2041. Eduardo

On April 16, 2021, four years after the birth of Alice the more-than-human, another offspring of the forest was born, someone who resembles her. Although human, Eduardo also left his mother's womb endangered, and by even more powerful predators. Like Gumercinda the turtle, Eduardo's father was being hunted too. Not so they could turn him into a commodity, but because he was fighting to keep the forest from being turned into one. In the Brazil of Bolsonaro, whose main power project has been the marketing of the Amazon, Eduardo was born into exile inside his own country.

Eduardo's father, Erasmo, was born in Altamira to a migrant couple; his mother, Natalha, is the daughter of quilombolas. Just months before Eduardo came into the world, his parents had to abandon their home and the region of Anapu and Volta Grande do Xingu to save their very lives. With them went Natalha's three small children (whom Erasmo also considers his) and a high-risk pregnancy. Erasmo had found the best possible partner in Natalha, a dauntless woman and plainspoken feminist. It was the second time that death threats had come so close to actual death that Erasmo was forced to disappear to stay alive.

Born in hiding in the midst of the COVID-19 pandemic, Eduardo was also destined to be a forest warrior. Not by choice, since his innocence still protects him from this horror, but by contingency. Children like Eduardo can't choose between fighting and not fighting. It's either fight, or die by gunshot or with a rope around your neck. They come into the world fighting, and being born alive is their first victory. Sometimes, the only one.

It's curious how so many Brazilians, cushioned inside their bubbles, don't understand that in the Amazon (and I think in all the Brazils), we are always at war. This isn't a figure of speech, I literally mean war. For humans like Erasmo, waking up the next day is always a victory. Erasmo embodies another forestpeople, one still undergoing forestation and thus often made invisible, or even disdained, by socioenvironmental organizations: peasants, or the landless, or those who have in recent years been resettled under agrarian programs in the Amazon—poor people from all the Brazils in search of ground not to market but to live on, who eventually reach the many Amazons or sometimes find themselves left over there at the end of huge construction projects like Belo Monte.

In 2005, these people in the process of forestation became more visible when six gunshots killed Dorothy Stang, a US missionary. Stang was murdered for defending peasants who were part of agroecological projects and thereby threatening the interests of the region's land grabbers, or grileiros. They became more visible because a white nun, a citizen of the United States, was slain in the middle of the forest. But then these people went back to their obscurity and to being killable, with even more of them dying starting in 2015.

When I first met Erasmo Alves Theofilo, I was captivated by this person who scurried about in a cheap plastic deck chair, the stackable kind. Erasmo caught polio because there was no vaccine in the region where he lived, so he can't walk. But he leads. And fights for the lives of three hundred families of small farmers and fishers in Volta Grande do Xingu and Anapu. With his motionless legs, Eduardo's father moves more than most Brazilians to keep the forest standing.

To me, this person who moved so quickly through the forest in a white deck chair, and leading all the while, was remarkable enough. But then Erasmo surprised me a bit more, turning into one of the most extraordinary people I've ever known. I owe him (and others) an entire book. Erasmo announced he wasn't a man but a "being." When he filled out the form for the protection of human rights defenders, he put down "nonbinary gender." Natalha had taught him—no, them—the term. Before that, they had often introduced themself as "bisexual." I realized then that if this peasant leader from Anapu, one of the most violent, patriarchal, and *machista* regions of the Amazon, can be a "nonbinary being," it is possible for us to create another world, a world of livingkind.

Peasant leaders like Erasmo, Indigenous, beiradeiro, and quilombola, are not vulnerable because they're weak. The forest remains standing only because these incredibly resistant peoples place their bodies on the front lines, raising a human barricade against the advance of the grileiros. The problem is that they're practically alone in their fight to keep the forest alive and sustain it as a public, collective asset for humans and more-than-humans. And they're fighting against forces that are much more powerful than them—and armed.

In Anapu, the people who fall are family farmers trying to establish agroecological settlements in public areas that have been set aside for agrarian reform but are coveted or already exploited by the region's big grileiros. The people who support them also fall. The grileiros portray themselves as fazendeiros—owners of large farms or ranches—but their rap sheets show they are federal land thieves.

In late 2019, under the protection of Jair Bolsonaro and his administration, the grileiros in the Amazon were acting as if they were convinced they had official authorization to threaten, beat up, and kill. They were making trouble in public places, provoking their opponents, and proudly crowing: "No judge orders me around." I asked Erasmo, ever closer to an unnatural death and living in a house accessible on all flanks, if they believed in the law. Their answer: "I do. If I didn't, I wouldn't be here."

Erasmo lives in a land where the fittest person is the law.

Erasmo is the weakest in the land ruled by the law of the fittest. And Erasmo believes in the law, the law represented by the Brazilian Constitution, the law supposedly above individuals, which defends the collectivity. I feel like repeating this sentence dozens of times and writing it backward and upside down to see if the mystery reveals itself from some angle. Seated in the white plastic chair that serves as their legs, battered a thousand times over, Erasmo is a Brazilian who believes in the law. And also because they believe in the law, they have had to flee twice to stay alive. As of this writing, a network of allies is working with Erasmo to organize their third escape. Three months after their return, they and Natalha will have to take their children far away. Forcing someone to flee is an act of violence against an adult, but even more so against a child, who then cannot attend school. But grileiro aircraft have been flying over Erasmo's house at treetop level, both to intimidate and to do reconnaissance. And a gunman disguised as a farmer knocked on their door in hopes of getting in to identify Erasmo's face and map out the space.

To understand who Erasmo is, and also understand the Brazil where Eduardo was born in hiding because his father had a target drawn on their head, we must understand the context and history of Amazonians like him. As an agroecological peasant, Erasmo understands the act of planting as an intimate relationship with the forest, where ongoing regeneration is determinant and also bound up with community life itself. Peasants regenerate with the forest at each cycle. The forest is the commons, to be lived with in communion. Foresting themselves is thus an imperative that radically differentiates peasants from the predators of the forest, who hide under the convenient umbrella of "agribusiness"—where "business" is all about reducing the forest to a commodity.

The ceremony marking the fifteenth anniversary of Dorothy Stang's execution can be viewed as a photograph. It was February 12, 2020, and the community was planting a cross beside the missionary's tomb. On it, a list of the names of those executed because of land conflicts in Anapu since Dorothy's death: along with her, twenty-two men, according to a survey by the Pastoral Land Commission.

It is important to note that nineteen of these twenty-two executions took place after 2015. From 2006 to 2014, an eight-year period that began with the close of Lula's second term and ended with Dilma Rousseff's reelection, the region saw no murders related to agrarian conflict. The ceasefire was broken in 2015 and violence exploded, with seven murders. By then, Rousseff had appointed the ruralist Kátia Abreu as minister of agriculture, and the most influential portion of the Workers' Party inside the government was emitting eloquent signals of support for the ruralist bloc and an interest in undermining FUNAI. This position was defended publicly by Gleisi Hoffmann, one of the party's key organizers in Congress. Another six deaths occurred in 2016, the year Rousseff was impeached and Michel Temer sworn in. It hasn't stopped since. In December 2019, the close of Bolsonaro's first year in office, two men were murdered in just five days. More corpses were being sown—and impunity established. The signals emitted by Brasília find their first echo in the Amazon.

We must now expand the frame of this photograph to include the people paying their respects at Dorothy's tomb. These men and women knew they might be her next year, their existence reduced to a name. One more name on that cross. This is how it has gone. You transmute from one place to another without any of the state powers stepping in to avert the massacre. To the contrary, as Bolsonaro goes about turning the state into a militia, the boundaries are increasingly blurry.

Where will each of them be on the next anniversary of Dorothy Stang's death? Every year, this becomes a more menacing question in Anapu, a municipality that emblematizes the intersection of the forest and grilagem. In other regions of the Amazon, the predators are sometimes members of organized crime who head up illegal mining operations on Indigenous lands or, other times, large transnational mining companies that crush the forest within the bounds of the law. They may likewise be loggers toppling trees to export timber without invoicing it, or loggers toppling trees to produce timber bearing certification stamps and false invoices. In Anapu, the bullets come from grilagem—and from timber.

Standing among the agroforested before the cross, I feel tears form rivers down my face, because this isn't the first time I've taken part in the ceremony and because I've been with living men who were reduced to corpses—and I've been with entire families who have fled so they wouldn't die, who couldn't even mourn their slain relatives. As I write this text, Erasmo sends me a picture of Eduardo, and a message: "I don't think it's fair for me to die fighting for what is right."

We must, however, look even farther. Look at who isn't there but who is still formally alive, like Father Amaro Lopes. Parish priest of Anapu and one of the people carrying on Dorothy's work, Father Amaro was criminally charged and detained in March 2018 during a ludicrous operation by the region's police forces: fifteen men and several squad cars arrived to arrest an unarmed priest who was preparing for the day's tribulations. The cleric was treated like Al Capone of the Amazon—but a gay Al Capone, in an effort to discredit him in the eyes of a conservative society. Some of the press thought it clever to make jokes about the title of a classic novel by the Portuguese writer Eça de Queirós: *The Crime of Father Amaro*. A more discerning mind would realize the facts pointed in the other direction: the crimes *against* Father Amaro.

The cleric spent three months in the Altamira penitentiary, the same one where fifty-eight detainees were decapitated or burned alive in July 2019. His cell was near that of Regivaldo Galvão, nickname Taradão, one of the men behind Dorothy Stang's execution. Although Father Amaro was later released while awaiting trial, his arrest effectively neutralized his pastoral work, which was the goal of those who had engineered his criminalization. He was not allowed to attend the tribute to his longtime friend.

Likewise excluded from this photographic scene are dozens of peasants who are afraid of being spotted and then attacked on their way home, because there are spies standing around the cross that lists the dead and among the people under the threat of sharing the cross with the dead in the near future. In 2019, the administrative region known as the Legal Amazon was the stage for 60 percent of the land conflicts in Brazil. Brutality is worse in the forest as well: 84 percent of homicides involving land conflicts were committed there. This is no accident, nor is it because this is a lawless land, a cliché belied by the facts. There has always been law in the Amazon. The question is, which law—and who is in charge of it.

These inflicted deaths are the most extreme act. Grileiros (by now familiar in these pages) operate with gunmen to carry out crimes against human bodies. To carry out crimes against the body of the forest, they operate by co-opting personnel inside the state's security forces and Judicial Branch, as well as notary publics and their staff, who forge the documents needed to appropriate land and sell it. (In a few paragraphs, I'll have to revise this information. But for now, it still makes sense.)

The grileiros learned something from Dorothy Stang's execution: certain murders draw a lot of attention. Some of the dead, even after they've stopped breathing, can force the state to fulfill its constitutional obligations. When these people become martyrs, they're more work dead than alive.

This is what began happening in 2005, when the six bullets that pierced Dorothy's body called the world's attention to Anapu and the Amazon—and state agencies then began taking action in the region, interfering with the grileiros' profits. In private conversations with third parties, certain representatives of this banditry in the form of public land theft and speculation admitted that killing off Dorothy had been a bad idea. Bad for business. From that point on, those who ordered the murders of peasants and people with ties to the peasant movement made sure they told their gunmen to do their killing in the city, in urban areas, so it would be harder to link the crimes to land conflicts.

The arrest, rather than murder, of Father Amaro Lopes heralded a new modus operandi: for the anonymous, death; for better-known figures and those with institutional ties, ruined reputations and criminalization. This tactic is an old standby for secret services in authoritarian countries—and also for militias and other organized political groups.

In the Amazon, the criminalization of Father Amaro was the precursor of what would happen to four firefighters in Alter do Chão, likewise in Pará, who were arrested in November 2019 under the farcical charge that they had been setting fires in the forest. Killing four upper-middle-class youth from São Paulo, even in Bolsonaro's Brazil, might get complicated, but criminalizing and publicly humiliating them has the effect of paralyzing them and setting an example for others who might be contemplating a move to the Amazon to fight to conserve the forest. Those who amass hefty profits by converting the woods into timber, soybeans, beef cattle, ore, and land for speculation don't want anyone getting in their way, much less those whose voices can reach farther, breaking through the barriers separating North from South.

In recent years, the grileiros have evidently realized even more than this. If murder is still a common method for stifling resistance, terrorizing people may be more efficient and leave fewer traces. Moreover, it draws less attention. For many leaders, fear is now as constant an element in their daily lives as air. Anyone who has lived with fear knows that inhaling fear along with oxygen is one of the most crushing experiences you can have. If you are conscious, you know you're alive because you feel fear. Sleeping, entering the oblivion needed to restore your body, eventually becomes impossible because you fear you won't wake up. Then come the hallucinations triggered by constant vigil.

This is how many leaders—peasants, Indigenous, quilombo-las, and beiradeiros—have been living in the Amazon. In recent years, there have been fewer movements of people occupying land for the purpose of living on it. It's easy to see why: greater risk. But even though there have been fewer actions and occupations, the violence has increased.

Christmas 2019, the first one with Bolsonaro in power, tells us much about this state of reality. While the advertising world was busy hailing the year's biggest family holiday, it was the season for Amazonian leaders to abandon their families in order to escape death. During the rest of the year, these leaders can still count on what is left of democracy in Brazil: basically, the Federal Public Prosecutor's Office and the federal and state public defender offices, agencies that can call in the Federal Police in extremely urgent cases. Or at least that is so in the few towns where these institutions have a functioning presence. The leaders also rely on nongovernmental organizations. But when public institutions enter their year-end recesses and NGOs go on collective holidays, the leaders have virtually no protection. The progressive absence of these institutions can already be felt early every November.

In 2019, the Bolsonaro effect prompted a mass exodus of those facing death threats. Some leaders traveled to places where they could count on someone else for support or had a minimal safety net. Others relied on nothing but the money raised when friends passed the hat, allowing them to vanish until the agencies resumed full-time operations. Upon returning home, one leader found their dogs shot to death, their chickens poisoned, and their calves with broken legs. "You're next." For another leader, spending Christmas and New Year's alone in a strange city where they couldn't walk around freely, since they were at risk anywhere in Brazil, was so hard on them that when they returned home, they clearly needed psychological support. It hasn't been hard to find psychologists, psychoanalysts, and psychiatrists who will see these people who are living under death threats. The problem is that there is no way to guarantee these individuals' safety on their way to the provider's office. If, on the other hand, the provider goes to a home being watched by the grileiros' militias, then one more person is at risk. And internet instability makes virtual visits hard in the Amazon.

Erasmo Alves Theofilo was first forced to flee during Christmas 2019. They returned only in February 2020, in time to join the community in remembering the fifteenth anniversary of Dorothy Stang's death, a moment of union and resistance for region peasants. Erasmo arrived late because they and several of their comrades had spent the night in vigil, since a grileiro had threatened to set fire to the whole settlement—things and people. Erasmo missed the mass but not the community luncheon. Two of the people in charge of the event have been strategic to interweaving life in the region: the missionaries Jane Dwyer and Katia Webster, members of the Congregation of the Sisters of Notre Dame de Namur, a religious order whose mission statement is to "stand with people living in poverty . . . in the most abandoned places." As friends and comrades of Dorothy Stang, they have carried on this work with tremendous personal courage. But they prefer to stay out of the spotlight.

The figure of Dorothy Stang—a martyr who is becoming a saint in peasants' eyes—is a strong unifying element in a region where your life hangs by a bullet. The white VW Beetle Dorothy once drove around the interior now sits next to her tomb. Today, her memory is a force that acts, a symbolic body that could not be killed. And Jane and Katia work to keep the martyr's memory present. Jane is more expansive, ironic, and talkative; Katia, more assertive, wary, and reserved, sometimes mordant. Jane, plumper, made of curves; Katia, thinner, formed of right angles. Both, very strong and determined not to retreat. "Being alive is a risk," says Jane, blinking her lively blue eyes, her mouth curling into a wry smile.

Up until 2020, a dog named Petica was the women's main source of protection (besides "the people's attentiveness," as Jane puts it) at the frugal wooden home where they live under enemy watch. Petica was a shorty with a dark, wheat-colored coat, and she was fierce. "She understood she was our protection, and she assumed her task diligently and with real grit," Jane says gravely, paying posthumous homage. Unlike the humans around her, Petica left this world by way of natural death. She was famed for only attacking men—and right where they are most sensitive. After Petica went to heaven, her daughter Sofia and granddaughter Dandara, graduates of the same school, took over as the missionaries' personal bodyguards.

Prior to 2015, the sisters had accompanied the more at-risk whistleblowers to the police station to lend their support. In recent years, the social fabric has grown so frayed in Anapu that the sisters' presence has become an excuse for criminalizing peasants. The scene at the improvised altar at the mass Erasmo could not attend was eloquent. Seven men at the pulpit: one bishop and six priests. Hovering above them, the image of a woman, Dorothy Stang. Jane's and Katia's gray heads stood out in the crowd, where they were subtly weaving the threads of the events.

It was on that same February 12, 2020, that Pope Francis's exhortation Querida Amazônia, or Beloved Amazon, hit the news, with its refusal to allow women to serve as deacons. Officially, women would remain on the church's periphery. Disappointment, anger, and scorn ensued. "We only have to wait another one hundred years," scoffed one Catholic nun at the ceremony. At the Amazon Synod, a major event in 2019, regional bishops and community leaders had recommended that women be allowed to serve as deacons and that married men of "exemplary lives" be ordained, as a way of addressing the region's tragic dearth of priests. But Francis gave in to chronic conservative misogyny. The section of the exhortation that explains why women will continue in their subaltern position is a disturbing affront:

That approach . . . would lead us to clericalize women, diminish the great value of what they have already accomplished, and subtly make their indispensable contribution less effective. . . . Women make their contribution to the Church in a way that is properly theirs, by making present the tender strength of Mary, the Mother.

This papal claptrap prompted anger but also guffaws during the ceremony to honor Dorothy Stang. Given the abject way some clerics use the figure of Mary, she must often roll over in Catholic heaven. And it comes hand in hand with an abusive view of motherhood that enslaves women and leaves them frozen in place. These days, some are starting to see this as moral harassment.

The Catholic hierarchy is not familiar with the Amazon and prefers to remain deaf to those who are. Neo-Pentecostal Evangelicals are advancing throughout the region. This might be just another religious war, mattering little to those who fight like forest, were it not for an alarming fact: a portion of these Evangelicals have joined in the spoliation project. Market Evangelicals and predatory agribusiness have strengthened their ties inside the Bolsonaro government.

Francis's step backward at the Amazon Synod has undermined the women missionaries and community leaders who are on the front lines of the forestpeoples' struggle in regions like Anapu, one of the few areas where the Catholic Church remains strong. The Vatican's retrogression has stained the forest with blood. Even during the pandemic, Jane and Katia ignored the overlapping risks—not just bullets but the virus as well—and continued to stand alongside those under greatest threat. Whenever news of an attack reached the peasants, the nuns moved to the home of those targeted by the grileiros. Nobody would sleep, sometimes not even the children. With the gunmen ready to pounce, nights moved slowly in vigil, nourished by storytelling circles. At the time, Jane was past eighty, Katia nearly seventy. They belonged to a lineage begotten by liberation theology, later eroded under John Paul II's lengthy papacy and almost destroyed by the ultra-conservative Benedict XVI. With the weakening of Catholic base communities, there are no worthy successors in training.

The Amazon Synod sent an important signal to the world, and the climate crisis has been a central theme in Francis's papacy. But this betrayal of the women missionaries and Catholic laypeople who risk their lives in the forest was a historical missed opportunity that will have major repercussions for the church in Rome, already in sharp decline in the region. In Northern Brazil, Evangelicals are now tied with Catholics in number. In this setting, Anapu is a stronghold of resistance thanks to the work of the Pastoral Land Commission—embodied by two women born in the United States who adopted the Amazon as their motherland.

The conflicts in Anapu, where Eduardo will grow up watched over by his brave missionary grandmothers, are products of the Transamazonian Highway. In the 1970s, the dictatorship divided the region into two poles, called Transa-West and Transa-East. Extending from Altamira to Placas, the first stretch was earmarked for official settlement and agricultural production, and the majority who settled there were from Southern Brazil. Along Transa-East, between Altamira and Marabá, settlement was predominantly spontaneous, attracting those who are always forgotten by official public programs, mostly migrants from Northeast Brazil. The latter didn't receive any government support when they settled these lands that had been deemed less productive. It must be remembered that for centuries all this land, from east to west, has been the home of Indigenous peoples and peoples of other species.

This history began with the genocide of various peoples, human and more-than-human, perpetrated by the dictatorship when it gashed through the forest to build the Transamazonian

Highway. That was one part of it. The other was the continuation of the country's whitening policy, initiated more than a century earlier, during the imperial period. When the Transamazonian was built, new colonizers were brought from Southern Brazil, mostly descendants of the European immigrants who had colonized that region. Things weren't easy for the European immigrants who reached Southern Brazil in the nineteenth century, nor were they easy for their descendants when they reached the Transamazonian in the 1970s. It was a saga. But it was much harder for the Northeasterners who landed in the Amazon aboard flatbed trucks, no invitation and no government support, pursuing their dream to have some ground so they would no longer have to rent their bodies to the rural barons.

In the same region, the dictatorship enacted a land concentration policy that answered to the bureaucratic name Contracts for the Alienation of Public Lands. These contracts defined the terms and conditions for selling three-thousand-hectare lots of public lands, offered primarily to people outside the Amazon region. The contracts often were accompanied by financing through the Superintendency for the Development of the Amazon, or SUDAM, an acronym made famous by its corruption scandals.

According to the terms for converting these Contracts for the Alienation of Public Lands into definitive titles, applicants were supposed to pay a stipulated amount and then, within five years, prove they had opened an agricultural or livestock-raising company. But many of the properties were sold to third parties long before that. In a good number of cases, the government didn't even cancel the title when the purchaser failed to set up the required company in time. Moreover, instead of registering the papers as pledges to buy and sell, which is what they effectively were, deed registrars filed them as actual land titles. By way of this tortuous path, public lands and public financing generated and fed a land speculation market in the Amazon, accompanied by a cycle of grilagem and gunslinging that endures today—and is the major culprit behind the destruction of the forest and its human and more-than-human peoples.

The deaths registered on the cross in Anapu, and the threats experienced by leaders like Erasmo Theofilo in recent years, are a direct product of the forest exploitation project forged during the twenty-one-year business-military dictatorship and never adequately reformed under the democracy inaugurated in 1985. When Bolsonaro arrived, he and his militarized government found a structure already in place for expanding predation of the forest. They didn't invent anything; they just picked up the pace and guaranteed official support to the criminals.

The predators' manual was written under the dictatorial regime and never shredded by the ensuing democratic governments, because power never left the hands of the predatory elites who have ruled Brazil since the beginning of its invention as a nation-state. The elites have never seen their privileges seriously threatened. On the few occasions when they have felt their status quo slightly disturbed—through concessions to other sectors of the population or victories by parts of society they deem subaltern, such as during the government of João Goulart (1961–1964) and under the Workers' Party (PT) administrations of Lula and Dilma Rousseff (2003–2016)—there had been a coup.

To stanch the blood being spilled in the disputes over lands in the Amazon that belong to the federal government, constitutional obligations would need to be met, and that would mean demarcating all Indigenous lands and expanding conservation areas, while adequately staffing and funding inspection agencies. This much is obvious. It would likewise be necessary to enact the agrarian reform that never was, ensuring the formal settlement and safety of the peasants who are already in the forest with the purpose of living there without expropriating it and who also commit to planting according to the principles of agroecology. And this is less obvious.

A portion of environmentalists still maintain a mistrustful, sometimes biased distance from family farmers, who tend to have closer ties to organizations like the Pastoral Land Commission and Landless Workers movement as well as to leftist unions. This distance hurts everyone. Exchange, mutual support, and the forestation and reforestation of bodies are needed. The dynamics of these conflicts have proven that without agrarian reform, blood will continue to flow in the Amazon. And without agrarian reform, there will be no climate justice.

After Brazil's return to democracy, the best chance to stop the blood came under the PT, which held the presidency from 2003 to 2016. The party listed agrarian reform on its government program, and family farmers and landless workers were relevant forces within its base. While some actions and policies were implemented, the reform was never concluded. And the historical window closed once again.

The Sustainable Development Projects defended by Dorothy Stang were established on lots that INCRA declared nonproductive in the late 1990s. Drafted at peasant assemblies, these projects blended family farming and plant extractivism, as the beiradeiros of the Amazon do. They were agrarian reform projects that guaranteed land to those living from and on it, incorporating the concept of environmental conservation. Rather than simply abandon public lands in speculators' hands, the government would earmark these areas for family farming and the settlement of thousands of people who would live on the land, and off it, while also producing a surplus to feed the country. This represented a choice about what to do with public lands allocated for agricultural production. Instead, these public lands were used for speculation and profiteering, engendering more destruction of the forest and the forestpeoples.

During Lula's first term as president, four Sustainable Development Projects were opened in the Anapu region for the settlement of six hundred families. Those who had taken possession both of public lands and of fat public financing reacted violently, resorting to gunslinging, arson, and deforestation. Dorothy Stang documented and denounced every one of the attacks and demanded that the authorities step in. She defended the idea that land tenure regulation was the requisite first step to forest conservation. She was executed.

During the PT's thirteen-plus years in power, its administrations formed ever closer ties to latifundiários and made concessions to the agribusiness sectors of soybeans and cattle, the latter for export as animal protein. During Lula's first term, however, the administration had still shown a strong commitment to peasants in practice. Not strong enough for effective agrarian reform, but strong enough for the state to be sent into the region following Dorothy's murder.

There were compelling signs that the missionary's execution had been determined by the "death consortium," a pool of grileiros that decided which people to erase whenever someone hampered their assaults on the forest. While the existence of this death consortium has never been proven, hardly anyone in the region doubts it. Whether in partnership or not, the grileiros kept at it persistently, if discreetly, through 2014. From 2015 on, the violence in Anapu reflected the increased power enjoyed by ruralists not only in Congress but also in the Executive Branch, which brought a resurgence in murders of peasant leaders and people with ties to them, culminating with the election of Jair Bolsonaro and his avowedly pro-predation government.

In 2018, a list of individuals marked for death was circulating in Anapu like a list of back-to-school supplies. Shortly before he was killed, on June 3 of that year, Leoci Resplandes de Sousa went to check whether his name was on the list. One of the heads of the local gunmen guaranteed he wasn't. He even said that if Leoci were, he'd scratch his name off. That's how things went. And still go. We don't know if the head man was lying, because not only was Leoci murdered, so was the head man, sometime later. The list—or lists—are still in place.

So far, three members of the Resplandes family—three rural workers who wanted their own land—have been murdered: Hércules, seventeen; Valdemir, forty-seven; and Leoci, twenty-nine. All in 2018. When Leoci was murdered inside his home after returning from the fields one day, the family fled Anapu. That's how the Resplandes live: bouncing around the map of Brazil, fleeing, without any support. And they are found. In November 2019, another Resplandes was shot but survived. It is uncertain whether this attempted homicide had anything to do with events in Anapu, but it's likely. Grileiros who call themselves "rural producers" and tear around in lavish 4x4s produce very little other than human bodies.

Iracy Resplandes dos Santos has lived at bay since losing three family members. When I last spoke to her, she was in hiding and clearly suffering from depression. They told her she could appease her pain by knitting. But Iracy would start knitting and then just couldn't go on. Her only dream had been to have a little plot of land to live on. She ended up planting her son, brother, and nephew in tombs she cannot visit now. And there are no indications that the sowing of human bodies will stop.

In November 2019, the tension was so great that whenever I went to Anapu, I was anxious to cross back over the river, and even more anxious until the barge finally kissed land. Márcio Rodrigues dos Reis, thirty-three, father of four young daughters, was murdered on December 4. The killer pretended to be a customer wanting a ride on Márcio's motorcycle taxi, and then killed him by stabbing him in the neck. As they say in the city: a slit throat means the victim "died because they talked too much."

Márcio was one of Father Amaro Lopes's key defense witnesses. He was also someone who knew a lot about what was happening in the region. Five days later, on December 9, Paulo Anacleto, former city council member for the PT, was executed in front of his young son on the city's central square. According to witnesses, he and the child were in a car when he was targeted by two men on a motorcycle. As Márcio's personal friend, Anacleto had been upset enough about the murder to go around the streets of Anapu saying he knew the instigator's name.

There were growing signs that the violence would only get worse. With Bolsonaro encouraging the advance on the forest and with the legalization of public land thefts a possibility, the grileiros continued their assault on peasants, while they also began fighting among themselves over the loot. Brazil was founded on the destruction of the original peoples in order to usurp land and violate nature. So the laws that regulate the ownership and use of the loot were invented by those who did the usurping and violating. This logic has been perpetuated throughout the evolution of capitalism. In other nations, certain adjustments have been made to appease contemporary sensibilities. Not in Brazil. Even in recent history, the system continues to reproduce itself—now laundered in the bleaching agent of democracy.

Both Lula and Michel Temer signed provisional measures that went into law, wielding their official pens to turn public land thieves into law-abiding citizens—an even greater miracle than Jesus Christ turning water to wine at the Cana wedding. In 2009, Lula legalized the theft of plots of public land not exceeding 1,500 hectares, as long as they had been "occupied" before 2004. In 2017, Temer legalized the theft of plots of public land not exceeding 2,500 hectares, as long as they had been "occupied" before 2011. From the outset of his government, Bolsonaro tried to surpass his predecessors by legalizing public land stolen before 2018, the year of his election—since the spree would be guaranteed after he took power. But given strong pressure inside and outside Brazil, the provisional measure did not come to a vote and the draft law that replaced it pushed the deadline back, while maintaining the expansion of self-declared land "regulation." In short, since there's no oversight, you simply declare yourself the owner.

The mere possibility that Congress might pass this law led to an explosion of land invasions and violence. Expectations have been destroying the Amazon forever. Suffice it to announce the construction of a road or railway or hydro plant—or the drafting of a law benefiting grilagem—and the map of deforestation and land invasion undergoes immediate changes dramatically for the worse. The predators move swiftly and savagely—and leaders like Erasmo fall.

Since the end of the business-military dictatorship, Bolsonarism has offered the best chances for the Amazon's big destroyers to transform themselves into "upstanding citizens" and duly legalized latifundiários. Bolsonaro's rise to power therefore requires us to update the concept of grilagem. With the crime now legalized and criminals rewarded, grileiros no longer need to corrupt a single government employee, since land grabbers are progressively morphing from outlaws into law-abiding citizens and steadily becoming the law itself. Indications are strong that in some cases the police are playing the role previously assigned to gunmen—not working with them, as in the past, but replacing them.

The grileiros, who for decades have gotten themselves elected as mayors and held seats in municipal legislatures in Amazon cities, have also come to hold office in the federal Congress and Executive Branch in Brasília. Under Bolsonaro, the phenomenon attained a new scale and space-probe speed. Taking the path of militias, grilagem in the Amazon is shifting from being a parallel form of power with branches in the state to being the state itself, something true of Rio de Janeiro militias for some time now, with the support of the Bolsonaro clan.

Ever since major criminal factions—like First Capital Command (PCC), with roots in São Paulo, and the Red Command (CV), from Rio de Janeiro—reached Amazonian cities, there have been concerns that grilagem, whose interest is land speculation, will form an alliance with organized urban crime, whose realm of action is the trafficking of drugs, arms, and a constantly growing list of other goods. All signs are that criminal factions have already begun entering the forest, via mining. In 2021, increased violence plus the quality and quantity of weapons used by wildcat miners in Yanomami territory, on the border with Venezuela, have been linked to the First Capital Command. There is evidence that this powerful criminal faction controls some twenty thousand miners now working in the region, presenting an unprecedented level of risk for this forestpeople. These "prospectors" are willing to take on the Federal Police and the army.

Artisanal mining, which is much less predatory, has been steadily replaced by reliance on large machinery, the extensive use of mercury and other toxic products, and the exercise of control through armed violence. When the global crisis of 2008 drove the price of gold up, this trend surged, eventually achieving its early 2020s level thanks to the active participation of members of Congress and even ministers. In early 2020, Bolsonaro proposed a law to legalize mining on Indigenous lands, keeping a promise made to his voter base, which comprises predators of the Amazon.

As we can readily see, crime and criminal land speculation are deforesting the forest, much as what we have witnessed in favelas and periphery communities in cities like Rio de Janeiro. Bolsonaro, friendly both with the militias that control much of organized crime in Rio de Janeiro State and with public land speculators in the Amazon, embodies this bridge like no other figure in Brazilian history. When he was still serving in the army, he tried his own luck with illegal mining, drawn by gold lust and the promise of getting rich quick. He hadn't yet discovered he could accomplish this as a lazy but noisy politician and by putting his whole family into the business.

To address this monstrous situation, where the machinery of the state has played an ever-greater role, unarmed peasants, one pair of elderly nuns, and a leader in a white plastic chair—because a chair equipped with wheels can't always get around in the forest or on the city's rough streets—have occupied Anapu's front lines. These people's courage and personal strength surpass that of any fictional character. But if they continue having to confront an attack of this magnitude all alone, there will be no way to keep the Amazon from reaching the point of no return.

This was the Amazon where Eduardo was born.

On the eve of September 7, 2021, Independence Day in Brazil, Eduardo and his family were once again forced to leave their home to keep from being killed. The intervals of relative safety had grown shorter. Eduardo wasn't even five months old and already had to flee for the second time. When I said goodbye to them all, his father, surrounded by dozens of peasants who had answered the summons, was wearing delicate blue fingernail polish. Courage lies in the details as well. For me, those blue nails augured that I would see my godson Eduardo again.

2042. amazon center of the world

I had first met Erasmo Alves Theohlo during an extraordinary moment in Amazonian life. It was November 18, 2019. I was on the opening panel at the meeting of the Amazon Center of the World movement, in Altamira. To my left was an Indigenous man of the Canela people. To my right, Erasmo. In front of us, Kayapó warriors in ritual formation, there to provide security for Raoni—the Indigenous Amazon leader nominated for a Nobel Peace Prize—and in fact to protect all of us. Some local grileiros, politicians, and businesspeople tried hard to disrupt the meeting, shouting at everyone who spoke. They were incited by an anthropologist who works for the predatory agribusiness sector and whose father is an Evangelical pastor accused of Indigenous genocide. The grileiros chose their spot in the audience and then announced: "We're sitting to the right." The Catholic missionaries Katia and Jane responded by sitting down among the grileiros—without uttering a word, they showed through their gesture that they would not be intimidated. At least one of those seated next to the sisters was suspected of belonging to the "death consortium" said to have decreed the executions of Dorothy Stang and other peasant leaders. A bit earlier, Silvério Fernandes, the noisiest member of one of the region's main grileiro families, had interrupted Juma Xipaia while she was talking; he shouted and came at her, practically poking her in the chest, this woman who is one of the forest's most amazing warriors. He was surrounded by Kayapó and Xipaya people and invited by the Federal Police to leave the campus of the Federal University of Pará. The police had been called in because grileiros were summoning Brazilians from all over to head to Altamira, and these threats had left the city tense for days. The scene was a precise portrait of how we live in the Amazon; its ending was not. There are no Federal Police in the deep rain-forest to protect the original peoples. Instead of words, there are bullets, and the grileiros (almost) always win.

Erasmo picked up the microphone. Since they couldn't rise to speak, they raised their voice. And raised it high. "I apologize to the Indigenous community for what our people have done!" Erasmo spoke and cried. It was a catharsis. When they had finished, they were surrounded by the Indigenous, quilombolas, and beira-deiros. The first hand to cover theirs was Kayapó, and then hands of all earth tones piled atop. The alliance for the Amazon was consummated at that moment, spontaneously, by people who had until only recently kept a cautious, at times even hostile, distance from each other, people who had killed each other in the past but who now joined forces as allies in the name of the forest, well be-yond any geopolitical sense. It was an alliance of forest-humans against predator-humans, of life against all forms of death. It was an alliance invoked in the name of resistance. My hand—still so white—was part of this scene.

Amazon Center of the World is a concept—and a movement. When I and others assert that the Amazon is central, we are not playing with words or making some rhetorical appeal but are de-manding a true displacement—or demanding the recognition of what *is*, but is treated as if it were not. Who decides what is cen-ter and what is periphery? And why? Based on what? The politi-cal dispute over centralities is strategic. And it is imperative to retake the center.

Now I need to retrace the movement traveled in these pages in order to establish this concept. The banzeiro is twisting round again but now in the sense of *òkòtó*, the word from the Yoruba language found in the title of this book. This word was given to me during a *jogo de buzios*—divination using cowrie shells—that I did with Rodney de Oxóssi, a *babalorixá*, anthropologist, and writer. The word arrived and took hold of both my perception of this movement and the title of this book. Whispered by the *orixá* Exu, it was more than another turn. *Òkòtó* is a helix, a snail shell, holding an ossified history; it spirals upward, twisting away from its base like a toy top. With each revolution, the *òkòtó* expands "ever more, until transforming into a circle opened to the infinite." Amazon Center of the World is the banzeiro transfiguring into *òkòtó*.

When our way of life altered the planet's climate, when we became a geological force capable of ripping ourselves from the Holocene and into the Anthropocene (an argument made by a growing number of scientists), and when we triggered the sixth mass extinction of species, we put ourselves up against the greatest challenge in human history. After deleting thousands of species from Earth and endangering thousands of others, we've brought our own species to the brink of extinction. This is our now, our expanded present. But as I wrote in earlier chapters, there is a logical problem in treating what is legitimate from a biological standpoint as an all-encompassing truth.

For the field of biology, we are one species, the one we call "human," pursuant to a set of genetic, morphological, and other criteria. But we have stretched this classification into a philosophical concept, that of humanity. However, while all of us with certain biological markers may be part of the same species, we aren't necessarily part of the same humanity. This "we, humans," simply doesn't exist. Because when we utter the word *we*, we are speaking of something not limited to biology; we have entered the realm of philosophy, social science, and—mainly—politics. And politics is a realm of ongoing dispute.

Stating that the human species caused the climate catastrophe is not only imprecise; it is erroneous. If, as the Indigenous thinker Ailton Krenak proposes, humanity is an exclusive club restricted to the dominant minority, it is accurate to say that humanity has caused the climate collapse, global heating, and the sixth mass extinction. And while the subhumanities, as Krenak calls them—formed by those who have been left outside the electrified walls of the "exclusive humanity club"—never caused these catastrophes or the destruction of the only house we all share, they are the first to suffer the consequences of these disasters.

In formulating the Amazon Center of the World movement, we have endeavored to be as clear and precise as possible, because the topic is still new and challenging for many and, unfortunately, not yet addressed much in schools. Repeating: the climate catastrophe and sixth mass extinction have been caused by a dominant minority composed of the financially wealthy within consumer countries, especially billionaires and supermillionaires, and by the financially wealthy within consumed countries, especially billionaires and supermillionaires. This dominant minority has a color—mostly white—and it also has a sex and a gender, since these decisions have almost always been made by men who present themselves as cisgender.

Yet those hardest hit by the climate crisis are those who haven't produced it, like Black and Indigenous peoples; women; those who have clung to the land, like forestpeoples; and those dispossessed of everything, including their identity, and reduced to the generic category "poor." The hardest hit are also the more-than-human peoples. The United Nations has called this inequality, which will increasingly define all others, "climate apartheid." But perhaps the term *apartheid* assumes that those on the outside want to be let in. And this is neither the point nor their desire.

The belief that the greatest desire of anyone and everyone who isn't currently consuming is to sit down at the consumer table, just like the belief that the only thing a "nation" can want is to grow infinitely (as if that were possible), is part of the dominant minority's mentality. However, the majority of the Others who are called original peoples and traditional communities, as their elders and ancestors point out, don't want to come in and become further devourers of worlds. What they *do* want is to keep the house they belong to alive—a house they neither own nor wish to own. They only want to live in it and with it, on their own terms. Because they are part of it, they are Other and the same. As previously stated in this book, we're not all in the same boat; this "we," which conceals asymmetries, doesn't even exist. The majority, who haven't produced the climate crisis, have but a tiny paper boat. Or the big canoe an Araweté told us about.

Responsibilities must be established so we can identify both the front lines of the climate war as well as the possibilities of life for the majority, who will remain outside the bunkers in New Zealand and the other, new postapocalyptic paradises exploited by billionaires and multimillionaires. Now that we've established that this "we" is a ruse used to blame those who were never to blame and to posit as part of the humanity club those who have never had either the privilege of belonging to it nor the desire to belong, our ability to imagine a future where it will be possible to live is determined by displacing what is center and what is periphery.

As we reach the turning point of the human-caused climate collapse and sixth mass extinction, the world's largest tropical rainforest is the center of the world. Or, more precisely put, the Amazon is one of the centers of the world, along with other enclaves where nature and nature-peoples resist capitalism, primarily, but also communism as implemented in regions of the globe like the former Soviet Union and China, the latter now in the process of cementing its position as the world's new superpower. Today the Amazon is as central as Washington, London, Paris, Frankfurt, Hong Kong, Moscow, Beijing. Or more so.

Those who intend to convert the forest into commodities—and the forestpeoples into the poor or into corpses—are aware of this. And they are in the forest. From local deforesters to transnational mining companies, from huge animal protein producers to China's state-owned energy companies—they all understand the centrality of the Amazon, but they understand it from the logic of predatory exploitation. The Amazon is one of the centers where the climate war is being waged—but waged as a massacre, given the disproportionate forces involved.

When I say "climate war," I'm not talking about a war on global heating or a war on the climate. What we are experiencing is a war between humans. On one side, the minority who eat up the planet, on the other, the minority who are eaten up along with the planet. It is a war between humans, but not between nations—and this is a crucial difference. This is also why we have witnessed the eruption of neonationalism throughout the 2010s, embodied in figures like Trump, Bolsonaro, and the rest.

Elected despots like Trump have manipulated the idea of nationalism so they can build walls. And who should be left outside these walls? Climate refugees, forced to leave their lands, devastated by drought or flood. The wave of Central American immigrants who headed toward the southern US border in late 2018 may have been the first great march of the climate diaspora. When journalists probed deeper with their questions, in many cases they discovered that major droughts lay at the root of this exodus. And then, provoked by climate transformation, came hunger, abject misery, and violence, the immediate reasons why masses of people abandoned their homes and countries, but not the primary reason. And we can all remember how these immigrants were treated.

Despots like Trump aren't the least bit concerned about the nation, or anything that anchors this concept. What Trump did (and will still do, if given the chance) was use nationalistic appeals to repress movements that are uniting humans above national flags and redefining today's impasse by defining who and where the enemies are. The rise in Black-led protests against racial inequality, which have intensified in the United States, Brazil, and other countries, is one example, as are the uprisings prompted by the new feminisms.

The climate war is a war of survival, but like every war of survival involving humans, it is a political one. And it must be waged politically. Amazon Center of the World is a political movement whose first proposition is to displace what is center and what is periphery, re-placing the Amazon and other enclaves of nature at the geopolitical centers of the human world on the planet.

In establishing the Amazon and other hot spots as centers of the world, the movement shifts the "we." We who? We, those who have clung to the earth and those who have chosen to stand alongside those who have clung to the earth, we affirm the centrality of the Amazon, much beyond "Amazon" in the current geopolitical sense. The Amazon is the planet's largest tropical rainforest and, at the same time, the symbol of a radical shift in thinking, and in thinking about humanities (now in the plural) *as* the planet. Not only in our way of thinking but in the very structure of thought. To Amazonize oneself is both an active and a reflexive verb that demands a shifting of geopolitical centers and also a transformation in the very structure of thought—a transfiguration of language.

The climate collapse is the product of a way of understanding the world that has been overwhelmingly defined by the white, Western, male, binary mode of thought. This way of understanding the world has not been conflict free. But even these conflicts—at least when they have been conflicts and not massacres—transpired as part of the same thought structure. The climate crisis cannot be confronted using the same mode of thought that generated it. The future depends on our ability to radically transform the way our species relates to itself and to what it calls nature. To this end, we need to generate not just new knowledge but also another mode of thought and even of language.

This is the second proposition of the Amazon Center of the World movement, as I understand it: to shift centralities in the realms of race, sex, and gender. And, very importantly, also to shift centralities in the realm of species, establishing an alliance between nature-humans and more-than-humans against predator-humans. The struggle of in-betweens and beings versus the planet eaters is not some fictional best seller—it has been happening for a long time now, and the original peoples who continue resisting today can tell us all about it.

The third proposition is to forge an alliance of forestpeoples and deforested peoples—or, to expand on this, between naturepeoples and converted-into-poor. Restoring the centrality of those called urban peripheries is as necessary as restoring the centrality of nature-peripheries. The majority of human peoples who have been reduced to the generic poor live in these enclaves, surviving solely through their desire to resist and their tremendous creative ability to invent solutions amid scarcity. It is vital to recognize the centrality of those on the margins who are fighting processes of genocide. Amazon Center of the World, as I see the movement, does not call on the "marginalized" to be let into the center. It is neither a request for permission to enter nor a request to be included in the system that led to the climate catastrophe. Rather, it is about recognizing the margins as what they are: centers of resistance against all forms of death and for the creation of possible lives, even amid the impossible. The margins not as exclusion but as insurgency. Only this alliance is capable of destroying the system that has corroded the planet, has converted the majority of human persons into the poor, and is now exterminating the more-than-human peoples.

In a city like São Paulo, the centrality of life and of processes of creation lies not in geographically central areas, where income is concentrated, but in outlying centers, like Paraisópolis, Brasilândia, and Capão Redondo. In Rio, centrality is not found on the financially wealthy South Side, near the beach, but in distant enclaves like Complexo da Maré and Complexo do Alemão. In Brasília, the federal capital, centrality is not found in the so-called Pilot Plan, but in satellite cities like Ceilândia.

Confronting the climate emergency means recognizing this centrality as the power to achieve a radical transformation in our way of life. Affirmative action, access to positions in the job market previously restricted to whites, and a presence at art exhibits and biennials are not enough. Perhaps these measures, tremendously tardy in Brazil and various other countries, would have been more meaningful in the past. Now the climate collapse demands that we be radical. It is not enough to remodel capitalism, as some would like; we must recast the human person. Amazon Center of the World argues that this recasting can only happen through the alliance of forestpeoples and deforested peoples.

The urban centralities known as peripheries were formed over centuries of deforestation, a process initiated when European monarchies launched their ships and sailed off to despoil new worlds by extracting resources from the bowels of Earth.

Despoiling nature in parts of the globe like Brazil and everywhere now known as America was a determinant of capital accumulation for the Industrial Revolution and the inauguration of the fossil fuel era, a process that has steadily corroded the planet and put us at risk of extinction.

Amazon Center of the World recoups the ancestry shared by the young urban Black man in a Rio de Janeiro favela—shot to death before turning twenty, at the hands of a militia or the police, always the same hands, or at the hands of nonmilitia organized crime—and the quilombola in the Amazon Forest— likewise shot to death, at the hands of loggers and grileiros, with growing ties to militias, or by mining, with growing ties to organized crime, or by the transnational companies that poison the earth and the rivers, under the cover of a perverse legality and the sanitizing jargon employed by major corporations to exterminate nature-peoples. This is the same genocidal process initiated centuries ago. When I declare that Brazil, as a nation-state, was founded atop human bodies, this is not a figure of speech, it is a historical fact. First the bodies of the Indigenous, then of enslaved Africans. Building this bridge out of shared memories and multiple identities is strategic to reforesting bodies and Amazonizing humans.

Marielle Franco—Black, lesbian, raised in the marginalized community of Complexo da Maré in Rio de Janeiro—shares the same ancestry as the quilombolas murdered in the forest. And she was slain by bullets for the same reason: because she dared occupy centrality with her body. The sorrow is the same—and so is the struggle.

I chose my side in the climate war, and this led my body to Altamira, one of the planet's multiple front lines. As I stated earlier, my challenge as a white woman is to learn to think, and to think about myself, in terms of radically different relationships with humans and more-than-humans. My challenge is to unwhiten myself—or, more specifically, make the movement toward unwhitening, something I'll never fully achieve. This is the journey you have taken with me on the slow walk through these pages. I've tried to share the process that brought me to now, that cast me into the banzeiro and will perhaps cast me into the òkòtó.

Many might think what I am saying is crazy, drug-induced, or just plain foolish. I'd like to point out that what is absurd, insane, and perverse is that a minority of humans dared overheat the planet and promote the sixth mass extinction. Think just how absurd this is: the temperature of an entire planet raised by degrees through the action of a minority of humans. Think how horrific this is: thousands of species of mammals, reptiles, amphibians, fish, birds, and insects vanishing thanks to a minority of humans. In the words of Greta Thunberg: "How dare you?"

The climate collapse and sixth mass extinction are inconceivable—and happening right now. It is the responsibility of the generations of humans alive today to rapidly change their way of inhabiting the planet. And this will not be accomplished merely by recycling trash, driving electric cars, or eating vegan. Today's challenge is to realize a much more radical transformation, consonant with the radical nature of what we have caused and are confronting. We must alter what it means to be human in our era, and with the generations now here. We must Amazonize ourselves. It is either that, or a terribly hostile future awaits us, right around the corner.

The COVID-19 pandemic, brought on largely by the destruction of the natural world, marks the moment when we reached this intersection. We are there. What is up for grabs right now is what we will find when we turn the corner. Neutralizing the novel coronavirus and all other future viruses is easier than overcoming the humans who act like viruses against their own species—with the crucial difference that the virus has no consciousness nor any intentions beyond its own survival, whereas the human minority now destroying the planet knows what it is doing, destroying worlds merely to maintain its unsustainable way of life, guarantee its enormous privileges, and accumulate more capital to keep this aberrant wheel spinning. If the virus had any type of consciousness along the lines of ours, it would be horrified to be compared to this breed of people.

Many conspiracy theories say the coronavirus originated in a Chinese laboratory, but evidence points to pathways much more terrible and real. In a way, the novel coronavirus, as well as the microorganisms that will spark the next pandemics, were and will be created by humans in the laboratory of capitalism, by disrupting the climate, destroying natural systems that support life, and pushing entire species to extinction, thus producing a deadly imbalance. The predators of nature are human viruses, and our war is against them. They too have the chance to stop killing their own species and reforest themselves. We, who are being killed, can neither wait nor merely hope. We must act.

Now. Yesterday.

Amazon Center of the World is a proposal to recast humans in order to create a future where it is possible to live with humans and more-than-humans. This idea moves, this idea is a word that acts.

2019. caravels of decolonization in terra do meio

The Amazon Center of the World meeting and movement were born together. First, through imagination. I don't think it would have been possible to imagine a meeting of climate activists from Fridays for Future and Extinction Rebellion with forest shamans in the deep Amazon—instead of some capital city in Europe, the United States, or Brazil—had I not been living between-worlds. Jair Bolsonaro had just been elected, and people who work with the security of human rights defenders and environmentalists had advised me to spend some time outside Brazil until we had a clearer idea of how likely it was for threats to turn into acts. I had already planned to visit my boyfriend in London, so I simply went a bit early. Jon and I have become a rather odd couple, who met and fell in love because of the Amazon and the climate collapse. While I was in England, the first thing I would do when I woke up was go to my social media accounts and post my tally of the number of days since Marielle Franco's murder: "X days. Who ordered Marielle's killing? And why?" The first thing Jon would do was check Donald Trump's Twitter feed, a kind of masochistic compulsion that left him devastated for the rest of the day. After that, life began, much of it taken up with conversations about the climate emergency and the horror to come.

When I began my daily demand for justice for Marielle Franco and Anderson Gomes, murdered on March 14, 2018, in Rio de Janeiro, I never imagined this denunciation would end up defining my every morning—despite my familiarity with the Brazilian police and legal system. For more than three years now, it has been my first act of the day. I will stand beside Marielle until the instigator or instigators of the crime are identified, tried, and sent to prison. As to Trump, fortunately he was banned from Twitter and lost the US presidential election, and this had an immediate beneficial effect on Jon's mental health and our shared daily lives.

In early 2019, during my stay in London, Jon and I were both excited about the young climate generation. He had just interviewed Greta Thunberg for the *Guardian*. When I listened to those adolescent girls, I heard echoes and intersections with the speech of nature-peoples. Their movement in the streets, especially in Europe, had many points of connection with the resistance on the forest ground. I thought to myself: they're Indigenous but don't know it.

For even longer, I had been advocating the idea of an alliance among the peripheries who are demanding their legitimate place as center, an alliance of nature-peoples with the art and resistance movements formed in the favelas of Brazil's large cities. When I listened to the adolescent girls from Fridays for Future, I realized it was also fundamental to forge an alliance with the climate youth, overwhelmingly white, European, and middle class. If all the ends were tied together, the world's geopolitical map could be transformed.

This had actually been going on for decades. Sting's tour with Raoni in the late 1980s had been a gesture in this direction. Strategic leaders like Sônia Guajajara, Davi Kopenawa, and Raoni often traveled to Europe and the United States to denounce the destruction of the Amazon and attacks against original peoples. My idea drew inspiration from my own experience traveling in the other direction, when I moved to Altamira. I firmly believe bodies must displace themselves. Bodies must literally be placed in the Amazon because some knowledge can be accessed only through embodied experience.

If the idea was to affirm the centrality of the Amazon, we had to reverse the path, because an idea must be lived to be realized. This meant inverting the flow: Europeans needed to displace their bodies to the Amazon. And not to its large cities or its towns, but to the deep rainforest, to the territory of beings and in-betweens. I wanted European activists, as well as Brazilian scientists and intellectuals from major Brazilian cities, to move through space and brave another approach to time, where distances are traveled by experiencing them. This would signal who should lead this movement—and what kind of thinking should inspire our side in the climate war if we want to recast the human.

Months earlier, I had had coffee with Iara Rolnik and Andre Degenszajn, heads of the Instituto Ibirapitanga, which focuses on two interlinked questions: food and race. When I began dreaming about the Amazon Center of the World meeting-movement, I contacted them both and, wonderful as they are, they immediately volunteered to help with funding and conceptualization. They took part in the weaving of every moment of Amazon Center of the World.

At the same time, I scheduled an interview with Anuna de Wever, the Belgian leader of Fridays for Future and one of the main faces of the climate youth. I tried Greta too but couldn't get past her aides. In Anuna's case, I had the good luck and enormous pleasure of talking to her mother, Katrien Van der Heyden, a very interesting sociologist, for whom I felt an immediate affinity. I interviewed them both, mother and daughter, in Antwerp for a story I was doing, and then I presented my idea, which they accepted on the spot. Katrien was essential to stitching up all the arrangements with European activists.

I was euphoric on my return from Antwerp—until I reached the immigration post at the train station. British agents detained me because they thought I wanted to immigrate to England— after all, who could possibly resist the charming Boris Johnson and all the Brexit supporters? Because of my constant comings and goings, I was made to wait in a little cordoned-off area for hours, no water and no bathroom. I was carrying a letter from Jon that explained that my comings and goings were motivated solely by love, but he was at a climate conference in Tromsø, Norway, and they couldn't track him down. On an earlier occasion when I had been detained by immigration, Jon was in Tanzania doing an investigative story, and once again they couldn't locate him. I suspect the agent thought my boyfriend didn't exist. They finally authorized me to return to London, after checking my information with the Federal Police in Brazil—and, of course, not before my train had left. I was warned that next time I would be deported.

I returned to Brazil and the Amazon a few weeks later and arranged to have coffee with my friend and partner in imaginings Marcelo Salazar. A native of São Paulo, Marcelo converted to the Amazon while he was still in college. He opened the office of the Socioenvironmental Institute in Altamira in 2007 and never again left the city. My main point of affinity with Marcelo is his unshakable certainty that the craziest ideas are fully achievable. His enthusiasm, which quickly transforms into action, is hard for the more levelheaded to take, but it's precious to me. And so Marcelo was in, even before he knew what it was all about. His ability to make things happen, his ties to the forestpeoples and social movements in Altamira, and his knowledge of the territory were essential to turning the idea into an event.

Months later, we were joined by Raquel Rosenberg, one of the founders of Engajamundo, a pioneering climate-activism organization led by young people in Brazil. Along with the ISA team— one of the gathering's collaborators—and her partner, Miguel Caldeira, Raquel took over the complex production of a gathering between worlds. Raquel moves so fast and with such joy that sometimes I'm afraid she'll turn into a forest spirit and I won't be able to see her anymore.

But the most important was yet to come. Leaders of the forestpeoples and social movements in the Middle Xingu region needed to consult with their communities and jointly decide whether they wanted the meeting and then, on this basis, assume it. This happened. We then became collaborators in spreading an aspiration through Terra do Meio and Altamira, so much so that two events ended up taking place together: in the deep rainforest, in early November, a gathering with a limited number of people—to respect the forest's delicate ecosystem—and immediately thereafter, in Altamira, an open gathering for all the Brazils and the world, which drew the wrath of grileiros and their cohorts across the country. Given the promise of violence broadcast across social media days before the event, certain illustrious white people, like Princess Marie Esméralda of Belgium, an environmentalist, were advised to withdraw at the last minute.

On the first day, carbon emissions from air travel were offset with the reforestation of 1.8 hectares. We held a *muvuca*, a direct planting technique in which a selection of seeds is cast over a deforested area prepared to receive them. Some seeds are born first and have shorter lives, serving as shade so larger trees can grow. Coordinated by Marlison Borges, the *muvuca* was ingenious in design and beautiful to watch. Each hectare is expected to give birth to thiry-five hundred trees. There are few creatures more artistic than seeds, with their colors and shapes. When they fly from your hands into prepared soil, it's almost better than climaxing.

Amazon Center of the World displaced centralities through this movement itself, first by displacing whites to another territory and to other peoples and bodies, effectively decolonizing thought and action. It was also a gathering of the Indigenous— those who knew they were, those who were just discovering it. The event realized the idea. As an aesthetics and an ethos. And also realized its contradictions.

Amazon Center of the World was such a powerful happening that it needs a whole book of its own to thoroughly explain. Here, I will just say that the gathering on the Rio Iriri Extractivist Reserve in Terra do Meio began with a *pajelança* rite by the Yanomami shamans who accompanied Davi Kopenawa. If we want to displace centralities, language must change as well, which means changing the ritual we understand as a meeting. During those days, it was not only humans who spoke, but also jaguars and ants, all the enchanted beings and *xapiripë* who were traveling with the bodies. The forest was the one who spoke.

Personally, I had an epiphany when I saw the shaman Davi Kopenawa alongside Pussy Riot's Nadya Tolokonnikova; the quilombola Socorro de Burajuba; Robin Ellis-Cockcroft, Alejandra Piazzolla, and Tiana Jacout, all of whom were Extinction Rebellion (XR) member activists; Raoni; Anuna de Wever and Adelaïde Charlier, Fridays for Future leaders; Elijah Mackenzie-Johnson, British activist; Assis Porto de Oliveira, a beiradeiro and our host; Tânia Stolze Lima, anthropologist; Yakawilu "Anita" Yudjá, a young Indigenous woman; Antonio Nobre and Tasso Azevedo, scientists; Raimunda Gomes da Silva, beiradeira; Eduardo Neves, archaeologist; Ísis Tatiane, quilombola; and Manuela Carneiro da Cunha, anthropologist. The list is long in the alliance of fierce life that began in November 2019.

Anuna and Adelaïde, from Belgium, embodied the image-symbol of this displacement to Amazon Center of the World: since they refuse to travel by plane because of the carbon emissions, they journeyed instead—from Europe to Brazil on a sailboat. Just five weeks to reach the coast of Brazil, followed by another brief saga to reach Altamira and then Terra do Meio. There they arrived, reinventing the voyage by caravel taken five centuries earlier by Pedro Álvares Cabral of Portugal—this time to decolonize themselves. They came to talk, but mainly to listen and to begin understanding the forest with their bodies. They disembarked from themselves in the deep rainforest to begin their long process of Amazonization.

Amazon Center of the World is a living idea, alive and therefore free. In the Middle Xingu region, it rewove the social movements broken apart during the process of inflicting Belo Monte on the land and came to designate an alliance between different organizations and leaders of forestpeoples, an alliance that has proved crucial since then in responding to the string of teen suicides in Altamira, the COVID-19 pandemic in the region, and all major actions to defend the forest. It is an ongoing forum of ideas and actions. Globally, it prompted new exchanges between movements generated within the various Brazils and international climate activism movements, like XR and Fridays for Future. It has been important in pressuring European parliaments to demand that the Brazilian government commit to reducing deforestation before signing trade agreements, like the one between the European Union and Mercosur.

There is no way to either control or measure the paths traveled by ideas. An event takes place inside each person it touches, and inside each person's others—and it takes place outside, too, one with the other and also with the others' others. It drives transformations and actions in a chain, inside and outside bodies. The report by the earth scientist Antonio Nobre triggered movements within me that translated into creations outside me. The words spoken by beiradeiras like Raimunda Gomes da Silva and Indigenous leaders like Davi Kopenawa destructured the language I inhabited. Greta Thunberg's boldness and what she caused to move fired new synapses in my thinking. The experience of living in—and with—the forest radically changed my body and my experience of body. And that is just me.

Amazon Center of the World is a powerful movement, provocative and the creator of me + 1 +. It has followed the most surprising paths as it circulates the planet. Amazon Center of the World is an idea that acts.

00. #freethefuture

The Indeterminate nature of the future haunted our human ancestors. At the outset of our species' adventure on the planet, what we now call the future was probably the day that followed night, but we have little to no idea how these humans interpreted the passage of time (or even themselves). Their ongoing concerns were to survive without being devoured by other, sharp-toothed peoples, or by humans from other groups, and likewise to obtain food, water, and shelter. Thousands of years later, for the portion of humanity whose next day is to some extent guaranteed, the future is ever more often planned according to each society's or community's values. That is, it is about learning a trade or guaranteeing land ownership; continuing your father's or mother's work or attending college; building up assets and forging alliances through marriage; or simply guaranteeing that your family lives on—these are some of the ideas of future shared by a part of the world's humans. Large doses of determination notwithstanding, our ancestors had to grapple with myriad variables, including early death (a constant possibility prior to the invention of penicillin) and major natural disasters, for which they were ill prepared.

Later, the future became a matter up for discussion: What future do we want? Who has the power to plan and define it? The king, president, or prime minister, the head of the clan or tribe, the family patriarch, or a religious or revolutionary leader? Social class or caste, race, and gender became determinants of what you could expect or desire for the next day. Revolutions were fought in the name of other possible futures and to win the power to determine the future.

Over the centuries, the future gradually shed its uncertain nature to become a matter of possibility, of dreams, even of utopia. People began calling for indetermination as a possibility and contesting the determinations imposed by groups wielding power. This fueled many of the nineteenth- and twentieth-century revolutions.

Throughout much of the twentieth century, it was each generation's ethical responsibility to do better than the previous one. The opportunity to plan the future gradually played into each society's sense of well-being, while also coming to be an aspiration at the individual level. Furthermore, the ability to plan the future became a value monetized and marketed by capitalism—the future might be Apple's next release or a more comfortable material life.

But not for everyone, it must be stressed. The very idea of future conforms to a way of understanding time that is supposedly universal but in fact is not. In a way, today's hegemonic concept of future is yet another imposition of the dominant minority. For some peoples, *future* is a word that exists in neither their tongue nor their language—or at least not as we understand it. For still others, *future* is a concept whose meaning derives from another way of understanding the world, and of understanding oneself in the world. But for most twentieth-century generations, the consensus is that the future is tomorrow, what lies ahead; it is indeterminate, open-ended—and should be better.

In the expanded present where we live, however, this has changed. And it has changed without most people realizing it, at least not consciously—though they still react somewhat. The climate emergency and sixth mass extinction may be transforming our perception of the future more than at any other time since the notion began circulating among some human societies: for the first time, the future has become determined well beyond human will—or at least the will of the individual, who has been convinced by capitalism to believe they hold their fate in their own hands. Even if most people don't sense this change, it exerts its effect on our bodies and it is my hypothesis that it triggers sickness and even suicide.

While the majority have paper boats (or big canoes, in the Araweté conception) and the dominant minority have ultra-luxurious high-tech yachts, everyone is going to live on a worse planet for humans. We already do. The COVID-19 pandemic is our first unequivocal global warning. Even the most obtuse, whether they admit it or not, can intuit what is happening. The spread of the novel coronavirus has shown us how much better shielded the dominant minority is, because it has more resources not only to protect itself from the virus but also to fight the disease when they are infected. Yet everyone is affected to some extent— and life gets worse. The pandemic has given us a sneak preview of what the future will be like.

What is still up for grabs is not if the planet is going to heat up—it already has and continues to do so. What is up for grabs is how many degrees hotter it will get, and this will define whether the future will be only worse or frankly hostile for the human species and for most of the more-than-human species. There's an enormous difference between a worse future and a hostile one. We may soon run out of time to reverse the acceleration of global heating and other devastating processes now underway. Parts of the Amazon rainforest itself have already crossed the point of no return—the forest as a past that will not return as a future. *Irreversible* is the word for this reality that is ever closer.

This is the first time in history that children and adolescents can be certain their lives will be worse than their parents', no matter how hard they fight. This conviction has fed the movement initiated by Greta Thunberg, as well as other collective gestures in the fight against extinction. This is also the first time whites have begun paying true attention to the fact that, in other ways of understanding the world, space-time, and ourselves, the end of the world might be the middle, and a means, at least collectively. The millions who lost their lives in the COVID-19 pandemic reached their end as individuals. For each one of them, this is irreversible. The question is: How will those who had the chance to survive move forward collectively?

Grounded in the idea that the possibility of a future must be recreated in order to confront the climate crisis, some of those who helped generate the Amazon Center of the World movement decided to conceive another action: the #liberteofuturo, or #freethefuture, movement. At the core of this movement lies the idea that we must fight, together, so the future will once again be indeterminate and open to possibilities. This movement can only become action if we are capable of imagining a future with all peoples, human and more-than-human, visible and invisible.

On July 5, 2020, we launched a Free the Future manifesto on a platform designed by Christiane Martins and Yannick Falisse to host virtual demonstrations—or "deminars"—similar to the street rallies lost to us with the pandemic. Posters, photographs, and slogans can be displayed during a deminar, as an active way of responding to the physical isolation needed to help contain the spread of COVID-19. We wrote: "We have launched this movement because we don't want to be slaughtered like cattle. Whether in rural areas or in cities, we want to live like the forest—standing tall—and we want to fight."

I wrote an article in which I introduced the movement as a fight for the future of our present, in the present. Those who have proven so skillful at imagining the end of the world—from the biblical apocalypse to zombie movies, from viruses to alien attacks, from domination by artificial intelligence to the nuclear holocaust, and now the climate holocaust—must learn to imagine the end of capitalism. Above all, we must learn to imagine a future where we can and do want to live. Imagining is political action. Imagining is a tool of resistance. Imagining the future means acting in and on the present.

How did this movement begin? Out of fear and desire, as almost everything does. The pandemic was taking hold across the world. Italy was living out scenes from the plague while Brazil was announcing its first case. But some were already talking about the "return to normal." This was our fear. Because we were fully aware of the climate collapse, the accelerated destruction of biodiversity, and the existence of unfathomable inequality, we had been expecting the time of pandemics. There is, however, a huge difference between foreseeing what is going to happen given the persistent destruction of nature, based both on the knowledge of forestpeoples and on scientific research—and actually experiencing it. Experiencing the pandemic was our fear, but we also dreaded what was looming before us as the post-pandemic "return to normal." Normal for whom? That was our first question.

With the impending recession, we knew the corporations now dominating the world—along with the rulers and politicians, economists and business executives who are financed by them—would crack the whip on the backs of the human cattle we've been converted into by neoliberal capitalism. They would spew a phantasmagoric discourse about the need to resume production and even accelerate it. And the abnormal we had already been experiencing before COVID-19 might become an even deadlier abnormal, further brutalizing human and more-than-human bodies.

At that moment in time, March 2020, we were concentrating our efforts on devising actions and campaigns to protect those the pandemic would hit hardest. We were taking action to attenuate suffering in the immediate present, passing the virtual hat on the internet to buy food baskets containing items planted by family farmers and traditional communities without the use of pesticides, and demanding that Brazil bolster its national health care system, known as SUS. But we realized more had to be done. We would have to dispute the future in the present.

The movement started with Raquel and me talking over WhatsApp. Then artists and climate activists like Eugênio Lima, Paloma Costa, Marcelo Salazar, Gabriela Carneiro da Cunha, and

Benjamin Seroussi joined us for weekly meetings. Three months later, we were many, each of us doing what we knew best and all learning to do what we didn't know how to do, because these are the times. Me + 1 +

As some thinkers have pointed out, it's not just the virus that can spread at lightning speed, but ideas too. Word of mouth. To make this idea go viral, we invited everyone to join in a movement to free the future. If so many keep saying the world will never be the same, and it won't, then what other world do we want?

The public health emergency made it imperative to fight for the human lives threatened by the virus. But something even harder had to (and still has to) be done: fighting for the post-virus future—or possibly for the future-with-pandemics. When the coronavirus shattered what is normal for a few but abnormal for most, it may have afforded an opportunity to design a society based on other principles, capable of attenuating the climate catastrophe and promoting racial and interspecies justice. The worst that could happen after the pandemic would be a return to the abnormal that is crushing the lives of the majority. This is what many are calling the "new normal"—but what we understand as the "new abnormal."

At the outset of the pandemic, even bastions of the liberal press like the *Economist* and *Financial Times*, born in the cradle of capitalism, said it would be necessary to take a step backward. Suggestions for the new, postpandemic social contract included greater state intervention, a guaranteed income, and the taxation of large fortunes—measures once considered exotic by players of this ilk. Conceding a little to ensure that nothing essential will change is an age-old trick. We quickly realized that the old forces were not only regrouping to try to keep everything as it was, but also preparing to further exploit the same people as ever—the majority.

We know people cling to what is familiar in a crisis. Even if the familiar is very bad, they find greater comfort in known deprivation than in risking the unknown, which might bring a misery they aren't acquainted with. The feeling of helplessness is a hard one to bear.

So it was, and is, quite likely that many or all of the "good" intentions—be these personal, corporate, or governmental (in the case of minimally decent governments, which is not the case for the Brazilian people)—would vanish with vaccination, and people would go back to their posts inside their regular cages. Until the next pandemic or the next challenge presented by the climate emergency now underway. Or worse: people might put up with losing more rights and granting more power to their oppressors in an effort to save themselves from the next virus or next catastrophe. Which will come, if there is no radical change in our way of living.

The virus, however, revealed a secret, as pointed out by the French philosopher Bruno Latour in an article that went viral. Through the virus, we have discovered that those who claimed it is impossible to quit producing, fly less, boost government investments, and radically change our habits were simply lying. The world changed in a matter of weeks when life demanded it. It is also for the sake of life that we must hold on to the good practices we developed during this period and push like never before to weave another type of society from other threads.

The planet, which is supposedly at consumers' disposal, has been consumed by capitalism, just as entire species have been driven to extinction and others subjugated so industrial production can devour their bodies (in a monstrously literal sense). In this system, everyone is born to be consumed and consume themselves, by consuming their bodies and their time. Since the Industrial Revolution, which unleashed a process of steeply rising carbon dioxide emissions through the burning of fossil fuels, the dominant minority of humans has converted the species into a force of destruction.

The big corporations that control the world, along with those who do their bidding, are finding themselves under pressure as nature collapses at their doing and evidence shows there will be more pandemics. And so now, as they have done in the past, they are trying to remodel the destructive system to maintain control—and reap further profit. And they have a good chance of succeeding. During the pandemic, billionaires increased their wealth while the majority grew poorer.

The Free the Future movement is an uprising born during a time of pandemic, with the goal of undermining any attempt to reshuffle the abnormal. It is an unarmed uprising that invokes the radical tool of imagination. Its power lies in recouping our ability to imagine other possible worlds.

Those of us who launched the movement believe the future has been hijacked by the neofascists that are ruling part of the world. As already stated in these pages, Jair Bolsonaro, Donald Trump, and others got themselves elected by peddling a past that never existed. This horde of liars has been selling a return to what never was, to a past where there was peace and everyone passively accepted their place—meaning Black people passively accepted their subaltern place, the Indigenous passively accepted their subaltern place, women passively accepted their subaltern place, and everyone passively accepted that gender was binary, or else deviant. They've been selling a past where everything was in its place, and everyone knew everything's place and everything was settled—settled, of course, for those at the top of the ferocious food chain enforced by the dominant minorities. The past they peddle is their biggest lie.

It must be repeated yet again that there never was peace in the past. We know the past was rife with conflict, subordination, erasure, and extermination. Elected despots like Trump and Bolsonaro have "cleansed" the past of its conflicts and deaths and packaged it up to offer it to a population frightened by a shifting world—a population frightened by the insurrections of those who have always been considered subhumanities, those who have always been on the margins of public and private life and have now begun disputing the center.

But why do these elected despots offer up a past that never existed? Herein lies another secret. The answer is that they have no future to offer. The future is the climate collapse, which they try hard to deny, but it is happening. The future is bad. To win power and hold on to it, they must sell a past that never existed and deny the future. It is vital to understand that they only win and hold on to power by denying the future and replacing it with neofascism's foundational lie. So the fight for the future is also by consequence a fight for the past.

They are deniers, but not because they doubt the climate crisis. They are deniers because they cannot offer a future and because they are at the service of the transnational corporations and local groups that are producing the climate crisis. This is the weak spot of the murderous far right that at the turn of the 2010s to 2020s was ruling Brazil and other countries: when their leaders deny the climate crisis, because they can do nothing but deny it, they must also deny the future.

The pandemic tore a hole in this strategy. Suddenly, the world stopped. When original peoples, scientists, and adolescents were screaming that we have to reduce production to save life on the planet, that it was impossible to persist with the dogma of infinite growth, and that it was imperative to change our way of living, rulers and big corporations said it was impossible. What did the pandemic show us? That it is indeed possible. And that it can be done quickly. In a few weeks, the impossible happened.

This is also why the half dozen people who embody the mystification known as the market rushed to reintroduce neoliberal discourse early on in the pandemic: the discourse about a "return to normal," to production and growth. It was strategic to say that everything can indeed change—but only for a brief time. And then we must restore and accelerate production and lost profits or, they threatened, a series of catastrophes would ensue.

Let us be clear, this return to "normal," as everyone knows full well, would be at the expense of others' bodies. "Sacrifice" is demanded from the majority so the minority can maintain their privileges. Or was there really a mass of contented, prosperous people prior to the pandemic, healthy and at peace, their time sequestered in a 24/7–model prison?

At the start of the pandemic, 2,153 people (sometimes we forget billionaires are people, with first and last names) held more material wealth than 60 percent of nearly eight billion other human beings inhabiting the planet. Billionaires represent such an insignificant fraction of the overall global population that percentages fail to render them visible: fewer than 0.00003 percent—or one billionaire for every 3.7 million people. But the racial, social, gender, and species inequalities they cause are brutally visible.

In early 2022, Oxfam International announced that during the first two years of the pandemic, the world's ten wealthiest men more than doubled their fortunes, from $700 billion to $1.5 trillion—at a rate of $15,000 per second or $1.3 billion per day. Meanwhile, the wealth of 99 percent of humanity dropped. According to the World Bank, more than 160 million people were pushed into poverty. "If these ten men were to lose 99.999 percent of their wealth tomorrow, they would still be richer than 99 percent of all the people on this planet," said Oxfam International's executive director Gabriela Bucher. "They now have six times more wealth than the poorest 3.1 billion people."

This says—no, screams—something about the system that brought us to the climate collapse and the time of pandemics. The Free the Future movement combats the return to an abnormal that is despoiling nature and condemning billions to poverty. We further believe that by freeing the future, we will no longer be hostages. As long as the future remains hijacked, we will be subjugated, jailed in a present continuous, an eternal loop, living convulsively.

We propose to remember every day the words of Ailton Krenak: "The future is here and now; there may not be a next year." Grounded in this mantra, we presented some foundations for the society we want to create, woven from nonnegotiable shared principles:

(1) There is no democracy if there is racism.
(2) There is no democracy if there is speciesism (racism against species).
(3) Racial, social, gender, and interspecies inequality must be abolished.
(4) Redeeming the future is the collective responsibility of everyone alive in this era.
(5) We understand ourselves as nature, and we want a world for the humans and more-than-humans who inhabit the planet.
(6) The Amazon, framed as a broad concept, is the center of the world.

We then invited people to imagine the future based on five proposals to postpone the end of the world:

(1) Antidotes against the end of the world: imagine how you want to live.
(2) Democracy: propose public policies and legislative and normative changes that will reduce racial, gender, class, and species inequalities and take democracy beyond the mere act of voting in every election.
(3) Consumption: suggest ways of eliminating the consumption habits that enslave our species and others as well.
(4) Climate emergency: suggest actions to stop the destruction of nature and guarantee the continuity of all forms of life on the planet.
(5) Insurrection: define the best form of civil disobedience for creating the future where you want to live.

Or you might answer just one question: What future do you want to free?

One-minute videos answering these five questions were posted to a giant display case of imaginings, accessible at https:// liberteofuturo.net/#/, a platform that can be used to inspire actions and serve as a research source on the imagination at this extreme moment in time. We then held imagination laboratories, divided into five starter topics, so that the ideas generated in a collective setting could become action in the world. The laboratories brought new protagonists into the uprising, which is now taking paths no longer traceable by those who launched the movement. Free the Future is not a group of people, or an organization, or even a collective, but an idea in action, acting to generate possibilities.

The Free the Future deminars, or virtual demonstrations, emceed by the deejay and theater director Eugênio Lima, re-placed centralities, consonant with the movement's proposal: most participants have been Black and Indigenous. The fourth virtual demonstration put Jair Bolsonaro on trial for genocide, since neither the International Criminal Court nor the Brazilian legal system had done anything. Designed by the artist Mundano for Bolsonaro, the Genocidist of the Year award was displayed by Indigenous leaders at the second big protest for Bolsonaro's impeachment, held in the streets of Brasília on June 19, 2021.

Imagining proved to be a more challenging action than we first thought. We discovered how much our imagination has been incarcerated, squared, formatted. Saying what world you really want, with clear proposals, is much more complicated than it seems for people who have been tamed to merely obey—or, at best, to live by reacting to attacks. The very exercise of breaking down the walls inside our bodies proved a powerful experience for everyone who risked it. If you think it's hard to free the future, it is indeed hard. But no harder than living in a present without a future.

In fact, it is no accident that neofascists attack art so much. Art fosters imagination and is always the first to be assailed by authoritarian governments and rulers, who need to control bodies to impose their power projects. Imagination is the art of thought. And it is through our imaginations that we can begin to ransom the future from captivity. Imagining is not a passive act. To the contrary, imagining is acting: imagin-action.

To cynics, I have nothing to say. Their world is the one right here. To skeptics, I'd like to say this: We combined what we knew and dared do what we didn't know how to do. We created something that didn't exist. The future we began to imagine became present during this action.

The idea of freeing the future is not a nice, inoffensive, cute, or cuddly one. It is an insurrection. Today, I don't know most of the people who have joined the uprising in Brazil and abroad. Nor do I agree with all of the proposals. In joining with others to weave this creation, my wish has been to place imagination about the future at the center of the political debate about the climate war. Ideas belong to their own movement of birthing worlds.

me + 1 + 1 +

between-worlds

When Lilo died, on April 15, 2021, I was making black beans. Making beans is how I magically process my life. Simmering them, drawing as much flavor as possible from what the earth gives me, using seasoning and herbs like a sorcerer. I received the news and went on dicing onions. I've never diced them so fine. I chopped away. And away. And away. *Whack whack whack.* Knife against cutting board. Then I sat down on the couch. And the horror intruded like dark night. Pitch black. The horror of the impossibility of Lilo's death, the horror of the impossibility of life without Lilo. Then I saw a jaguar. Not like in a dream. I saw him in the clarity of my horror, a true reality, white outline against a black background, like a Denilson Baniwa painting, moving. We, the jaguar and I, were in the room. He was outside me, and also inside. I lay down on the couch and felt him ripping my guts out with his teeth. Furious, his claws tearing into my body-earth. I felt a new kind of pain, the pain of being mauled to my depths. After writhing about for nearly an hour, I realized I'd have to let the jaguar go. He spun around, body and head, tensed his muscles, and plunged into the forest.

Since then, Lilo has walked with me through all forests. In the Amazon you don't die, you transform into another being. I always thought Lilo was a bird, but he's a jaguar. Some *buiúnas* in our Amazon network of women—the name *buiúna* comes from magical figures who inhabit the rainforest, half giant snake, half woman—told me I was the jaguar. I don't know, I'm still searching.

Lilo, my Lilo, companion during more than twenty years of reporting, the other half of my duo, "torn-out piece of me," was murdered by Jair Messias Bolsonaro. Putting Bolsonaro's and Lilo's names in the same sentence horrifies me, the horror of living in a country ruled by a genocidist. And of waking in the morning to find the genocidist still there, because the minority that is eating the planet still thinks they can profit from it. Lilo Clareto's death certificate lists his cause of death as COVID-19. But Lilo was murdered. Bolsonaro, Brazil's antipresident during the pandemic, carried out a plan to spread the virus to achieve what is called "herd immunity," supposedly to keep people working and the economy active.

At the time I write these words, Lilo is one of over half a million dead in Brazil whom we will never let be reduced to numbers. Innumerable. According to epidemiological research, four hundred thousand of these half million deaths could have been avoided if Bolsonaro had enacted available preventive measures, such as mask use, physical isolation, and lockdowns, rather than fighting the use of masks, encouraging crowds, and battling the governors who declared quarantines. Of this total, at least ninety-five thousand lives could have been saved if Bolsonaro had invested in vaccines when they were first offered to the government—and rejected by him. As I write, I know that tens of thousands more will die, and this awareness is unbearable. As I write, I am fighting with many others to see that Bolsonaro is ousted through impeachment and tried by the Brazilian justice system and the International Criminal Court for extermination—a crime against humanity—and for the genocide of original peoples.

In the Amazon, Bolsonaro's use of the virus as an unexpected biological weapon helped him intensify predation while simultaneously undermining resistance. While the people who fight for the forest tried to protect themselves by staying home and isolating to avoid spreading the virus, human predators advanced at will. To the point where this phrase became a cliché: "The destroyers of the Amazon aren't working from home." A year after the pandemic began, there was still no emergency plan to protect the forestpeoples, despite the fact that the Federal Supreme Court had ordered the government to formulate one. As mentioned earlier, Bolsonaro actually vetoed plans to provide the Indigenous with drinking water, emergency medical beds, and information campaigns.

Viruses and bacteria have always reached the original peoples via the bodies of whites. Admittedly, the European invaders of 1500 didn't know they were carrying microorganisms deadly to the Indigenous. The same cannot be said about the other colonizers who kept on coming, over the centuries and even into recent decades. Bolsonaro was not the first to use disease to eliminate people physically. Dozens of accounts from the enduring oral memory of the original peoples tell of smallpox-contaminated clothing being scattered in villages where the Indigenous were resisting white occupation and even of an airplane dropping flu-infected toys. Some of these accounts have also been recorded on the "paper skins" where words are imprisoned, white people's tree skin.

During the COVID-19 pandemic, Bolsonaro relied on two strategies: he left Indigenous lands open for the virus to enter, while at the same time fostering invasions by miners, loggers, and grileiros. The crime of genocide is evident. It wasn't just people who died, but also a substantial part of the resistance. Since the older population is more vulnerable to the virus, a number of elders fell—elders who had led the fight against their people's destruction, elders who were also the keepers of collective memory, culture, and ancestral knowledge. In some cases, they were the last speakers of their language. In other cases, like Aruká Juma, they were a people's last elder.

For forestpeoples and those in the process of forestation, like me, the perception that Earth's skin has been ripped open is so strong that it is now part of our body. The severity and effects of the crimes committed by Bolsonaro and his accomplices will make themselves felt for decades, perhaps centuries—forever, in a way, because the chain of events never ends. I feel the planet writhing like a living body of which I am part. My process of forestation has made me into a diverse, divergent, organically integrated being, and now whenever I visit São Paulo, I can hear rivers buried alive in the concrete tombstone that is the city. A city I love but know to be monstrous. We awaken other senses when we return to being nature. This isn't a matter of magic, or superstition, or witchcraft, or esotericism, or tree-hugging. It is an organic relationship with the planet, another way of being-and-becoming in the worlds—and of moving between them.

The rainforest is flesh woven from the threads of many lives, and today I find blood of a different color there. Bolsonaro, brutish murderer that he is, doesn't grasp the magnitude of what he has done. But for those who have learned to listen, this silence of another texture freezes them to their bones. As foreseen by Davi Kopenawa, many shamans have died and the sky is falling.

A new chapter has opened in the war of beings and in-betweens against the world eaters. These chapters don't open as they usually do in books. This is different. Each new chapter encompasses all the earlier ones by devouring them, expanding the narrative in open, infinite circles. For the first time, however, if whites—whites in the broad sense—are unable to become Others, there may be an end that is not a middle for what we call humans. The planet will then continue on, carrying with it our extinction.

A few days after Lilo died, I read a scientific article about butterflies in the Amazon. In various parts of the rainforest, they are losing their color. They are no longer yellow, blue, red, orange, green, pink, purple . . . but brown and gray. Butterflies also want to survive and so are adapting to the end of the world, mimicking the ash gray of the incinerated forest and the concrete gray encasing Earth like a straitjacket, eventually asphyxiating all life.

Only then did my tears for Lilo become river, become water-fall, become banzeiro. Nothing is sadder to me than forest eaters also eating the colors of butterflies. Monster humans like Bolsonaro have stolen the rainbow. The story they told to the white child I once was, was wrong: the treasure was never the pot of gold, but the rainbow. And now the struggle of beings and in-betweens is also a struggle to restore all the colors of the worlds.

Now I continue on, to tell of what will come. In today's Amazon, you hear more and more Mandarin spoken on airliners. You still hear the classic gringos who darkened the forest with their white-ness during the years of the business-military dictatorship and in recent decades, but now these voices are more often those of jour-nalists from the United States or Europe on missions to cover the climate crisis. Many of the new gringos, the ones doing business, are from the Asian giant. China is not only the largest importer of what are called commodities but are in fact nature, or exact a price from nature; it is also expanding its strategic presence in the energy field.

The geopolitics of the deforested world has changed further still as a result of the pandemic and the dynamics of vaccine distribution to countries like Brazil. The vaccine produced in China was the first to reach Brazil. This is not a minor detail. As a global power, China recalls the United States during the Cold War, when the latter engineered dictatorships in Brazil and throughout Latin America. But there are many differences as well. China apparently is less interested in disputing ideologies and thought in countries like Brazil at the present time, concern-ing itself instead with buying and selling, but it is already begin-ning to work on what we call "soft power." With its vaccine, it advanced a few spaces across the global chessboard. Directly and indirectly, China is also buying nature in the Amazon.

Recent research has shown that the rainforest, the world's largest carbon sink, has already started emitting more gases than it absorbs. Assassinated day after day, the Amazon is taking with it the moisture that regulates the climate and has begun to poison the air we breathe. Besides being the worst of all rulers, Bolsonaro and his stridency have served to camouflage what is in fact the most stable, persistent group, which has merely changed names throughout the history of Brazil-the-nation and which will continue to obliterate the rainforest using subtler techniques than those employed by the brutes of Bolsonarism. In the war between humans, the fight in Amazon Center of the World will grow more heated in the coming years and decades of the climate collapse. And each one of us will have to decide which side we are on. Not with our words but with our bodies.

As the forestpeoples have pointed out, this is also a war between those who espouse development and those who espouse involvement. Between those who have uninvolved themselves from nature, placing themselves outside of it, turning nature into a commodity-producing commodity—and those who know they are deeply involved because they are an organic part of the planet.

I have become an inhabitant of the between-worlds. This book tells the story of how I came to be *in-between* through a singular process, of which I only recently gained full awareness. My home is this place between places, perpetually traversing, perpetually journeying. Before, I understood myself as a displaced no-where, a misfit. Today, my long journey into the rainforest has shown me that between-places is also a place, that displacement allows me to see from other angles, and that being a misfit lets me escape all the boxes they'd like to fit and imprison me in. When I feel like I'm suffocating, I simply displace my limbs, dislocate my bones, and disappear like a snake.

Between-places is my place of speech. Between-languages and between-language is how I exist. I am gradually becoming trans-world, translingual, and translanguage. I am the movement of action. Bit by bit, I am leaving the banzeiro to (r)evolutionize into *òkòtó*.

I resist to exist to resist . . .

This book is anything but definitive about the Amazon (or about me, for that matter). My writing transpires by traversing—fields of knowledge, experiences, geographies, peoples, sensibilities, times. Bodies. My writing is transpirational.

I end this book in the middle

My thanks

My profound thanks to Fiona McCrae. The story of this book's publication begins with her, at a bookshop café in London in late 2019. Fiona said: "I want another book of yours. What would you like to write?" Those weren't her exact words, but that's how I understood them. Fiona said what any writer wants to hear, but what a writer of another nationality, like myself, rarely hears from a US publisher. As all of us non–English speakers know right from the very first sentence in the very first book that the walls of the Anglophone literary world are high—and not very open to realities that don't fit in with their certainties about the worlds of Others. Being translated into English is a rare thing. Having a US publishing house ask me to write the book I wanted to write—that seemed a little like a miracle. And the fact that the publisher was Fiona and the publishing house Graywolf made it even more of a miracle. Since I only believe in miracles wrought by people, I dug my claws into Fiona's words and immediately said I wanted to write about the Amazon, this pluriuniverse that extends well beyond the geopolitical outline of the world's largest tropical rainforest. Right then, I didn't know exactly what or how, because if I had known, I would have lost interest before I'd even started, but I knew I wanted to. And Fiona said yes.

My thanks to Diane Grosklaus Whitty, my English translator, who has become one of those people you've always loved even though you've never met them in bodily flesh. Diane and I share intimacies that fly across the internet, and we've become real friends. How could I not love someone who fights for my words as much as I do? Who discovers intentions in my text that I hadn't realized were there? Who often knows my interlines better than I could? Who worries about my pain and is patient with my absences? Along with Diane, there is Michael, her companion, first reader of my words translated into English, who suggests whether the writing flows like a river or encounters some dam that must be destroyed straightaway—my gratitude to him as well.

My thanks to my love, Jon Watts, to whom I dedicate this book, for seeing me, loving me, and daring to Amazonize with me and in me. For wanting to reforest a small piece of the forest with me and build a house-world together, and for leaving behind a lovely apartment in a charming district of London to live with me, and in community, in the Amazon's most violent city. For never having hesitated in the face of ideas that many would consider insane. For holding me each night as if nothing bad could happen to me inside his long arms. For an idealism as deep as mine and a desire to change the world that only grows bigger over the years. For his intelligence, which has helped guide me in recent years, when the world here needed to find the world there to build bridges he knew more about than I did. And also for his careful reading.

My thanks to the forest-communities who opened the doors of their homes to tell me their stories and teach me about other worlds—especially the beiradeiros of Riozinho, in Terra do Meio.

My thanks to Cristiane Fontes (Krika), who stopped by my desk one day at the collective newsroom where I worked in old downtown São Paulo and asked what she could do to help me. And who did it. To the Ford Foundation in Brazil, and especially to Graciela Selaimen, who believed in my endeavor and understood what it meant in the medium term, well beyond conventions and bureaucracy, and who financed my work during my first year in Altamira. To the entire Graywolf team, especially Anni Liu, who embraced this book written in crazy times and cared for it as if it were a living thing, because it is, and who dared maintain a title whose words were born in other worlds. To my agents Lucia Riff and Julia Wähmann, who take care of me and help me find trails to pursue in this labyrinthine world.

My thanks to photographer Lilo Clareto, for being the best reporting partner a reporter could dream of, to the depths of what it means to narrate worlds. For believing in me with an unconditional surrender. For trusting in me more than I trusted in myself. For more than twenty years of companionship along roads and rivers, giving me the shelter and support I needed to venture into the many Amazons and, throughout this mystery, merge myself with them. His eye, imprinted on mine, pierces every page of this book. The photograph on the cover, announcing the vortex just beyond, is his. Death doesn't separate us, and now Lilo walks beside me like a jaguar.

My thanks to the more-than-humans who humanize me, especially Frida, Capitu, Bentinho, Flora, and Babaju.

My thanks to all those, human and more-than-human, who defy the world eaters and weave the uprising.

Translator's Note

"*Banzeiro Òkòtó?* What language is that? What does it mean?" Perhaps you asked yourself that when you spotted this book on display. The answer to the first question is straightforward: Portuguese. And Yoruba. As to the second, on page one you'll begin learning the meaning of *banzeiro*, but it will probably take you the whole book to have a real feel for this three-syllable word, which is unfamiliar and undefinable even for many Brazilians. And you'll only learn the meaning of *òkòtó* toward the end of the journey. Yes, this book does not give up its secrets easily; it demands patience. You are entering foreign territory, and from the book's very title, you have been forewarned.

You also need to know that while the words you will be reading are English, the English language can't always capture an experience so foreign to itself. Translation is an imperfect act, undertaken by very stubborn individuals who insist on committing it anyway. As the old saw goes, it can become an act of betrayal— and that is even more the case with this book, which in its original Portuguese is already a fierce act of translation: Eliane Brum's effort to translate the other-languaged universes of the Amazon to outside readers in a way that their "ears will be able to hear to understand."

Throughout the book, Eliane makes clear that understanding someone else's language is a formidable challenge, one we can never fully meet—particularly when the speaker is part of the more-than-human world, as she points out in the chapter entitled "in-betweens of the forest": "A while back, someone asked me what the river would say if it could talk. But when the river does talk, we don't understand. You have to inhabit the river's skin to hear it." Further on: "I tell the stories of dammed-up lives because I don't understand the river. My stories are born out of this impossibility of grasping the language of the Xingu."

Then this struggle to comprehend is followed by the task of transmitting what has been received. In "confession," Eliane tells us:

> When I listen, I "lend" my body to the other's words. It resembles the experience of possession, but it is not. My body, me, is an active mediator of the other voice. Of course, when I turn this voice into my written word, this delicate mediation will be present. It is the other's narrative, the other's experience, the other's words, after passing through my body. But my body is not an absolute vacuum, through which the other's narrative passes without being altered by the experience of passing through me.

Now indulge me please, and reread the above paragraph, replacing "When I listen" with "When I translate." In portraying her work as author, Eliane has unwittingly depicted mine as translator.

So let the buyer beware: the words you read in these pages, the voices they try to echo, the experiences they hope to convey, have all voyaged far—from their origins not just in the Amazon but in human and more-than-human bodies in the Amazon, traveling next through the body of Eliane Brum and then, adding another layer of distance, through this translator's body. Who knows how the experience of "passing through" me has altered the other's narrative? To the extent that I had conscious control over the process, I would like to offer a few glimpses into it.

First, as with most translators today, my overall goal was to provide Anglophone readers with much the same experience as the one enjoyed by the Lusophone readers of the original. Because Eliane's banzeiro takes us into spaces where scars are words, where language "is not clothing but a way of inhabiting your own body," and where *now* is a place, *where* is a being, and *forever* is a noun, this reading experience is at times unsettling. Eliane "persistently breaches" the grammatical constraints of Portuguese, repeatedly drawing the reader up short. Following her lead, I often had to wrestle the English language into something a little bigger, a little stranger, to replicate this experience, producing sentences and phrases like these: "What are those whites?"; "Hope unmattered to me"; "My insomnia sails me along"; and "Everything that spoke English was better" (again, in this book, you don't need to be a human person to speak). By prodding us to rethink our words, Eliane prods us to rethink our worlds, and I attempted to mirror this effort.

As I endeavored to remain true to the original—to the reading experience and the book's voices—I didn't always smooth the way for you, reader, as another translator might. I wanted you to know you were in foreign territory not only through geographical references and the like, but by the way the English text (mis)behaved. Take, for example, this sentence: "The boy had been born in a city on the banks of the Xingu and he had never been on the river. He had been born on the river but amputated from it." This could have been translated "born on the river but cut off from it"—some might say a more fluid translation. However, this alternative would imply three losses: the link Eliane draws between the boy's separation from the river and his grandmother's amputated foot, the opportunity to mimic how Eliane stretches linguistic boundaries, and, lastly, the organic, corporeal link between the human-person and river-person, where the river is part of the boy's body (or maybe the other way round?).

Another example where I chose not to predigest everything for the reader: in the chapter entitled "the soccer ball," Eliane says a certain priest is "no more like a movie star than a piranha is like a pirarucu." Most Anglophones have heard of piranhas, and syntax tells the reader that a piranha must differ greatly from a pirarucu—but for anyone unacquainted with the latter, there is no way to know how these two fish differ. I could have replaced "pirarucu" with "sturgeon" or "shark" (yes, we translators can do that) or added a brief explanation, like this: "pirarucu, the largest South American freshwater fish." But as Eliane writes, "every word is tied to meanings and values that can't be corralled into a dictionary." A fish is color, movement, smell, feel, flavor, folklore, songs, memories—things a translator can never give you, no matter what word they choose. And so by opting for "pirarucu," I hoped to remind you that these realms are filled with creatures, who despite their English-language names, lie well beyond your immediate reach.

That said, I must be equally transparent about how I sometimes facilitated the reader's journey, adding a tidbit of information familiar to Brazilian readers but not necessarily to Anglophones. Talking about Rio de Janeiro, for instance, the "South Side" became the "South Side, near the beach" while the "enclaves" of Complexo da Maré and Complexo do Alemão became "distant enclaves." Elsewhere, the term *municipality* has been explained parenthetically as "roughly akin to a county or parish." At the same time, what might look like a translation gloss may actually be just a translation, as in this case: "*mucajá*, a fruit that tastes like candy to the turtles." This is because the worlds of *Banzeiro Òkòtó* are often as foreign to its original audience as they are to foreigners, prompting Eliane to do her own glossing.

Conversely, in the course of the translation and editing process, decisions were occasionally made to cut references to Brazilian events or personalities easily recognized by the average reader of the original book but obscure to most Anglophones. Such cuts were made only if the deleted material was not central to the author's argument and, primarily, if an explanation would have distracted, or detracted, from the flow of Eliane's text and ideas. And always with her approval.

One final point: As a consummate transgressor of semantic and syntactic conventions, Eliane went a step further in the original book, adopting forms of inclusive, gender-neutral language in certain instances. As she warned her Lusophone readers, they might at first find this jarring or even disturbing, but "what doesn't disturb us doesn't transform us." Unfortunately, there is little chance that you, English reader, will be disturbed in the same ways, since English is not a gendered language—that is, while English pronouns are marked for gender (him/her), nouns are not. For example, the equivalent to *humans* in standard Portuguese is *humanos*, marked as masculine by the letter *o* but nevertheless standing in for all genders—the infamous male default, as in *mankind*. Eliane chose to replace the masculine *o* ending with a neutral *e*, thus de-gendering the word. Similarly, she used not *todos* but *todes* for *everyone* and not *outros* but *outres* for *others*. This approach is among the alternatives proposed by Brazilians working toward a gender-neutral Portuguese. While you will often see this neutral *e* form (as well as *todxs* and *tod@s*) on social media, it is rarely found in print and, for many readers, not easily absorbed. With this in mind, Eliane did not adopt gender-neutral language across the board, instead maintaining the default masculine for gendered nouns such as *beiradeiro/beiradeira* and *gaúcho/gaúcha*. As she told her Lusophone readers, she is "still figuring it out."

While I likewise adopted inclusive, gender-neutral language in my translation, this rarely entailed any drastic changes to English as we know it. After all, *humanos, humanas, humanes*, or even *human@s*—it's all *humans* to us. This is an undeniable translation loss because the reader misses out on the intermittent jolt of written words doing battle with gendered power structures. My answer was to incorporate usages where the English language can likewise question these structures, for example, *themself* in combination with the use of *they* as a third-person singular pronoun. In extending inclusive language to the more-than-human world, very much in keeping with Eliane's goal, I was also purposeful in employing *who* rather than *that* as the relative pronoun referring to fauna. Another way I found to express Eliane's intent was the introduction to the translation of the neologism *livingkind* to refer to both humans and more-than-humans. But in the case of the few gendered nouns that I borrowed from Portuguese, I decided to retain the default masculine (e.g., *beiradeiro, gaúcho, fazendeiro*), not only to be consistent with the Portuguese original but also so the curious reader would have no trouble accessing the terms in a dictionary or search engine. Perhaps tomorrow I would do it differently; perhaps, referring to the forest, I would not write "it has been" but "*ki* has been sculpted over the course of thousands of years," embracing Robin Wall Kimmerer's suggestion that we be more respectful of the more-than-human world by replacing the objectifying pronouns *it* and *they* with *ki* and *kin*, drawn from the Anishinaabe language. The banzeiro evolving to òkòtó.

I hope I have hinted here at what Eliane leaves crystal clear in the pages of this book: her language is not separate from either message or journey. She writes to re-center power, and this includes taking back power over language. The ultimate result is a book that is not meant to be an easy read. Maybe it should come with a warning label: "If you want easy, if you want your comfort zone, read elsewhere." Instead, I hope this English translation of *Banzeiro Òkòtó* will stir its readers, as it did me, to follow the pull of the banzeiro.

To close with words of gratitude: my deepest thanks to Eliane, first for writing this book and then, in the same breath, giving me the opportunity to revel in the "terror and joy" of carrying her words across more worlds, a perpetual learning experience. Eliane is my translator's dream come true: voice and substance, poetry and fierceness, passion and integrity. I know that being translated burns word-scars into her, and I am humbled every time she trusts me with letters that are very much of her flesh.

My deep thanks as well to everyone at Graywolf. To Fiona McCrae—who solicited a manuscript for translation before it had even been written in Portuguese—for her passion and daring. To Anni Liu, for her thoughtful commentaries and feedback. To both women, for their readiness to contemplate translation conundrums with me and, above all, for their abiding respect for Eliane's voice. To Katie Dublinski, for helping wrap up the loose ends. To Steve Woodward, who was missed. The proof that *Banzeiro Òkòtó* found the perfect home in Graywolf begins right with its title. Thank you all for your courage and care.

Thank you as well to Thais Passos, dear friend, translation colleague, and super sleuth, for helping me puzzle out myriad enigmas. And to Jonathan Watts for his careful reading and suggestions.

My enduring thanks to Michael, my husband, hearth, and first reader, poet-soul of perpetual joy and kindness, for the countless ways in which he keeps me where we both seem happiest: just this side of sane. In ways big and small, he makes everything better, including this book.

Lastly, a debt of gratitude to all those who fight for this planet-home and especially to the beiradeiros, quilombolas, and Indigenous people who entrusted their stories to Eliane.

Glossary

APIB, Articulação
dos Povos Indígenas
do Brasil

Brazil's largest Indigenous organization.
Alternately translated as Articulation
of Indigenous Peoples of Brazil and
Association of Brazil's Indigenous People.
http://apib.info/apib/?lang=en

beiradeiro (m.);
beiradeira (f.)

A member of a traditional forest community who lives in close relationship
with the Amazon's rivers; also known as
a *ribeirinho*.

bombachas

The baggy riding breeches that are a traditional male garment worn by *gaúchos* in
southern Brazil and other parts of southern South America.

Collective Urban
Resettlement

Reassentamento Urbano Coletivo (RUC).
Standardized neighborhoods built to
house people expelled from areas flooded
by the Belo Monte hydroelectric power
project.

demarcation

A lengthy legal process by which land
is officially recognized as Indigenous
territory.

fazendeiro

An owner of vast tracts of ranch or
farmland.

FUNAI, *Fundação
Nacional do Indio*

Brazil's federal agency of Indigenous
affairs.

gaúcho (m.); *gaúcha* (f.)	As used in this book, a demonym for someone native to Rio Grande do Sul, Brazil's southernmost state. The term draws from the image of a traditional itinerant inhabitant of the vast plains of the biome known as the pampas, where the horse, *bombachas*, and yerba mate are fundamental constituent elements.
grilagem	A term used for the illegal theft of public land, often by force and/or through the falsification of deeds and other documents.
grileiro (m.); *grileira* (f.)	An individual who practices *grilagem*; land grabber.
IBAMA, *Instituto Brasileiro do Meio Ambiente e dos Recursos Naturais Renováveis*	Brazilian Institute for the Environment and Renewable Natural Resouces, Brazil's environmental protection agency.
INCRA, *Instituto Nacional de Colonização e Reforma Agrária*	National Institute for Settlement and Agrarian Reform, Brazil's land and agrarian reform agency.
ISA, *Instituto Socioambiental*	Socioenvironmental Institute, a nongovernmental organization whose mission is to build sustainable solutions that guarantee collective, diffuse rights and valorize socioenvironmental diversity. https://www.socioambiental.org/en
latifundiário (m.); *latifundiária* (f.)	A large landowner.
orixá	A deity, or spirit god, in the Afro-Brazilian religion of Candomblé, intermediary between humans and the supreme being. Word of Yoruba origin.

pajelança	An Indigenous ritual conducted by a *pajé*, or shaman.
pariwat	Munduruku word used to refer to non-Indigenous people and also to their enemies.
piranha	A carnivorous freshwater fish native to South American rivers and lakes, which typically measures six to eight inches.
pirarucu	One of the largest freshwater fish in the world (also known in English as arapaima or paiche).
quilombo	A settlement formed by enslaved Africans who rebelled and fled to form strongholds of resistance, some of whose populations numbered in the tens of thousands during Brazil's period of slavery. The rebels' descendants hold legal title to these traditional lands, still known as quilombos. The term is often extended to refer to antiracism and other antioppression initiatives in present-day Brazil.
quilombola (m. and f.)	Descendant of the enslaved rebels who settled in quilombos.
Regional Recovery Center of Altamira	*Centro de Recuperação Regional de Altamira*. A penitentiary located in Altamira, in southwestern Pará, where fifty-eight inmates were massacred on July 29, 2019.
ribeirinho (m.); *ribeirinha* (f.)	Synonym for *beiradeiro* (which see).
RUC	See Collective Urban Resettlement.

ruralist	Member of the powerful rural bloc in the Brazilian Congress, aligned with agribusiness interests. Historically, ruralists have had ties to grilagem (which see), the pesticide and GMO industries, and violent actions against Indigenous peoples and traditional communities in biomes such as the Amazon.
tabuleiro	Nesting beach for river turtles.
tracajá	Yellow-spotted river turtle (*Podocnemis unifilis*).
voadeira	A rapid, motorized metal canoe used in the Amazon. Literally, "flyer."
xapiri (sing.); *xapiripë* (pl.)	A central figure in Yanomami cosmology, *xapiri* spirits materialize for shamans in the form of animals, trees, water, and all else in the earth-forest.

Notes

1. destructuring

11 **the concept of "existing violently"**: Eliane Brum, "De uma branca para outra," *El País*, February 27, 2017. https://brasil.elpais.com /brasil/2017/02/20/opinion/1487597060_574691.html

11 **the best white person . . . a nice slave master**: Eliane Brum, "No Brasil, o melhor branco só consegue ser um bom sinhozinho," *El País*, May 25, 2015. https://brasil.elpais.com/brasil/2015/05/25/opinion /1432564283_075923.html

12 **"paper skin" where words are imprisoned**: Davi Kopenawa and Bruce Albert, *The Falling Sky: Words of a Yanomami Shaman*, trans. Nicholas Elliott and Alison Dundy. Cambridge, MA: Belknap Press of Harvard University Press, 2013, p. 64.

2. the clitoris and the origin of the forest

15 **"Landscapes are . . . imprinted in the environment"**: William Balée, "Sobre a indigeneidade das paisagens," Simpósio de Arqueologia e Ecologia Humana no século 21 do 6ª Congresso Mundial de Arqueologia, July 3, 2008. https://revista.sabnet.org/index.php/sab /article/view/248

16 **"The Amazon has been occupied . . . thousands of people"**: Eduardo Góes Neves, *Arqueologia da Amazônia*. Rio de Janeiro: Zahar, 2006, p. 10.

16 **It's impossible to understand . . . a cultural history**: Neves, *Arqueologia da Amazônia*, pp. 10–11.

17 **In the forest, we human beings . . . surrounded by fences yet**: Davi Kopenawa and Bruce Albert, *The Falling Sky: Words of a Yanomami*

Shaman, trans. Nicholas Elliott and Alison Dundy. Cambridge, MA: Belknap Press of Harvard University Press, 2013, p. 393.

17   **"The center of what the white people call ecology"**: Kopenawa and Albert, *Falling Sky*, p. 393.

17   **"Since the beginning of time"**: Kopenawa and Albert, *Falling Sky*, p. 393.

17   **This is why . . . evil beings get closer**: Kopenawa and Albert, *Falling Sky*, p. 393.

18   **In the past . . . protect the forest**: Kopenawa and Albert, *Falling Sky*, p. 394.

18   **"The white people's thought remains full of forgetting"**: Kopenawa and Albert, *Falling Sky*, p. 255.

18   **"Has a heart and breathes"**: Davi Kopenawa in an interview with F. Watson of *Survival International*, Boa Vista, July 1992. In Davi Kopenawa and Bruce Albert, *A queda do céu: Palavras de um xamã yanomami*, trans. Beatriz Perrone-Moisés. São Paulo: Companhia das Letras, 2010, p. 468.

18   **"What it is to *be* . . . and environment"**: Kopenawa and Albert, *Queda do céu*, p. 16; foreword by Viveiros de Castro.

21   **His full name is Juarez . . . God bless you, Transamazonian**: *Amazônia*, special edition of the magazine *Realidade*. São Paulo: Editora Abril, no. 67, October 1971.

22   **"more and more, Indians are becoming human beings just like us"**: Jair Messias Bolsonaro, weekly live statement, January 24, 2020. https://www.youtube.com/watch?v=WX7Xrs2Y3QY

22   **"the conquest of this gigantic green world"**: Plaque commemorating the start of work on the Transamazonian Highway, in Altamira, Pará, October 10, 1970. http://almanaque.folha.uol.com.br /brasil_10out1970.htm

23   **"He [Médici] broke ground . . . How is that possible?"**: Eliane Brum, "Lula e Dilma passarão para a história como predadores da Amazônia," *Época*, June 4, 2012. http://elianebrum.com/opiniao/colunas -na-epoca/dom-erwin-krautler-lula-e-dilma-passarao-para-a-historia -como-predadores-da-amazonia-2/

26   **the machine of the world**: Allusion to the poem "A Máquina do Mundo" (Machine of the world) by Carlos Drummond de Andrade.

15. the amazon is a woman

30   **"Brazil . . . every foreign pervert wants"**: "'Brasil é uma virgem que todo tarado de fora quer,' diz Bolsonaro ao falar sobre Amazônia," G1, July 6, 2019, https://g1.globo.com/politica/noticia/2019/07/06/brasil -e-uma-virgem-que-todo-tarado-de-fora-quer-diz-bolsonaro-ao-falar -sobre-amazonia.ghtml

31   **"Whoever wants to come here to have sex with women, feel free"**: "'Quem quiser vir ao Brasil fazer sexo com mulher, fique à vontade,' diz Bolsonaro," *Pragmatismo político*, April 25, 2019. https:// www.pragmatismopolitico.com.br/2019/04/jair-bolsonaro-brasil -paraiso-gay.html

34   **"Our ancestors are more ancient than Jesus Christ"**: Mundukuru and other original peoples in a letter to the authorities when they occupied the Belo Monte Hydroelectric Power Plant job site, Fórum Brasileiro de Economia Solidária (FBES), June 11, 2013. https://fbes.org.br/2013/06/11/cartas-da-luta-dos-povos-indigenas -no-canteiro-de-belo-monte/

34   **"Our inspiration is . . . we'll cut off some heads"**: Maria Leusa Munduruku, at a meeting of the Amazon Center of the World movement, Altamira, Pará, *Atmos*, April 28, 2020. https://atmos.earth/amazon -rainforest-indigenous-activism-history/

35   **We rescued the fish's mother . . . our pajés know to be our ancestors**: Munduruku people in a letter to the authorities, Ipereg Ayu movement, December 30, 2019. https://movimentoiperegayu.wordpress .com/2019/12/30/resgate-das-itiga-pelo-povo-munduruku/

37   **"Because of the government, our forest is shedding tears. Tears that fall like milk from our breast"**: Jonathan Watts, "'The forest is shedding tears': the women defending their Amazon homeland," *Guardian*, December 21, 2019. https://www.theguardian.com/envi ronment/2019/dec/21/mother-with-a-price-on-her-head-defending -amazon-forest

45. rape. and reforestation

42   **"image skin"**: Davi Kopenawa and Bruce Albert, *The Falling Sky: Words of a Yanomami Shaman*, trans. Nicholas Elliott and Alison Dundy. Cambridge, MA: Belknap Press of Harvard University Press, 2013, p. 13.

43   **"Because I want to *unwhiten* myself"**: Eliane Brum, "Vivendo o fim no centro do mundo," *Córtex*, November 30, 2019. https://www.youtube.com/watch?v=ghIL7ExjaxQ

45   **"sustainability is personal vanity"**: Ailton Krenak, "On Time," trans. Alex Brostoff, *Critical Times: Interventions in Global Critical Theory*, July 13, 2020. https://ctjournal.org/2020/07/13/on-time/

45   **We've formed such an immense constellation . . . produce anything in equilibrium?**: Krenak, "On Time."

7. fierce life

49   **"I'd never seen silk . . . I saw this land butchered"**: Rosa Acevedo Marin, "Quilombolas de Burajuba: lutas identitárias e territoriais," anthropological report by the Quilombola Community of Burajuba, Center for Amazon Advanced Studies (Núcleo de Altos Estudos Amazônicos). Belém: unamaz, UFPA, September 2013.

24. confession

56   **"becoming other"**: Davi Kopenawa and Bruce Albert, *The Falling Sky: Words of a Yanomami Shaman*, trans. Nicholas Elliott and Alison Dundy. Cambridge, MA: Belknap Press of Harvard University Press, 2013, pp. 30; 302; 343; note 5, ch. 24.

0. resistance

60   **"wouldn't demarcate one more square centimeter"**: Gabriel Hirabahasi, "'Não demarcarei um centímetro quadrado a mais de terra indígena,' diz Bolsonaro," *O Globo*, December 12, 2018. https://oglobo

.globo.com/epoca/expresso/nao-demarcarei-um-centimetro-quadrado
-mais-de-terra-indigena-diz-bolsonaro-23300890

60   **"What I'm worried about . . . five hundred years"**: Ailton
Krenak, "Somos índios, resistimos há 500 anos. Fico preocupado é se
os brancos vão resistir," *Expresso*, October 19, 2018. https://expresso
.pt/internacional/2018-10-19-Somos-indios-resistimos-ha-500-anos
.-Fico-preocupado-e-se-os-brancos-vao-resistir

60   **The Indigenous population . . . won't rattle us**: "Expresso:
'Somos índios, resistimos há 500 anos. Fico preocupado é se os brancos
vão resistir,'" Fundação Astrojildo Pereira, November 29, 2019. https://
www.fundacaoastrojildo.org.br/expresso-somos-indios-resistimos-ha
-500-anos-fico-preocupado-e-se-os-brancos-vao-resistir/

62   **While there is some dispute . . . the history of humanity**:
Marcio Goldman, "Quinhentos anos de contato: por uma teoria
etnográfica da (contra)mestiçagem," *Mana* (Rio de Janeiro), no. 3,
December 21, 2015. https://doi.org/10.1590/0104-93132015v21n3p641

666. the end of the world isn't the end. it's the middle

67   **"The Indigenous are experts . . . their world ended in 1500"**:
Eliane Brum, "Diálogos sobre o fim do mundo," *El País*, September 29,
2014. https://brasil.elpais.com/brasil/2014/09/29/opinion/1412000283
_365191.html.

67   **Researchers calculate . . . aboard the invaders' bodies**:
Alexander Koch et al.,"Earth system impacts of the European arrival and
Great Dying in the Americas after 1492," *Quaternary Science Reviews*,
v. 207, March 1, 2019, pp. 13–36. https://doi.org/10.1016/j.quascirev
.2018.12.004

68   **"Indians? . . . You won't come across a single one"**: Claude Lévi-
Strauss, *Tristes Tropiques*, trans. John and Doreen Weightman. New
York: Modern Library, 1997, p. 43.

69   **"My grandson . . . The whitening of the race"**: Breno Pires, "'Meu
neto é um cara bonito, viu ali? Branqueamento da raça,' diz Mourão,"
O Estado de S. Paulo, October 6, 2018. https://politica.estadao.com.br

/noticias/eleicoes,meu-neto-e-um-cara-bonito-viu-ali-branqueamento
-da-raca-diz-mourao,70002535826

69   **When COVID-19 hit . . . to the virus:** Senado Notícias, July 8, 2020.
https://www12.senado.leg.br/noticias/materias/2020/07/08/bolsonaro
-sanciona-com-vetos-lei-para-proteger-indigenas-durante-pandemia

5. forestpeoples: the alliance of the beings and in-betweens

90   **The symbol of this alliance . . . side by side:** Amazon Watch
press release, November 5, 2014. https://amazonwatch.org/news/2014
/1105-defying-brazilian-government-indigenous-group-proceeds-with
-demarcation-of-amazonian-territory

92   **"a sub-humanity, a people who clings to the land":** Ailton
Krenak, *Ideias para adiar o fim do mundo.* São Paulo: Companhia das
Letras, 2019, p. 22.

92   **How have we . . . the same language:** Krenak, *Ideias,* pp. 10–23.

94   **walking in shoes of arrogance . . . with their own feet:** Allusion
to the song "O mundo é um moinho" (The world is a windmill) by samba
composer and singer Cartola.

87. between-worlds

97   **This is an unprecedented challenge . . . that will fundamen-
tally reshape society:** Carola Rackete with Anne Weiss, *The Time to
Act Is Now: A call to combat environmental breakdown,* trans. Clair
Wordley. Berlin: Rosa Luxemburg Stiftung, 2021, p. 115.

98   **We don't need to discuss . . . create a more just society:** Carola
Rackete, *É hora de agir.* Porto Alegre: Arquipélago Editorial, 2020.

101   **On September 10, 2021 . . . in the coming years:** See permanent
peoplestribunal.org and campanhacerrado.org.br

12. the conversion of the forestpeoples into the poor

103   **"for theirs is the kingdom of heaven":** Beatitudes, Luke 6:20–23,
Revised Standard Version of the Bible.

109   **"On the river, I was king . . . to get there**: Eliane Brum, "They owned an island, now they are urban poor: the tragedy of Altamira," *Guardian*, February 6, 2018. https://www.theguardian.com/cities/2018 /feb/06/urban-poor-tragedy-altamira-belo-monte-brazil

33. flying rivers

115   **"The Future Climate of Amazonia"**: Antonio Donato Nobre, "The Future Climate of Amazonia: Scientific Assessment Report," Articulacão Regional Amazônica, October 2014. https://wwf.panda.org/?232041 /The-Future-Climate-of-Amazonia

120   **electron capture detector . . . about the universe**: Bruno Latour, "This is a global catastrophe that has come from within," *Guardian*, June 6, 2020. https://www.theguardian.com/world/2020/jun/06/bruno -latour-coronavirus-gaia-hypothesis-climate-crisis

121   **"We must live in terror and joy"**: Donna Haraway, interviewed by Juliana Fausto, Eduardo Viveiros do Castro, and Débora Danowski, August 21, 2014. https://www.youtube.com/watch?v=1x0oxUHOlA8

122   **The forest has survived . . . mere human beings**: Nobre, *Future Climate of Amazonia*, p. 25.

123   **"Dialogues on the End of the World"**: Eliane Brum, *El País*, September 29, 2014. https://brasil.elpais.com/brasil/2014/09/29/opinion /1412000283_365191.html

126   **a report about the first climate initiative . . . included thirty children**: Urgenda Foundation, "The Urgenda Climate Case against the Dutch Government," December 20, 2019. https://www.urgenda.nl/en /themas/climate-case/

127   **When the strategic lawsuit . . . already been forgotten**: Greenpeace, ADPF Climática, November 11, 2020. https://www.green peace.org/brasil/publicacoes/acao-judicial-amazonia-clima/

127   **But I prefer to call it "collective responsibility"**: In the sense used by Hannah Arendt, *Responsibility and Judgment*. New York: Schocken Books, 2003.

127   **"This shitty world is pregnant with another"**: Isabel Coutinho, "Escritor Eduardo Galeano sobre o estado do mundo na Acampada de

Barcelona," *Público*, June 14, 2011. http://blogues.publico.pt/ciberescritas
/2011/06/14/escritor-eduardo-galeano-sobre-o-mundo-na-acampada
-de-barcelona/

10. the soccer ball

135   **In 2014, I was to cover . . . the Brazilian national team**:
http://elianebrum.com/desacontecimentos/os-outros-lados-da-copa
-do-mundo/

138   **Castelo de Sonhos is Amazonian . . . At gunpoint**: Eliane
Brum and Solange Azevedo, "À espera do assassino," *Revista Época*,
November 25, 2015. http://elianebrum.com/reportagens/a-espera-do
-assassino/

140   **"In generic terms . . . issuance of land ownership"**: Maurício
Torres, "Grilagem para principiantes: guia de procedimentos básicos
para o roubo de terras públicas," in M. I. M. Marques et al., *Perspectivas
de Natureza: geografia, formas de natureza e política*. São Paulo:
Annablume Editora, 2018, pp. 285–314.

142   **"that totally sick . . . tapper who got fucked"**: Igor Felippe Santos,
"Maior grileiro do mundo," *Caros Amigos*, September 2005. https://
www.viomundo.com.br/denuncias/deputado-do-pt-homenageia-o
-maior-grileiro-do-mundo.html

143   **The designation intended . . . chemicals, and explosives**:
André Vargas, Projeto de Lei n. 6.167-c, 2009. https://www.camara.leg
.br/proposicoesWeb/prop_mostrarintegra?codteor=1065689

144   **"The best way I can . . . centre of the earth"**: https://www
.gutenberg.org/files/219/219-h/219-h.htm

121. overlords, vassals, and serfs

155   **In 2011, I traced this intricate genealogical tree**: Eliane
Brum, "A Amazônia, segundo um morto e um fugitivo," *Revista Época*,
January 28, 2012. http://elianebrum.com/opiniao/colunas-na-epoca/a
-amazonia-segundo-um-morto-e-um-fugitivo/

155 **João Chupel Primo, murdered on October 22, 2011**: "Rainforest Mafias: How Violence and Impunity Fuel Deforestation in Brazil's Amazon," Human Rights Watch, September 17, 2019.

156 **Until not long ago, Brazil . . . in the Amazon**: Maurício Torres, "Grilagem para principiantes: guia de procedimentos básicos para o roubo de terras públicas," in M. I. M. Marques et al., *Perspectivas de Natureza: geografia, formas de natureza e política*. São Paulo: Annablume Editora, 2018, pp. 285–314.

171. the amazon locusts

169 **"horizontal vertigo"**: Pierre Drieu de la Rochelle and Victoria Ocampo. https://sul21.com.br/colunasfranklin-cunha/2017/01/362859/

182 **I'll never forget . . . in 2001**: Eliane Brum, *O olho da rua: uma repórter em busca da literatura da vida real*. Porto Alegre: Arquipélago Editorial, 2017.

183 **"I'm going to pose like an Indian killer"**: Naira Hoffmeister, "O Pioneiro," *Intercept*, July 13, 2020. https://theintercept.com/2020/07/13/quartiero-fazendeiro-bolsonaro-amazonia/

185 **"cowboy economy" and "spaceman economy"**: Kenneth E. Boulding, "The Economics of the Coming Spaceship Earth," in H. Jarrett (ed.), *Environmental Quality in a Growing Economy*. Baltimore, MD: Resources for the Future/Johns Hopkins University Press, 1966, pp. 13–14. https://www.laceiba.org.mx/wp-content/uploads/2017/08/Boulding-1996-The-economics-of-the-coming-spaceship-earth.pdf

4.0. the children of altamira

207 **President Jair Bolsonaro . . . I'll answer you"**: Talita Fernandes, "'Pergunta para as vítimas dos que morreram lá o que eles acham,' diz Bolsonaro sobre massacre no Pará," *Folha de S.Paulo*, July 30, 2019. https://www1.folha.uol.com.br/cotidiano/2019/07/pergunta-para-as-vitimas-que-morreram-o-que-eles-acham-diz-bolsonaro-sobre-massacre-no-para.shtml

207   **"I've read in the paper . . . mothers are there crying"**: Fabiano Maisonnave, "Não é resposta que um presidente dê a essas famílias," *Folha de S.Paulo*, July 31, 2019. https://www1.folha.uol.com.br/cotidiano /2019/07/nao-e-resposta-que-um-presidente-de-a-essas-familias-diz -bispo-de-altamira-sobre-bolsonaro.shtml

207   **"Problems come up"**: Gustavo Uribe, "'Problemas acontecem,' diz Bolsonaro sobre presos mortos em transferência no Pará," *Folha de S.Paulo*, July 31, 2019. https://www1.folha.uol.com.br/cotidiano /2019/07/problemas-acontecem-diz-bolsonaro-sobre-presos-mortos -em-transferencia-no-para.shtml

207   **Kayapó Tuíra . . . José Sarney**: "Índia Tuíra, a heroína indígena que mudou a história," Museu de Imagens. https://www.museudeimagens .com.br/india-tuira/

2018. the first generation without hope

220   **"Our house is on fire"**: Greta Thunberg, Svante Thunberg, Malena Ernman, and Beata Ernman, *Our House Is on Fire: Scenes of a Family and a Planet in Crisis*. Penguin Books, 2018.

220   **"You grown-ups don't give a shit about my future"**: Emily Witt, "How Greta Thunberg Transformed Existential Dread into a Movement," *New Yorker*, April 6, 2020. https://www.newyorker.com /books/under-review/how-greta-thunberg-transformed-existential -dread-into-a-movement

221   **"Since our leaders . . . taken long ago"**: Greta Thunberg, COP24, Poland, December 4, 2018.

222   **Some people . . . group of people**: Greta Thunberg, World Economic Forum, Davos, January 24, 2019.

224   **"I don't want . . . I feel every day"**: Greta Thunberg, *No One Is Too Small to Make a Difference*. Penguin Books, 2019, p. 19.

225   **Greta is vocal about having Asperger's . . . "superpower"**: https://twitter.com/gretathunberg/status/1167916177927991296

68. hope is overrated

227   **my first (and so far only) novel**: Eliane Brum, *One Two*, trans. Lucy Greaves. Seattle: Amazon Crossing, 2012.

229   **"I don't want your hope . . . I want you to panic"**: Greta Thunberg, *No One Is Too Small to Make a Difference*. Penguin Books, 2019, p. 19.

232   **In May 2019, the *Guardian* announced:** "Why the Guardian is changing the language it uses about the environment," *Guardian*, May 17, 2019. https://www.theguardian.com/environment/2019/may /17/why-the-guardian-is-changing-the-language-it-uses-about-the -environment

233   **Perhaps the challenge . . . constructing unprecedented shiftings**: Peter Pál Pelbart, "Negros, judeus, palestinos: do monopólio do sofrimento," *Revista Percurso* June 2018.

234   **The best answer still lies . . . but not for us**: Pelbart, "Negros, judeus, palestinos." [Translator's source for the Kafka quote: https:// timesflowstemmed.com/2011/08/24/an-infinite-amount-of-hope/]

235   **Perhaps the time has come . . . an ethical imperative**: Eliane Brum, "Em defesa da desesperança," *El País*, December 21, 2015. https:// brasil.elpais.com/brasil/2015/12/21/opinion/1450710896_273452.html

236   **"The Indigenous are experts . . . their world ended in 1500"**: Eliane Brum, "Diálogos sobre o fim do mundo," *El País*, September 29, 2014. https://brasil.elpais.com/brasil/2014/09/29/opinion/1412000283 _365191.html

236   **"Indigenous peoples cannot not . . . neologism *rexistir*"**: Eliane Brum, "A potência da primeira geração sem esperança," *El País*, June 5, 2019. https://brasil.elpais.com/brasil/2019/06/05/politica/1559743351 _956676.html

1937. self-extermination as a gesture

241   **the concept of "psychological wage"**: W. E. B. Du Bois, *Black Reconstruction in America, 1860–1880*. New York: Free Press, 1998.

243 **suicide rates among youth ages fifteen to twenty-nine rose 8.**3 **percent**: Secretaria de Vigilância em Saúde, "Perfil epidemiológico dos casos notificados de violência autoprovocada e óbitos por suicídio entre jovens de 15 a 29 anos no Brasil, 2011 a 2018."

244 **Writing this story was a very painful personal process**: Eliane Brum and Solange Azevedo, "Suicídio.com," *Época*, n.d. http://revistaepoca.globo.com/Revista/Epoca/0,,EDR81603-6014,00.html

245 **rates of vulnerability to violence among youth**: Secretaria de Governo da Presidência da República, "Índice de vulnerabilidade Juvenil à Violência 2017." https://forumseguranca.org.br/wp-content/uploads/2020/10/fbsp-vulnerabilidade-juveni-violencia-desigualdade-racial-2017-relatorio.pdf

246 **"They say we are the country's future . . . don't have a present?"**: Eliane Brum and Clara Glock, "A cidade que mata o futuro: em 2020, Altamira enfrenta um aumento avassalador de suicídos de adolescentes," *El País*, April 27, 2020.

1987. belo monte refugees

247 **the Belo Monte Refugees movement. . . . Care Clinic**: https://www.latesfip.com.br/clinicadocuidado

254 **"João loved Tereza who loved Raimundo who loved Maria"**: Carlos Drummond de Andrade, *Multitudinous Heart: Selected Poems*, trans. Richard Zenith. New York: Farrar, Straus and Giroux, 2015.

100. about ties

261 **As I wrote in my article about this series of suicides**: Eliane Brum and Solange Azevedo, "Suicídio.com," *Época*, n.d. http://revistaepoca.globo.com/Revista/Epoca/0,,EDR81603-6014,00.html

261 **The main [suicide] risk factors . . . happening now, in 2020**: Eliane Brum and Clara Glock, "A cidade que mata o futuro: em 2020, Altamira enfrenta um aumento avassalador de suicídios de adolescentes," *El País*, April 27, 2020. https://brasil.elpais.com/sociedade/2020-04-27/a-cidade-que-mata-o-futuro-em-2020-altamira-enfrenta-um-aumento-avassalador-de-suicidios-de-adolescentes.html

262 **To understand these suicides . . . our future generations:** Brum and Glock, "A cidade que mata o futuro."

9. pigeon claws on the roof

267 **In the short book where I narrate the history of my relationship with words:** Eliane Brum, *meus desacontecimentos*. Porto Alegre: Arquipélago Editorial, 2017.

69. translingual

289 **"place of speech":** "Place of speech" is a term that has gained popularity in contemporary discussions in Brazil, especially since the 2010s and particularly among intellectuals and activists within Black movements, such as the philosopher Djamila Ribeiro. Given the evidence that certain sectors of the population are oppressed by racial, gender, and sexual orientation inequalities and that their voices are ignored, the notion of "place of speech" expresses the importance of guaranteeing that those who experience certain realities are heard, and this consequently shifts power relations. For example, a Black woman is better positioned than a white woman to speak about what a Black woman experiences, and a woman is better positioned than a man to speak about what a woman experiences. This does not mean a white woman cannot speak about what Black women experience or that a man cannot speak about what women experience, but it means we must listen to those who have lived experience with the realities in question if our discussion is to be valid. For more, see this interview with Djalma Ribeiro: "'Ain't I a Woman Too?': Djamila Ribeiro on Social Justice, Black Feminism and the Place of Speech," by Johanne Affricot, *GRIOT*, September 21, 2020. https://griotmag.com/en/aint-i-a-woman-djamila-ribeiro-on-social-justice-black-feminism-and-the-place-of-speech/

290 **Thais says that in the Mebêngôkre language . . . heard in my ear":** https://site-antigo.socioambiental.org/pt-br/blog/blog-do-xingu/nossa-terra-e-uma-so

291 **a lament for strings:** Alexandre Guerra, "An Elegy for String Orchestra inspired on the drama lived by the Amazonian tribe 'Araweté.'" https://www.youtube.com/watch?v=i14WwbKpCGA

293 **the biggest open-pit gold mine in Brazil**: Marcel Gomes, "As veias abertas da Volta Grande do Xingu," *Repórter Brasil*, October 2017. https://reporterbrasil.org.br/wp-content/uploads/2017/11/as_veias _abertas_da_volta_grande_do_Xingu-1.pdf

294 **FUNAI's first census of them registered 120 survivors**: Instituto Socioambiental, Povos Indígenas no Brasil. n.d. https://pib .socioambiental.org/pt/Povo:Arawet%C3%A9

294 **What Norte Energia did . . . impact mitigation measures**]: Guilherme Heurich, "A barragem e a canoa de Jawitï," Povos Indígenas no Brasil, 2013. https://pib.socioambiental.org/files/file/PIB_verbetes /arawete/osaraweteeoplanoemergencial.pdf

296 **"What does our name . . . we are of this river"**: Instituto Socioambiental, Povos Indígenas no Brasil, Yudjá/Jurana, n.d. https:// pib.socioambiental.org/pt/Povo:Yudj%C3%A1/Juruna

296 *bïde*, **which means "us," . . . "enemies," "foreigners"**: Instituto Socioambiental, Povos Indígenas no Brasil, Araweté, n.d. https://pib .socioambiental.org/pt/Povo:Arawet%C3%A9

298 **You, whites, have no soul**: Jorge Pozzobon, *Vocês, brancos, não têm alma*. Rio de Janeiro: Azougue Editorial, 2013.

2041. Eduardo

305 **nineteen of these twenty-two executions took place after 2015**: https://www.cptnacional.org.br/downlods/category/41-conflitos -no-campo-brasil-publicacao

310 **"stand with people living in poverty . . . in the most abandoned places"**: https://www.sndden.org/who-we-are/our-mission/

311 **Pope Francis's exhortation Querida Amazônia**: Pope Francis, "Post-Synodal Apostolic Exhortation Querida Amazônia," February 2, 2020. https://www.vatican.va/content/francesco/en/apost_exhortations /documents/papa-francesco_esortazione-ap_20200202_querida -amazonia.html

311 **At the Amazon Synod**: "Final Document, The Amazon: New Paths for the Church and for an Integral Ecology," February 2, 2020. http://secretariat.synod.va/content/sinodoamazonico/en/documents /final-document-of-the-amazon-synod.html

312   **That approach . . . Mary, the Mother:** Ch. V, Items 100 and 101 of the apostolic exhortation. https://www.vatican.va/content/francesco /en/apost_exhortations/documents/papa-francesco_esortazione-ap _20200202_querida-amazonia.html

313   **In Northern Brazil, Evangelicals are now tied with Catholics in number:** Anna Virginia Balloussier, "Avanço evangélico no Norte explica preocupação católica em encontro de bispos," *Folha de S.Paulo*, October 8, 2019, https://www.folha.uol.com.br/poder/2019/10/avanco -evangelico-no-norte-explica-preocupacao-catolica-em-encontro-de -bispos.shtml

319   **Lula legalized the theft of plots of public land:** Medida Provisória 458, February 10, 2009. https://www.planalto.gov.br/ccivil _03/_ato2007-2010/2009/mpv/458.htm

319   **Temer legalized the theft of plots of public land:** Lei nº 13465, July 11, 2017. http://www.planalto.gov.br/ccivil_03/_ato2015-2018/2017 /lei/l13465.htm

319   **Bolsonaro tried to surpass his predecessors by legalizing public land stolen:** Agência Câmara de Notícias, "Deputados apro- vam texto-base de projeto sobre regularização fundiária," August 3, 2018. https://www.camara.leg.br/noticias/789100-deputados-aprovam -texto-base-de-projeto-sobre-regularizacao-fundiaria

2042. amazon center of the world

325   **"ever more, until transforming into a circle opened to the in- finite":** Juana Elbien dos Santos, *Os nàgô e a morte: pàdê, àsèsè e o culto Égun na Bahia.* Petropolis: Vozes, 2012.

333   **This idea moves, this idea is a word that acts:** According to the anthropologist Spensy Pimentel of the University of São Paulo's Center for Amer-Indian Studies: "Words are the core of resistance. They take action in the world; they are words that act. They make things happen, they make the future. The boundary between discourse and prophecy is tenuous." Eliane Brum, "Decretem nossa extinção e nos en- terrem aqui," *Época*, October 22, 2012. http://elianebrum.com/opiniao /colunas-na-epoca/decretem-nossa-extincao-e-nos-enterrem-aqui/

#freethefuture

346   **"We have launched this movement . . . and we want to fight"**: https://liberteofuturo.net/#/movimento

346   **I wrote an article in which I introduced the movement**: Eliane Brum, "#liberteofuturo," *El País*, July 5, 2020. https://brasil.elpais.com/brasil/2020-07-05/liberteofuturo.html

352   **At the start of the pandemic . . . inhabiting the planet**: "World's billionaires have more wealth than 4.6 billion people," Oxfam International, January 20, 2020. https://www.oxfam.org/en/press-releases/worlds-billionaires-have-more-wealth-46-billion-people

352   **In early 2022, Oxfam International . . . poorest 3.1 billion people"**: "Ten richest men double their fortunes in pandemic while incomes of 99 percent of humanity fell," Oxfam International press release, January 17, 2022.

352   **"The future is here and now; there may not be a next year"**: Ailton Krenak, *Ideas to Postpone the End of the World*, trans. Anthony Doyle. Toronto: House of Anansi Press, 2020, p. 1.

between-worlds

357   **"torn-out piece of me"**: From the song "Pedaço de Mim" by singer-songwriter Chico Buarque.

358   **And of waking in the morning to find the genocidist still there**: A reference to "The Dinosaur," a short story by Augusto Monterroso, which in its entirety reads: "When he awoke, the dinosaur was still there."

358   **a plan to spread the virus to achieve what they call "herd immunity"**: Eliane Brum, "Pesquisa revela que Bolsonaro executou uma 'estratégia institucional de propagação do coronavírus,'" *El País*, January 21, 2021. https://brasil.elpais.com/brasil/2021-01-21/pesquisa-revela-que-bolsonaro-executou-uma-estrategia-institucional-de-propagacao-do-virus.html

358   **over half a million dead in Brazil**: See the website INUMERÁVEIS (Innumerable: memorial dedicated to the history of each victim of coronavirus in Brazil). https://inumeraveis.com.br/

358   **According to epidemiological research, four hundred thousand of these half million deaths could have been avoided**: Marcela Mattos, Beatriz Borges, and Sara Resende, "Epidemiologista diz à CPI da Covid que cerca de 400 mil mortes poderiam ter sido evitadas," G1, June 24, 2021. https://g1.globo.com/politica/cpi-da-covid/noticia/2021/06/24/epidemiologista-diz-a-cpi-da-covid-que-cerca-de-400-mil-mortes-poderiam-ter-sido-evitadas.ghtml

360   **a scientific article about butterflies in the Amazon**. Ricardo Luís Spaniol et al., "Discolouring the Amazon Rainforest: how deforestation is affecting butterfly coloration," *Biodiversity and Conservation*, vol. 29, June 3, 2020, pp. 2821–38. https://doi.org/10.1007/s10531-020-01999-3

361   **the rainforest . . . has already started emitting more gases than it absorbs**: Luciana V. Gatti et al., "Amazonia as a carbon source linked to deforestation and climate change," *Nature*, vol. 595, July 14, 2021, pp. 388–93. https://www.nature.com/articles/s41586-021-03629-6

Eliane Brum is a Brazilian writer, journalist, and documentary filmmaker. A selection from her previous books of nonfiction was published in English as *The Collector of Leftover Souls*, which was longlisted for the 2019 National Book Award in Translated Literature and the 2022 Jan Michalski Prize. She is also the author of the novel *One Two*, which was a finalist for the São Paulo Literature and Portugal Telecom Literature prizes. She has received more than forty awards and honors at home and abroad, including the Inter American Press Association and King of Spain prizes, making her Brazil's most award-winning journalist. In 2008, she received the United Nations Special Press Trophy for "everything she has done and is doing in defense of justice and democracy." In 2021, she received the Maria Moors Cabot Prize from Columbia University for her body of work. She is a columnist for the international section of *El País* and also writes for other European and US newspapers and magazines. She is a founder of Sumaúma: Journalism from the Center of the World, a trilingual journalism platform based in Altamira, in the Amazon rainforest, where she lives.

Diane Whitty has translated over a dozen major nonfiction books from the Portuguese, including *The Collector of Leftover Souls* by Eliane Brum, *Activist Biology* by Regina Horta Duarte, *The Sanitation of Brazil* by Gilberto Hochman, and *Our Immoral Soul* by Nilton Bonder. Her translations have appeared in the *Guardian*, the *New York Times*, *Granta*, the *Paris Review*, *Harper's*, *Atmos*, *Glossalia*, and *Litro*. She spent twenty-three years in Brazil and now lives in her native Wisconsin with her husband.

The text of *Banzeiro Òkòtó* is set in Warnock Pro.
Book design by Rachel Holscher.
Composition by Bookmobile Design and Digital
Publisher Services, Minneapolis, Minnesota.
Manufactured by Versa Press on acid-free,
30 percent postconsumer wastepaper.